Lincoln's Fifth Wheel

TO
MY SANTA BARBARA FRIENDS
1944–1949

Lincoln's Fifth Wheel:

The Political History
of the
United States Sanitary Commission

by
WILLIAM QUENTIN MAXWELL

Preface by
ALLAN NEVINS

LONGMANS, GREEN & CO.
NEW YORK · LONDON · TORONTO
1956

LONGMANS, GREEN AND CO., INC.
55 FIFTH AVENUE, NEW YORK 3

LONGMANS, GREEN AND CO. LTD.
6 & 7 CLIFFORD STREET, LONDON W 1

LONGMANS, GREEN AND CO.
20 CRANFIELD ROAD, TORONTO 16

LINCOLN'S FIFTH WHEEL

PUBLISHED SIMULTANEOUSLY IN THE DOMINION OF CANADA BY
LONGMANS, GREEN AND CO., TORONTO

FIRST EDITION

LIBRARY OF CONGRESS CATALOG CARD NUMBER: 56–6506

Printed in the United States of America

Preface

D R. MAXWELL'S book fills a place which has too long been
left vacant. It is the result of a vast labor in the huge neglected archive which the United States Sanitary Commission,
long ago placed in the Astor Library, and which was taken into
the New York Public Library when the Astor, Tilden, and Lenox
foundations were united. With scholarly thoroughness and penetrating judgment, yet with unfailing narrative interest, it treats
of almost the darkest side of the Civil War—the sufferings of the
wounded and sick—and of the great philanthropic organization
which did so much to save lives and alleviate agony during the
four years of conflict. Yet its range is wider than these two
themes. It furnishes fresh material of the first value on many
aspects of the war: on camp arrangements, on the diet of soldiers,
on home relief, on drill and morale, on sutlers, recreations, and
the traits of officers high and low. A broader work than George
Worthington Adams's *Doctors in Blue*, it takes its place alongside
that volume as an essential contribution to our understanding of
the struggle.

"The Sanitary Commission," wrote Katherine Prescott Wormeley in a little book of that title which she published anonymously
in 1863 in Boston to aid a Sanitary fair, "is the great artery which
bears the people's love to the people's army." Miss Wormeley, an
active worker in the Hospital Transport Service of the Commission, wrote another volume called *The Other Side of War*, mem-
orable for its ghastly pictures of the human debris of the Peninsular campaign, and its admiring portrait of that remarkable
administrator Frederick Law Olmsted. Until now her two books,
fragmentary as they are, the dry if very useful official compen-
dium by Charles J. Stillé, and the vivid glimpses of Sanitary
Commission work in the diary of George Templeton Strong, its
treasurer, have been our only dependable sources for the work
it did. Dr. Maxwell, using sources never before scrutinized by a
historian, has brought together all the important facts, and made
of them a story as moving as it is instructive.

What a story it is! The title Lincoln bestowed on the Sanitary Commission, the "Fifth Wheel," was not truly accurate. The Army wagon always requires four wheels: the quartermaster's services, the commissary, transportation services, and medical and surgical care. This wagon after Fort Sumter was limping along on three wheels and a pole—the pole being the little, rickety, antiquated, incompetently led Army Medical Bureau. After weary months of shoving and pulling, the Army Medical Bureau was greatly strengthened. The appointment of the redoubtable William A. Hammond as surgeon-general was a decisive turning point in its history. To the end, however, the Sanitary Commission remained absolutely indispensable. All told, it raised not less than twenty-five millions in money, goods, and personal help, much of it coming from poor farmers, mechanics, and clerks who could give but a dollar apiece. In a nation which had no medical association, no nursing schools, no apparatus for meeting a sudden strain on hospital facilities, it mobilized the best talent available for the war emergency. It was truly a fourth wheel, and the labors it performed under Dr. Henry W. Bellows and Olmsted were as important as the equally neglected labors of Montgomery C. Meigs as head of the Quartermaster's Bureau.

The Civil War was one of the bloodiest conflicts of history, the total deaths in the Union and Confederate armies being authoritatively computed at about 625,000. The butchery began on an unexpectedly heavy scale in the early part of 1862. One of the facts which most appalls the student is the enormous amount of suffering on the field and in the hospitals. Armies the world over were probably worse provided in 1860 with medical and surgical resources than European armies had been when Napoleon's wars ended in 1815; the standard had deteriorated. The work of Pasteur and Lister lay, so far as any application to surgery went, well in the future. Almost every abdominal wound meant death. Any severe laceration of a limb meant amputation with a good chance of mortal gangrene or erysipelas. The North systematically prevented shipments of drugs and surgical instruments to the South, a piece of barbarity which did not shorten the war by a day, but on the Confederate side added greatly to its sufferings. Little was known about the best means of erecting field and base hospitals. So rudimentary was the knowledge of hospital sanitation that surgeons marveled when tent hospitals, open to the clean winds and sunshine, proved healthier than wooden buildings with dirty walls and filth-soaked floors.

Any careful reader of the literature of the war is stricken by the often casual but cumulatively horrifying notes he finds on battlefield scenes. Story after story is the same. Night would fall on a field ringing with cries of anguish: Water! Help!; if in winter. Blankets! Fire! Yet water, blankets, help did not come. Frequently they did not come for long days. Shiloh was fought on a Sunday and Monday. A cold April rain set in on Sunday night, and continued intermittently through Tuesday night. On Tuesday morning the great majority of the wounded lay where they had fallen. Some had been there forty-eight hours without attention; many had died of exhaustion or shock; not a few had drowned in rainfilled depressions from which they could not crawl. Every house in the area was converted into a hospital, where the floors were covered with wretches, sometimes with arms or legs torn off, who, after the first bandages, got no medical care, no nursing, not even nourishment. "The first day or two," wrote a reporter, "the air was filled with groans, sobs, and frenzied curses, but now the sufferers are quiet; not from cessation of pain, but mere exhaustion." Yet the war at this time was a year old.

Even more poignant versions of the same story might be given. The battle of Second Manassas was fought on Friday and Saturday so near Washington that people on housetops in the capital plainly heard the roar of cannon. The field, five miles long and three wide, was thickly strewn with dead and wounded. Pope retreated in confusion, while many in Washington feared the city might be taken. In these circumstances, as late as the following Wednesday one member of the inadequate body of surgeons on the field estimated that two thousand wounded had received no attention. Many had not tasted food for four days; they were actually dying of hunger and thirst. On Friday, a week after the battle began, a correspondent of the New York *Tribune* wrote of heart-rending scenes as the doctors searched among heaps of putrefying dead for men yet clinging to life—men who, if anyone approached, would cry: "Doctor, come to *me*; you look like a kind man; for God's sake, come to *me*." Let anyone who would understand what a great battle means, not in cheap pageantry and empty glory, but in agony and despair, turn to the pages in *Battles and Leaders* where General John D. Imboden describes the sufferings of the Confederate wounded after Gettysburg as they were transported back into Maryland.

The pain and anguish, the callous neglect, the needless loss of life, would have been far greater but for the heroic labors of the Sanitary Commission. Its leaders, agents, and doctors, few at first and inadequately financed, toiled indefatigably. According to the lights of their day, as Dr. Maxwell shows, they put a scientific temper into their exertions; their reports probed to the bottom of error and inefficiency; their recommendations struck basic principles in advance of their time. They accomplished their great results, as he also shows, not merely without proper government cooperation, but in the face of much government opposition. The generals in the field, quickly learning how unselfish and efficient their efforts were, raised a unanimous chorus of praise. Not a single leader of high rank withheld his commendation; not one officer so placed as to judge expertly of the Commission's work ever criticized it. Yet the War Department under Stanton continually impeded it. One of the unhappiest pages of Civil War history is that which records how Stanton, out of mere jealous prejudice, accomplished the downfall of Surgeon-General Hammond, who had been appointed at the instance of the Commission, and who had wrought an almost superhuman renovation of medical work in the Army. Other unhappy pages record his neglect and indifference in dealing with one of the most admirable creations of the war period.

For the Commission became an instrumentality in which Americans might well take the deepest pride. It was by 1864 the most powerful organization for lessening the horrors and reducing the losses of war which mankind had thus far produced. It was the forerunner, and to some extent the parent, of the American Red Cross. Its influence for the betterment of hospitals, nursing, and medical and surgical practice was felt long after the war ended. It did not a little, as its historian indicates, to nourish among Americans a more national spirit. Altogether, Dr. Maxwell, putting his own consecration of spirit into a task prosecuted against many disadvantages, has an almost epic story to tell.

ALLAN NEVINS

Contents

Introduction

A WORD about the files of the Sanitary Commission. Much pertinent material in the letter press books is still available. Back in the sixties and seventies clerks folded the letters written to the commission, put them in legal envelopes, labeled and numbered them; the clerks put about there hundred letters in each box. Because many boxes are falling to pieces, the numbered order is frequently meaningless. I found that a much surer way of checking references was to note the box number, the writer's name, the person to whom it was sent, and the date and place of writing; these facts are generally written in a large hand on the front of the envelope, together with a synopsis of the contents; this simplifies the job of examining masses of manuscript. The Bellows Collection (Boxes 638–42) is arranged alphabetically; in the other boxes letters are generally ordered according to the day of week and month. Microfilm proved especially valuable in examining immense collections; all that I gathered have been turned over to the Butler Library at Columbia University.

I wish to thank Mr. Robert Hill, Mr. Wilmer Leach, and Mr. Edward Morrison of the Manuscript Room in the New York Library for their help. Mrs. Mary B. Corning sent me microfilm of letters in the Bellows Collection at the Massachusetts Historical Society. Frederick Law Olmsted, Jr., let me see his father's papers for the Civil War years. Mrs. W. Crosby Roper and Mrs. Helen Bullock at the Library of Congress and Mrs. Helene Maxwell Hooker at the Huntington Library made it possible to dress this account with more than the bones of official transactions. By the help of Mrs. Henry Royal of Plymouth and Mr. Gersham Bradford of Washington I was able to examine the papers of F. N. Knapp. Miss Amy Steiner let me read the diaries and letters of her father, Dr. L. H. Steiner; these manuscripts are now the possessions of the Maryland Historical Society. At the Pennsylvania Historical Society I read the letters of C. J. Stillé and H. H. Furness; at the New York Historical Society I examined the A. J.

Bloor diaries and the Schuyler-Post correspondence. Mrs. Thorn-dike H. Endicott of Boston let me use the printed documents of her father, Dr. H. W. Bellows.

My debt to Professor Allan Nevins is large. Professors Henry Steele Commager and Richard Morris read and criticized my manuscript. The staffs at the New York Medical Association, the Butler Library of Columbia University, and Peabody Library of Baltimore, and the Medical Library of Johns Hopkins University were generous of time and interest in my behalf. Those who brought pertinent items to my attention were Messrs. Walter Plasted, James Rawley, Donald Bigelow, Richard Lowitt, Harry Wurtz, Joseph Raymond, A. H. Sulzberger of the New York *Times*, James Heslin, and Miss Helen Dunlop. To thank Dr. Alvin Johnson properly calls for a special tribute impossible to give in this brief space. Agnes and Sigrid de Lima were a steady source of encouragement. I profited from Miss Virginia Ackerley's warmth of friendship and advice. Without the aid of Miss Mary A. Reilly my life would have been a trial. What saints are to believers Miss Reilly is to the overwhelmed student.

A fellowship from the Social Science Research Council enabled me to study the history of medicine at Johns Hopkins University. By a grant from the John Simon Guggenheim Foundation I have been able to conclude this study.

WILLIAM QUENTIN MAXWELL

Williamsburg, Virginia
June, 1954

CHAPTER I

Making and Testing the Fifth Wheel

- 1 -

ON January 9, 1861, the Rev. Dr. Henry Whitney Bellows,* minister of All Souls Church Unitarian in New
York, wrote to his son Russell, a student at Harvard: " . . .
we can think of nothing else! *Nothing* is interesting but *the
papers,* and every night and morning I take them up eagerly
and carefully to see whether we have a country or not!" [1]
Republican victory in the election of 1860, Southern secession
and the formation of a Southern confederacy, Lincoln's in-
auguration, and the attack on Fort Sumter on April 12, 1861,
spelled civil war. The president called for 75,000 troops to
quell the rebellion. Emergency demanded participation of
all. Swept into action, women formed soldiers' aid societies to
cheer the recruit and furnish him comforts and necessities.
The first organization of that kind appeared at Bridgeport,
Connecticut, on April 15; similar groups sprang up at Lowell
and Charlestown, Massachusetts; Cleveland, Ohio, established what became a large and flourishing aid society, on
April 19.

This desire to succor soldiers in camp and field held Bellows' attention. Without concert of effort and a clear idea of
common goals these devoted women might waste their zeal
and produce as much harm as good from their excitement.

---

* Asterisk after a name means see Biographical Notes, which follow the
text.

[1] Bellows MSS. H. W. Bellows to R. Bellows, Jan. 9, 1861, New York.

1

As pastor of All Souls Unitarian Church, Bellows discussed the need for giving their enthusiasm a focus. He spoke in ringing tones, and his face and body could express a range of emotion; his manners ever cordial, Bellows represented good-fellowship with a sense of duty.

It was twelve o'clock on April 25, 1861. Bellows stepped out of the vestry, and met Dr. Elisha Harris.* Together they went to the New York Infirmary for Women. Some fifty or sixty women were meeting here to discuss ways and means of helping the soldiers. Bellows was called to the chair, and did most of the talking. He called for a general association of New York City and its neighborhood; he would invite all churches, schools, and aid societies to cooperate in the systematic work of supply. He drew up an address summoning the women of New York to meet at Cooper Institute on April 29; ninety-one of the most influential women signed it. After many conferences he drew up the constitution of what became the Woman's Central Association of Relief, secured a presiding officer and speaker, and arranged the order of business. When the meeting took place, Bellows met no opposition in calling it to order, nominating the committees, and reporting the constitution.

Women from city and country successfully launched the Woman's Central Association of Relief. From the outset it encountered petty jealousies in and around New York. Pride of locality took fright. Why should the little fishes of the sea enter the belly of a whale? The Woman's Central Association also suffered defeat when it tried to establish a connection with the army. At a conference Dr. R. C. Satterlee, military medical purveyor in New York, rebuffed Bellows' proposals. Bellows knew nothing of the ways of thinking in the medical corps and its habit of deprecating civilian help. Dr. Satterlee doubtless believed that the role of the public in giving relief to the army would be negligible. His small-scale experience on the Wisconsin frontier, in Florida, and in the Mexican

War had taught him the unimportance of civilians in succoring troops. Satterlee insisted that errands of mercy would inevitably prove troublesome. Love of novelty had joined with public anxiety to brew a sentimental storm, he thought, but the realities of drudgery and care would dispel their gusty enthusiasm. The best the Medical Bureau could do was to humor a fad and speed it to nothingness.

This conference left Bellows considerably flattened. The Woman's Central Association saved him from dropping the work as a fruitless duplication of government functions. Pressing needs were demanding satisfaction. Questions arose that proved futile; lint, for instance, exercised the public, but experience proved that almost anything was good enough for bandaging. But the possibility that lint might be important made supply organizations seek a satisfactory working basis with the government. Nurses were a more fundamental problem. Their training under Dr. Elizabeth Blackwell had been one of the original objectives of the Woman's Central Association. Would the government receive their nurses? What wages were to be paid them? Who would pay the transportation costs of applicants?

Washington had no answers to these questions. It did not know what supplies would be needed or in what quantity; it made no provision for suitable cooks in the regiments; it neglected the medical inspection of recruits. New York supply organizations joined forces. They chose a joint committee, whose members were Dr. Bellows and Dr. Harris, of the Woman's Central Association of Relief, Dr. W. H. Van Buren, of the Physicians and Surgeons of the New York Hospitals, and Dr. Jacob Harsen, of the Lint and Bandage Association. These four set out for Washington to learn at first hand what could be done. Bellows noted: "I hope I may do some good. At any rate, I shall see *some fun*, and perhaps something that won't be so *funny*; but I apprehend no peril." [2]

[2] Bellows MSS. H. W. Bellows to his sister, May 15, 1861, New York.

- 2 -

The train of May 15 was the first to leave New York for Washington after the Baltimore riots of April 19, when mobs had stoned Northern troops en route to the capital. (Maryland, though shaken by disloyalty, remained true to the Union.) There was much for the committeemen to talk about. Secession had flown from the grumbling hive of politics along with a horde of Southern drones. Valuable men like Colonel Robert E. Lee were leaving the United States Army to join the Confederacy. Washington was left to the incoming swarm of motley Republicans. Critics complained that the mood of compromise and procrastination made it impossible for the capital to understand the vigor of Northern temper. Greatness had been thrust upon the Republican party, but where was the resolute leadership? Leaders lacked energy and youth. Generals Scott and Wool were over seventy. Men who were anything but young made up the cabinet. Lincoln remained an unknown quantity. Those who knew him said the president was better fitted for crisis than carpers gave him credit for.

The committeemen talked about making war a little more tolerable by safeguarding military health. Citizen soldiery knew nothing about war and its rigors. The recruit's enthusiasm and recklessness revealed the spirit of the time; but personal independence, self-reliance, and ignorance counted as liabilities in a military machine. The recruit became easy prey to disease. The Medical Bureau could not meet the problems of sanitation and hygiene in an army numbering 75,000. Enlisted men traveled miles in cattle cars; they lacked even the crudest accommodations for human comfort; they found no preparations to receive them at their destination. Rations were often unwholesome and distasteful. Shoddy blankets were known to cover beds of rotting straw. The disease rate was beginning to rise, but the government was helpless to provide adequate precautions.

How could Americans best profit from the example of Crimea? asked the committeemen. The Crimean War (1854–56) disclosed the horrors attending inadequate preparation. Parliamentary investigations and newspaper accounts taught the public that it could not expect soldiers to fight on a defective diet. Doom befell offenders of the laws of health and sanitation. In April, 1856, the British Army had numbered 111,313, in officers and men. At the seat of war the total mortality came to 20,899—2,755 were killed in action; 2,019 died of wounds. Approximately one out of 4.6 lost his life; nearly 5,705 were discharged for disabilities. Losses from disease approached 16,323. Of this mortality 65 per cent took place in the first seven months, from September, 1854, to March, 1855. In July, August, and September, 1854 the death rate was 293 out of every 1,000. At one time more soldiers were in the hospitals than on duty.

Great Britain met disaster with measures of reform. The secretary of state gave broad scope to his instructions to the British Sanitary Commission. The issuance of orders was not enough, he said, for the point was to see them carried out. Few wars had heroes comparable to Florence Nightingale. She and her unit of thirty-eight nurses had established a new kind of war hospital at Balaklava and Scutari. Strict in discipline, Miss Nightingale was famous for cutting red tape and defeating entrenched opposition. The British Sanitary Commission had also produced astonishing results. With the establishment of sanitary operations in Crimea the death rate dropped to 250 out of every 1000 in May, June, July, 1855; by Janury, 1856, only 25 out of every 1000 were lost.

The four committeemen from New York debated plans. Bellows later recalled: "Dr. Harris says that the first idea of a Sanitary Commission, which certainly had not entered my

head when we left New York, was started between us in the
cars twixt Philadelphia and Baltimore—in a long and earnest
conversation . . ." [3]

Would Americans accept the British model with its sweeping powers? There was the rub. Committeemen thought not;
but they knew their countrymen would look kindly on the
use of persuasion and moral force to move official mountains.
The Crimea had dramatized the problem of sanitation; the
public seemed ready to profit from its experiences. The
Crimea illuminated other factors, such as military inflexibil-
ity, helplessness in the medical corps, and obstacles created
by official jealousy.

After some thirteen hours the train reached Washington
on May 16. The next day the committee visited Miss Dorothea Dix, superintendent of nurses. She was depressed. The
sick lacked nurses and provisions. Her absorption in duty
approached total self-sacrifice. Colonel (or Dr.) Wood,* the
acting surgeon general, was apathetic. The Medical Bureau
seemed unaware of the great crisis. At headquarters General
Scott, a corpulent model of military deportment, suggested
Dickens' Mr. Turveydrop; for, although he lay on a couch
quite unwell, he insisted on greeting the committee, and
called two aides to help hoist him to his feet. After courte-
ously hearing them, he promised to issue an order weeding
out recruits unfit for duty; but his command was never fully
carried out.

Never before had Bellows felt the impact of official Washington. He liked it. The flash of bayonets, sword knots, and
gaudy uniforms could not overawe one whose white cravat
carried the fame of his respectability. Statesmen considered
the committee of first importance; wealth, influence, and
fame bowed to let it take precedence. Civilian and military
listened respectfully, while Bellows harangued president,
cabinet, and generals. Lincoln lacked dignity and the nec-

[3] Bellows MSS. H. W. Bellows to C. J. Stillé, Nov. 15, 1865, New York.

essary presence to assure popular confidence, thought Bellows. His smile sweet, his mind patient, slow and firm, President Lincoln wanted largeness to his thinking. Appearance had caught Bellows in its snares. Secretary of State Seward looked "cunning, not frank, not gentlemanly"; Secretary of War Cameron seemed the most direct and businesslike; Secretary of the Treasury Chase apparently had a mental breadth and positive outlook that set him above his colleagues in morals and manners.

In a second session with Colonel Wood the committee broached the idea of setting up a sanitary commission. At first they tried to form an agreement between the New York organizations and the Medical Bureau; they asked Wood to admit that the bureau needed the intelligent and popular support which only a commission could supply. He knew nothing about this kind of device; there was no precedent for it in America. He refused to countenance this innovation. But that which had made him stubborn had given them drive; the committeemen pressed their demands with vigor.

Bellows composed a letter antedated May 18; it asked for the creation of a body of mixed civilians. Wood sent a supporting letter to Secretary Cameron, calling for a "Commission of Inquiry and Advice in respect of the Sanitary Interests of the United States Forces," on May 22. It would act as an adviser to the government. New York philanthropists and Miss Dix backed the scheme. The *Evening Post* urged its support, and later reported Washington in favor of it. The New York committee was obliged to stay in the capital more than a week. They had clearly worn out their welcome. Officialdom treated them like an ill-fated band of hope; the delays of office seemed never ending. Before the new body could be organized certain officers had to sign an executive order. Committeemen learned to bide their time, while the War Department gave its attention to others.

June 9 brought the reward of patience, when Cameron wrote out the order.

It rested on Lincoln's desk four days later. He showed no eagerness in signing. A novelty like this might become "a fifth wheel to the coach," he said. His skepticism spoke for officialdom. Neither good nor bad could come from this group. Destiny would give it a short life; at the end of its span this commission of inquiry and advice would stand in monumental mockery of well-intentioned philanthropists and silly women. President Lincoln wrote on the order: "I approve the above."

The Medical Bureau now viewed the Sanitary Commission with suspicion. Surgeon General Lawson had died. Dr. Wood stepped aside, and Dr. Clement Alexander Finley,* the next in line according to seniority, assumed leadership. Finley frowned on innovations. What saved the commission was his belief that volunteers would not make good soldiers. He gave approval only after receiving assurance that the commission would confine its activities to them and the navy. So the commission found itself excluded from the small regular army. The navy called on it only when stores were needed on the Mississippi River.

- 3 -

At their first meeting the commissioners elected Bellows president on June 12, 1861. Presiding over the meetings, he gave unity, method, and practical success to their counsels. Alexander Dallas Bache was chosen vice-president, and George Templeton Strong treasurer. Other members were George Washington Cullum, Alexander Eakins Shiras, Robert Crooke Wood, John Strong Newberry, William Holme Van Buren, Cornelius Rea Agnew, Oliver Wolcott Gibbs, Elisha Harris, Samuel Gridley Howe, Thomas March Clark, Joshua Huntington Wolcott, Mark Skinner, Ezra Butler McCagg,

John Healey Heywood, Theodore S. Bell, Charles Janeway Stillé, Fairman Rogers, and Horace Binney, Jr.* Those who received invitations but did not join the commission were the Hon. Joseph Holt, Dr. Jeffrey Wyman, and R. W. Burnett.

The executive order creating the Sanitary Commission gave no indication of its possibilities. Had its members been literal, the commission would probably have remained a body of inquiry and device. Bellows saw a "majesty" about its development. The commission, he said, moved according to a plan, one "based on the best study, the most devoted analysis of the facts, the most cautious and anxious regard to the laws of human nature." As it strove to do "the most good with the least pain," the commission became "a great governmental department." There was more to do than supplement the unavoidable defects of the Medical Bureau; the commission must also increase and improve the regular supplies and methods of the bureau. So the commission sent agents and stores to about five hundred bloody encounters; it developed relief corps for camp, battlefield, and hospital; it organized not less than seven thousand aid societies and from them drew various stores; it set up lodges where exhausted or convalescent soldiers could find a meal and a night's rest; it placed feeding stations on the route from battlefield to base hospital; it helped the veteran get his back pay; it kept the wounded soldier in touch with his family and friends through its directory; it distributed among the army surgeons medical and surgical monographs on recent advances in medicine.

Yet these were merely the outer show of the commission's work. The majority of men thought its internal machinery a "mystery," because it was "invisible"; few had the patience to understand the implications of Sanitary actions. Bellows said: ". . . all . . . local, state and other efforts of a benevolent sort are . . . mere trifles, ephemeral and inconstant efforts without method or philosophy as compared with our plan." They despised the Sanitary Commission for its fore-sight and caution, although their rush to do good often pro-duced confusion and harm. Bellows denied boasting when he said: "Our plans have a breadth and height and depth which no similar military philanthropic undertaking ever had, since the world began." [4]

Only men of highest intelligence could presumably under-stand the Sanitary Commission, its "scientific basis" and its "profound regard for politico-economic principles on which . . . a humane work must proceed." One of the elect was Frederick Law Olmsted. [*] Short, slight, and in his late thirties, Olmsted walked with a slight limp. Europe and America already recognized his books on the South prior to the Civil War as classics. Later generations have usually accepted Olmsted as a landscape architect; for his chief concern was the study of landscape and "its potentialities for advancing human morality and happiness." "The Yosemite Valley and the Mariposa Big Tree Grove (1865)," his preliminary report to the California legislature, "formulated a philosophic base for the creation of state and national parks." [5]

Throughout the war Olmsted demanded the dissolution of slaveholding as a social foundation. In the spring of 1861 he was "pining" to find his "mission." His training fitted him to manage the Negroes who had fled to Union lines and were caught in a "limbo" between slavery and freedom. As one of the landscape architects of Central Park, Olmsted had helped superintend some fifteen thousand workingmen; but in the summer of 1861 he became secretary general of the Sanitary Commission. Here he performed "his most impor-tant single public service," shaping the Sanitary machine and filling it with his drive. Bellows readily admitted that the Sanitary Commission would have died without Olmsted's "power of organization, his influence with his subordinates,

[4] Box 608. H. W. Bellows to R. B. Swain, Oct. 31, 1862, New York.
[5] *Landscape and Architecture*, Vol. XLIII, No. 1, pp. 12–13.

his experience in great undertakings, and his extraordinary powers of concentrated attention."

There were times when Olmsted worked "every night and all night." His letters were often voluminous and not always clear. He confessed:

I am an exceedingly labored and poor writer. I cannot write what I have thought. Writing is a laborious process of judgment with me. I never know quite what I think until I act, or write action." [6]

Olmsted not battling for his convictions would not have been Olmsted. He refused to compromise with popular prejudice. Philanthropic persons criticized the commission for paying its employees. Olmsted answered with a question: "How long could the war be carried on upon the theory that voluntary and unpaid services are the best or that a patriotic spirit is the best security of discipline?" For the daily performance of Sanitary business he insisted on "getting the best available talent and paying the market price for it." [7]

In theory the commission [8] enjoyed an intimate footing with the government, sharing observations. It chose to work through the Medical Bureau, because the interests of the two groups were identical. The soldier as a fighting unit concerned the bureau; the commission wanted to form a link between the recruit and the rest of the country, and to do the things the bureau could not perform. For both organizations to function properly meant that the one required the confidence of the other. The commission, moreover, stretched the meaning of relief to spare the government any extra burdens. To maintain military efficiency the commission acted

[6] Box 914, Vol. I, letter 268. F. L. Olmsted to J. S. Newberry, Nov. 5, 1862, New York.
[7] Olmsted MSS. F. L. Olmsted to Judge Mark Skinner, Nov. 25, 1862, Washington, D.C.
[8] For a description of the organization see Chapter XIV.

as public distributing agent; it also listened to the questionings of anxious friends and relations of soldiers. To secure greater cooperation Dr. Elisha Harris took care to approach Surgeon General Finley in July, 1861. He failed in his mission. As a person he pleased Finley, but the surgeon general never showed a spark of liking the other commissioners.

The Medical Bureau was averse to the language of sweet reasonableness while contemplating the object of its detestation. Preening and strutting in borrowed feathers, the upstart commission hawked its claims to sanitary light and boasted of cutting red tape! The Medical Bureau would not tolerate questioning or even implied criticism from this singular creature which bore no resemblance to any other governmental agency. It was like the bastard in the royal family; unable to enforce his rights, he must depend on the good will of others. But did the Sanitary Commission have any worth? None, for it could only be a nuisance.

Others before Finley had set the bureau's tone. The bureau had satisfied the peacetime needs of 15,000 men; its personnel largely included a surgeon general and twenty-six surgeons. Many of these were incapacitated, while one-third were unfit for service. To attract young doctors Congress had created the post of assistant surgeon in 1834. Finley apparently did little to change the bureau. Fearing the Sanitary Commission as a mischiefmaker, he did everything to make anxiety a reality. He refused the commission confidential footing, rejecting its counsels and offers of cooperation. The Sanitary Commission could assume no role but that of critic.

The difficulty, thought Bellows, boiled down to Finley's vanity, obstinacy, and conceit, his "conscientious narrowness and well-intentioned weakness." The surgeon general blocked plans that had been based on "the largest European experience, commended by the medical intelligence and the humane feeling of the great centres of knowledge and philanthropy throughout this whole country, and involving the lives and comforts of so many of our citizen soldiery." Finley was wed to the small scope of his service, clinging to antiquated ideas and procedures; death alone could part him from his love of settled arrangements and prejudice against change. Without medical reputation, the surgeon general was too old to win it, thought the commissioners.

They worked as closely as possible with the medical directors of the various armies. As General McClellan's medical director, Surgeon Charles Stuart Tripler * was important; but he too took an exaggerated pride in the prerogatives and privileges of military position. Both Finley and Tripler seemed to follow the tradition of Sir John Hall and Dr. Menzies, the British medical directors at Crimea. The Sanitary Commission was not the only critic of the bureau; other agencies thought it the most inefficient and ineffective of divisions in the War Department. Neither Finley nor Tripler could strike out alone, but abided by the letter that killed. They failed to understand the Unicorn's advice on cutting Looking-Glass cake: "Hand it round first, and cut it afterwards."

- 4 -

To the commission the journey between New York and Washington ran on rails of monotony. Changing seasons brought little variety. Winter turned the countryside into a flood of dreariness; summer meant the addition of dust to humidity. The crowded rowdy trip strengthened the commuter's stoicism, for he must endure the constant change from cars to ferryboats and back to cars. Then there was Washington. Crossing the muddy streets in winter coated one's boots and called for a bootblack's "assiduous attentions." Summer swarmed with flies, mosquitoes, crowds, and bad smells.

Sanitary headquarters at the Treasury Building was a large room. It held a long green-covered table and chairs ranged in order; a neat pile of stationery was set before each place. For George Strong the sight was enough to produce "sensations of dignity and red tapery." The commissioners stayed in these crowded quarters until October, when the government rented them the three-story Adams house at 244 F Street and a storehouse.

At board meetings the commissioners discussed organizational matters, formed general policies, and made decisions. Mrs. Henry Whitney Bellows remembered the first two weeks of Sanitary existence, when the commissioners met day and evening. She wrote: "The business itself is inspiring, but the accessories of battle, camp bed, dyspepsia, crackers . . . canteen men pulling constantly at our door bell belong less to the heroic and more to the irritating and self-seeking and annoying order of things." [9] Frequently some of the commissioners performed special services, but they were never obliged to follow prescribed duties. The commissioners rather looked to others for leadership. For a while their gospel was Olmsted, but long before the end of the war they were leaning on the executive committee.

In the classical lines of the federal buildings loyal Americans found the fullness and promise of grandeur they wished their country to embody. Commissioner Strong especially admired the Capitol's marbles and frescoes, but the paintings in the rotunda and the Mills equestrian statue of Jackson he would have thrown to the Confederacy. To a Marylander like Dr. Lewis Henry Steiner,* Washington was a stupid place. Who and where were its old families? The city mirrored national slovenliness. Olmsted saw the reflection of frontier indifference and the laziness of a slave society. The capital looked down at the heels, and for this Americans paid in loss of prestige abroad. A visitor saw the government

---

[9] Bellows MSS. Mrs. H. W. Bellows to Russell Bellows, June 23, 1861, New York.

buildings—those symbols of "moral grandeur of a great republic"—from the "unmitigated shabbiness and filth of the unsewered, unpaved, unpoliced streets of a collocation of houses," whose owners were powerless to remedy the evil. The total effect was an offense to good taste, "like precious stones on dirty hands."

What could have been more slipshod than the new Republican president and his Dickensian Congress? The sight of that lanky figure strolling with a couple of "loafers" was too much for Olmsted. Dressed in a cheap suit, Lincoln's person bore no connotations of great office. Olmsted's companion made a joke at the president's expense. Lincoln overheard the quip and "turned and laughed familiarly."

Congress, a group of poor provincial lawyers, developed the fugue of slovenliness. With no sizable practice, these men worked hard at lawmaking; they did nothing thoroughly and showed no signs of vigorous training; they depended on being shrewd, wary, decisive, and always open to anybody and anything. These public servants regarded all business alike. Petty or important, no matter; everything they squeezed helter-skelter into their calendars. Olmsted watched the chairman of an important committee leave his colleagues to talk with a visitor. The chairman spoke with conviction; but, expressing contrary views, the visitor said his own information was better founded. The chairman returned to committee. Five minutes later he rose and presented the visitor's argument as his own carefully reasoned opinion; his was the "official report from opportunities and duties of his chairmanship." Members of lobbies and interested citizens oppressed Congress, thought Olmsted; lawmakers got rid of these beasts of prey by tossing out promises with shameful carelessness. Congressmen lacked breadth of experience. New Englanders were apt to be reserved and silent. New Yorkers were sloppy and of little use to the Sanitary Commission; Senator Preston King did not study, but made the most of what he knew. Westerners were generally ill tempered and jealously local. Pennsylvanians were out for special interests. As ignorant as they were self-assured, Congressmen were fitful in discipline and consequently unreliable; their administration was irregular, lax, and feeble.

Olmsted observed: "Nothing was more evident during the whole war than that the members of Congress and most of the popular leaders never trod on any firm ground of conviction about the popular character." Too few of the most responsible officials knew the alphabet of administration. They treated administrative and executive as one and the same. Vague ideas floated in their minds about the "relations of authority and responsibility, of assignments of duty and accountability with reference to given assignments." Was there no "Euclid of Administrative Science"? Was there no axiom that read: "As is the measure of free will, so is the measure of responsibility" and its corollary: "In proportion as free will (authority or discretion) is restrained, responsibility is reduced"? But Americans cared little about fitness for office; they paid almost no attention to men who served ably in minor but important offices.[10]

Uncouth Washington was also a city of ease and informality. Summer band concerts made a difference for an hour and a half on Sunday afternoons. Average men watched the great and near great move among tides of mediocrities. Washington was the worst place in the world for ministers, thought Bellows. Sunday morning found lawmakers stuffing their bellies, when their souls should have been sharing a love feast. "Really the capital seems about the last place for seeing anything in a large way," said Bellows. "Things are

[10] Olmsted MSS. From "Notes on American Civilization," Mariposa, Calif., Private Book 226, F. L. Olmsted to Hurlburt, Jan. 31, 1863, Washington, D.C.

too much under your nose, and I am too busy with my own concerns to attend much to the people or the things which with more leisure I might see and enjoy." [11] Complaints reached the commission that the moral tone of the capital was suffering. Freed from home restraints, the citizen soldier was profane and obscene, swaggering and drunken, truculent and turbulent. Respectability could not pass him without a shudder. Would any good come out of Washington? Olmsted could find no great men, heroes, and philosophers, only the "mysterious strength of the free unenlightened people," to carry the Union through crisis.

- 5 -

The national government left the problems of raising and equipping troops to the states. State rights made discipline hard to achieve, especially with three-month enlistments. Training was almost impossible; federal supervision began when regiments had filled their quotas and were on the way to camp or firing line. Governors chose regimental and company officers, generally selecting those who would be helpful politically. Green at war, too many officers were self-seekers, their epaulettes covering carelessness and ignorance. They felt superior to *Army Regulations*. This military venture was temporary, they reasoned. Why take the trouble to master information they would never use again? Few officers knew more of their duties than they had learned in the peacetime militia. The captain, "the father of his company," went to the field unpracticed in his duties.

The citizen soldier hated to take orders, while his officer issued them with reluctance. A self-reliant private felt little respect for his superiors, whose extremes of domineering and easy familiarity made for weak discipline. Election of officers

[11] Bellows MSS. H. W. Bellows to R. Bellows, Jan. 12, 1864, Washington, D.C.

to fill vacancies set popularity before ability; the newly chosen captain fresh from village politics still looked like a hayseed to his men. Olmsted sensed an inherent weakness in army structure, but military authorities put off any criticism. Only through painful experience could men be taught, they told Olmsted. The Sanitary Commission soon learned that individual state action led to confusion and waste of energy. To avoid duplication, needless expenditure, and bad hygienic conditions, Sanitary leaders stressed strong central direction.

The human material assembled at Washington ought to make an admirable army, thought the commissioners. "Severely disjointed regiments" camped under canvas. Sanitary inspectors east and west reported stinking sinks, no sewage disposal, imperfect drainage, inadequate tents, bad discipline, no camp police, drunkenness, personal uncleanliness, overcrowding, clothing of bad quality, inadequate diet, and few trained cooks. To the Sanitary Commission these conditions confessed national uncertainty and unpreparedness.

Officialdom expressed interest in the commission, but almost no one gave it serious consideration. Government representatives on the commission gave scarcely five seconds to what demanded five hours' attention; they did little more than obstruct and discourage. Military men ignored Sanitary advice. Since sanitary improvement could only come with stricter discipline, the commission asked for power to enforce its decisions. It went before the Senate military affairs committee with a bill, providing that rations be given Sanitary inspectors stationed in or near camp and requiring officers either to comply with recommendations or assign reasons for not doing so. The president and the secretary of the commission would receive franking privileges. This last was enough to kill the bill, said Strong; but Senators Wilson, King, and Rice expressed such enthusiasm that they wanted to suspend any officer who refused to obey Sanitary commands. The commissioners protested against this "prerogative of mis-chiefmaking."

The bill met no opposition on initial passage; but it gave umbrage to military and medical officers, who launched their attack in mid-July, when the commissioners had left Washington and could not counterattack. Senator Wilson now refused to support a bill so offensive to the Medical Bureau. The commissioners set the senator down as a double-dealer. Eventually Olmsted placed him among abolitionist fence-jumpers, and liars, and "infernal gamblers" of armies. Only Samuel Gridley Howe tried to explain his position. Honest and earnest, Wilson was "very impressionable." The bureau had seized on this quality so admirably that he had given up the commission as useless.

Foe and friend stood boldly etched. In this experience President Lincoln and Quartermaster Meigs spoke of the commission with sympathy. On July 21 the commission advised providing comfortable accommodations for incoming and outgoing soldiers near the Washington railroad station, employing competent cooks in the army, issuing large quantities of fresh vegetables, and setting up an allotment system; but the government acted on none of this advice.

- 6 -

On Arlington Heights, General McDowell commanded some 35,000 men in five divisions. The thought of advancing on Richmond made men overoptimistic, thought Olmsted. Short of ambulances and stores, Surgeons W. S. King, medical director, and Dr. Magruder, his assistant, met problems by improvisation. Lacking power of enforcement, they could not make the surgeon of one state accept casualties from another state.

Federals and Confederates clashed at Manassas or Bull Run on July 21. Surgeons worked in an individual manner, the results of their toils understandably small. King packed instruments, dressings, and stimulants in his saddlebags, and used them to restrain hemorrhage and relieve exhaustion and suffering. The soldier usually received surgical attention on the spot where the wound was received. Surgeons made hospitals of Sedley Church, nearby houses, and barns. The wounded who failed to find shelter took refuge in groves and ravines.

Union defeat came at five o'clock in the afternoon. Fleeing soldiers, horses, and vehicles jammed the road back to Washington. The panic-stricken swirled past overturned wagons and their spilled contents. Vigorous officers fled on horses or in ambulances, leaving most of the wounded on the field. Caught in the retreat, Dr. King was unable to make provision for them. Union doctors who remained with the wounded were sent to Richmond as prisoners. The Confederacy released them later in 1861, and they returned home. The foe had clashed with one-eighth of the Union Army, and had killed 483. The list of the missing was large. Bull Run proved that an armed mob did not make an army; it showed that the individual exertions of doctors could not make a medical corps.

The commissioners feared for the safety of Washington, while Olmsted wandered through the streets of woe. Men at dawn slept on pavements, doorsteps, and in gutters; there they lay without blankets or overcoats. Those awake clustered together, "pale, grimy, with bloodshot eyes, unshaven, unkempt, sullen, fierce, feverish, weak, and ravenous . . ." They were wearing parts of different uniforms, soiled and dank with dew. No arms, no officers, these men who had been soldiers tore down fences to build fires and boil coffee "in black and battered vessels." Some sat bowed and silent in rows along the curb; others went from house to house begging for food. In striking contrast, the officers had flocked to Willard's Hotel. A few were ragged, dirty, or else drunk.

Occasionally one would display a bandage. His arm in a sling gave his body the excuse to occupy an entire sofa. None seemed to know the whereabouts of his regiment; none seemed to care. An officer of different character had spent the night in camp. His men were close to collapse; getting them food and supplies was his concern. But taken as a whole, concluded Olmsted, the breed of officers was mean and brutish.

The Sanitary Commission prepared seventy-five questions on the conditions of soldiers before, during, and after Bull Run. Seven inspectors examined thirty bodies of troops. Their findings formed the basis of Olmsted's *Report on the Demoralization of the Volunteers*, a scathing indictment of the Republican administration. Carelessly distributed rations, the needless waste of strength by marching four to twelve miles at double-quick time, indifference brought on by fatigue, heat, and no food and drink, and a general lack of confidence in the officers—all these points arranged themselves in a pattern of defeat. The soldiers had fought in "the most elementary and imperfect military organization"; their discipline was "little better than a mob" which did not know its leaders. They mistakenly believed the enemy superior in skill and numbers. False news spread about the size of Confederate reserves coming into battle; then panic ripped to tatters the shoddy military fabric, and the chickens of incapacity flew back to roost in Washington. Indolent, frivolous, and dissipated, they had learned nothing from disaster.

During the rout the soldiers felt no terror, but mocked and jeered at their officers. It was later that dejection set in. The New York Zouaves were the most demoralized. They had suffered exposure, fatigue, and exhaustion, and had never been paid. These reasons failed to account for their total collapse, thought Olmsted. He knew the Zouaves for hardiness, bravery, devotion, and self-sacrifice. In the light of defeat people saw only the absence of those qualities.

Everyone praised Rhode Island's 2nd Regiment, whose soldiers had good lodgings, clothes, and a variety of food; they enjoyed an excellent band, singing, dancing, social and athletic recreations; they observed daily religious ceremonies; they were known for the important names among their visitors. Rhode Islanders at Bull Run suffered with the rest, but retreated in good order.

What was the basic reason for demoralization? asked Olmsted. The citizen had identified his government with his country. He had offered his services with little thought of remuneration. Washington owed him suitable food and lodging; it was obliged to care for him sick or wounded. But what was the volunteer's lot? Hard bread and salt pork, green coffee, a shoddy blanket, and the damp earth to lie on. In the hospital the surgeon left him to the care of comrades, who generally refused to add nursing to their military duties. The recruit had come to the army expecting to fight a battle at once. Waiting became tedious and irksome. There was nothing to do but the "eternal" manual of arms and guard duty. Because he had answered his captain's insults, the recruit was set to work in filth. In one instance, noted Olmsted, the colonel kept his men at attention for one hour in the hottest summer sun, while he stood drinking at the bar of Willard's Hotel. Before electing their officers volunteers had no previous way of knowing that their captain was a "blackguard and a petty tyrant," their colonel a "politician," their surgeon a "quack," and their quartermaster a "knave." For lack of sports, the soldier chose the saloon; here he could give vent to his anger and escape into daydreams. When the drums began to roll, the army shoved an antiquated musket into his hands, and ordered him off to war. "War?" sneered Olmsted. "War without artillery and without cavalry?"

Simple appreciation of the citizen in uniform meant fair returns in regular rations, good blankets, and at least clean

straw for mattresses. For its own self-interest and self-pres-
ervation the government must treat him better than cattle.
As it was, neglect had made the volunteer "soul sick." The
Sanitary Commission had done all in its power to help him.
It requested limiting the number of absences from camp,
only to be told that the colonel knew his business; it suggested setting time limits on leaves of absence and forbidding the bringing of liquor into camp, only to be told that
such orders could not be enforced. In short, the army
snubbed all Sanitary proposals to improve discipline.

Within a week of Bull Run, Olmsted and his staff had thoroughly examined the causes of defeat, carefully preserving
their details and accurately noting their influence. The commissioners knew of no other achievement in history comparable to the *Report on the Demoralization of the Volunteers*; but it was nothing as compared to the shock it gave
them. Olmsted had carried their convictions. Yes, a new set
of imbeciles had moved into Washington, and the American
system of government met disaster poorly; but the commissioners dared not publish this philippic until later. Olmsted
ignored the part of the states in furnishing troops; this he
regarded the exclusive function of the national administration. Olmsted struck the commission's first plea for political
nationalism, meaning a strong central government for a
people living in a given area and conforming to similar cultural patterns.

- 7 -

The United States was in for a long war. On July 24, 1861,
Lincoln called General George Brinton McClellan to Washington to direct the armies. The country sensed relief, as the
slow work of reorganization got under way. McClellan's
remarkable energy increased popular confidence. The commissioners watched him tighten the reins of discipline and

infuse men with hopefulness; they knew that time and a dogged spirit would put the army in fighting trim. Indefatigable, McClellan visited every camp, and received new regiments to expand and strengthen his machine. By drill and review he brought his 50,000 troops a sense of pride. His purpose was to get volunteers to carry out orders, not to act like regulars.

With October came the test at Ball's Bluff, when Union recruits showed themselves better as soldiers than their officers as leaders. The Sanitary Commission at Washington sent hospital stores and blankets at once. Frederick Newman Knapp * and Dr. John Hancock Douglas * saw that the field hospitals were supplied. They gave clothing to soldiers who in the retreat had stripped off their uniforms to swim back across the Potomac. Knapp and Douglas could find no signs of demoralization. Patients in tent hospitals wanted to get well and meet the enemy again. Soldiers who had escaped unharmed were without the Bull Run blues. Lowell and Holmes, those favored sons of New England, were among the casualties. Holmes was well enough to sit up and smoke, but Lowell's wound was so serious that he could not be moved.

To get better officers McClellan reconstructed the general staff. He reminded those who liked to wander about Washington of the duties they owed their commands. His provost marshal closed the Washington saloons. A military commission examined volunteer officers and weeded out incompetents. Resignations of captains and lieutenants were numerous, but few majors and colonels gave up their posts. This examination requirement apparently discouraged indiscriminate appointments, but did not cause wholesale dismissals. During the Civil War there were 2,537 generals and a proportionate number of minor officers; a few hundred dismissals or resignations could not improve discipline. New appointees were not likely to be superior to the displaced. Schemers who became officers by election generally made indifferent leaders. Hard knocks taught soldiers to choose efficient and courageous officers.

Organization of the armies went on slowly in the West. In October, 1861, General W. T. Sherman argued that effective Western defense called for an army of 200,000. Mad! cried the newspapers. The War Department soon relieved Sherman and placed him in a subordinate position. General Don Carlos Buell, his successor, devoted attention to discipline and drill. His nature was studious and reserved; few surpassed Buell's knowledge of the various duties of officers and men. He gave small encouragement to his medical corps; perhaps he thought that soldiers were made for fighting, and anything extra was of no consequence. General Prentiss at Camp Defiance, Cairo, put his men in fighting trim. They had faults and deficiences, noted a Sanitary inspector, but no martinet's strait jacket could throttle the "rollicking independence" of the American soldier.

In September, 1861, the Sanitary Commission congratulated government and country on the forward strides in discipline, morale, health, provisioning, and supply. In December, Olmsted reported good morale in all regiments, except in four that had suffered unduly from Bull Run. The sick list was the key to morale, for a small sick list was associated with high spirits. The army neglected healthful recreation. Gambling was a major attraction for troops left to their own devices; it admitted the sharper and kept the soldier from outside exercise. Only 42 of 200 regiments engaged in sports systematically; 156 had no outdoor recreation, while there were no reports from 2. Out of 200 about one-fifth had libraries, mostly of religious books. Bands were an object of pride; out of 200 regiments, 143 had bands, while 53 were without; there were no reports from 4. To develop sound morale a military band was indispensable, said Olmsted. Soldiers needed one after defeat to restore the esprit de corps; they supported it by a self-imposed tax.

Sutlers were useful, if restricted by *Army Regulations*; but lacking supervision and proper control, they made for weak discipline. Some sutlers and officers formed "corrupt bargains," whereby the sutler made presents of wine to increase his influence. Both were known to engage in the sale of liquor, and so they kept the recruit from sending home his savings. Twelve out of 200 regiments had no sutlers in September and October. Of 188 sutlers 103 were appointed by colonels, 63 by the secretary of war, 14 by a board of regimental officers, 5 by state governors, and 3 by means not ascertained.

The sutler sold liquor in 31 regiments. Its sale was forbidden in 169, but in 177 regiments men had no difficulty in getting wine and spirits. More guilty than the sutler was the pie peddler, whose piecrusts hid a bottle of whisky. Drinking did not necessarily mean drunkenness, which was common in only 6 regiments; in 31 drunkenness occasionally took place; in 163 it was rare. Pay day and shortly after were times of jollity. The American volunteer was generally considered more temperate than the European soldier.

Olmsted defined discipline as "a habit of prompt and exact obedience under certain authority." He took issue with McClellan's double standard; to expect discipline of regulars but a weaker brand from volunteers gave rise to abuse and neglect. Admittedly the army had improved since Bull Run, said Olmsted, but laxity had by no means disappeared. The rewards of strong discipline came in lives saved. Strict enforcement of *Army Regulations* would prevent disease, and do more than the Sanitary Commission could ever propose. But administrative duties burdened the officers, who worked without clerical help, and frequently left him no time to push sanitary reform. Because the conscientious officer could

not do all he ought, the good of the country was bound to
suffer.

- 8 -

The Sanitary Commission slowly won the confidence of
others. General Mansfield had once turned down a Sanitary
offer to supervise a lodge for soldiers passing through Washington. Events forced him to change his mind. At first he
would not allow the preparation of food for soldiers fatigued
by travel; finally he allowed the serving of coffee and rations,
specifying that the lodge must be under military control.
Mansfield seemed afraid the commission would stuff the
travel-worn with "sugar-plums."

McClellan felt that the commission had not received the
favor it deserved. He expressed a wish to encourage it and
profit from its experience. Toward the middle of September
the general gave Bellows an interview in the presence of
Secretary of War Cameron. McClellan's head was not large,
but its proportions were harmonious. Constant exposure had
given his face a deep tan; his hair was brown, his features
regular, and his eyes "calm, direct, and powerful." The
young commander moved with an excessively catlike grace,
swaying and bending his "well-knit" and "perfectly balanced
form." He accompanied his talk by spitting a little on the rug
and playing with a dog. No one could call McClellan elegant,
polished, or scholarly; but he was unaffectedly self-possessed,
his complacency a blend of natural dignity and frankness.
He spoke to the point with earnestness, honesty, and intelligence. His humanity and sympathy fitted him to win the
"enthusiastic love of women and common soldiers." Mc-
Clellan's conversation was free from sentimental, speculative,
or religious references. Possibly he entertained a simple
faith, for the general seemed to base his understanding of
men and circumstances on intuition.

McClellan made small events yield large conclusions. He knew his place and its responsibilities. More conspicuous than "ingenuity, brilliancy, or originality" was the availability of his talents, his promptness and balance, his "superiority to routine and willingness to stand in the gap." He formed judgments quickly and struck at the heart of a matter. McClellan would do great things, but lacked the power to sustain true greatness; he had neither the "iron" of Wellington nor Washington's "reserved strength." This American, an intimate of success, was the "bright consummate flower of our railroad, telegraphic, and money-making system." [12]

Bellows, McClellan, and Cameron discussed the Medical Bureau and ways to cut tape. McClellan and Cameron declared their resolution to follow Sanitary advice. The general agreed to confer military status on inspectors; he said they should have authority to enforce health regulations. But as often as he kept the word of promise to Sanitary ears he broke it to their hopes. Inspectors discovered constant neglect and disobedience in camps; yet the commission accomplished much by pursuasion.

Catch-as-catch-can was the Sanitary policy. The commission was groping and feeling its way, assuming the nearest burden and heeding the loudest cries for help. But the Irish maxim—"When you see a head, hit it"—just would not do. Olmsted wanted a warlike tone and policy. Let the Sanitary Commission stand between the Medical Bureau and the people; let it be more "comprehensively humane" than the indifferent and bewildered community. The Sanitary rock must be a "large contingent fund," and its commandment should read, "Prevent rather than cure." Force indifferent Washington to do better, said Olmsted, even at the expense of some temporary cruelty.

All eyes inevitably rest on Lincoln in the history of the

---

[12] Bellows MSS. H. W. Bellows to Mrs. H. W. Bellows, Sept. 12, 1861, Washington, D.C.

Civil War. In the Sanitary story his presence is always
shadowy. During September, Olmsted asked him to recommend "the purpose of the Commission to the confidence of
the public." The president seemed shy about signing a circular; not until General Scott had set down his name did Lincoln add his. During October the commissioners held an interview with him. Looking older and more settled, Lincoln
received them kindly. He appeared awkward and ill at ease;
but he went straight to the point and spoke well. Frank and
direct, Lincoln overcame all disposition to cavil. Commissioners left the interview pleased with the president's compliment and full of the belief that they had reached an
important stage of development.

- 9 -

In the first months Sanitary expenses did not go beyond
$5,000. The commission depended on voluntary contribu-
tions. Because it believed the rebellion would be crushed
with comparative ease, it asked for $50,000; this amount
would permit a careful study of military hygiene.

Newspapers reminded the business community of the destruction that attended the Crimean and East Indian campaigns. They argued the case in monetary terms. Each
soldier was a costly piece of national property; his enlistment, equipment, and training came to some $200; his death
placed the burden of support on the citizens. The commission asked insurance companies for large amounts, for pru-
dence demanded their support. According to the argument,
the commission would save the nation thousands of men
and millions of dollars. Failure to back it would mean losses
in lives and the depression of property values. The nation
needed a system of sanitary defense to protect camps from
epidemics. Once disease had destroyed one army, the raising
of another could only be accomplished at fearful cost.

Through argument and appeal the Sanitary Commission raised a total of $12,807.95 by the end of June.

Government generosity made possible the curtailment of expenses. It furnished offices, storehouses, and the building occupied as the Soldiers' Home in Washington; it also provided horses, ambulances, and army wagons for Sanitary inspectors and agents; it gave them every facility for visiting camps, hospitals, and army posts. The commission took no money from the government; it was unwilling to ask for a Congressional appropriation. Moral rectitude was its pride and honor; government aid would apparently tar these very qualities. The moral power on which their usefulness depended would be weakened, feared the commissioners, if they appeared to beg from the public treasury; they shunned the suspicion of connection with political machines and intrigue. To the power that created it the Sanitary Commission said, "Noli me tangere"; to the public from which government derived its powers the commissioners passed the hat.

CHAPTER II

The Soldier and the Sanitary Commission, 1861

- 1 -

THE need for men created abuses in the enlistments of
1861. A recruiting agent without scruples would fill up
regimental quotas with the unfit. Doctors erroneously believed that volunteers did not have to meet standards set up
for the regular army. Physical examinations varied from state
to state; in southern Ohio they involved "little more than
opening and shutting the hands, bending the elbows and
knees, rotating the shoulder joint, with a casual glance at the
teeth and eyes and a question as to age and previous general
health." In Washington the army canceled the May order to
re-examine the volunteers, apparently for fear of losing too
many three-month enlistments. A general order in August
directed the examination of all recruits, but surgeons generally ignored it. As general secretary of the Sanitary Commission, Olmsted asked Northern governors to keep high
standards, because the army wanted men capable of with-
standing privations, fatigue, and exposure; those who became
disheartened on losing a meal or fell ill for want of domestic
comforts and tender care did violence to the army's idea of
what soldiers ought to be—"sound, tough, enduring, and long
suffering."

Faith in numbers alone was a delusion enjoyed by the un-
initiated. Tyros at arms quickly learned that real power did
not come from indiscriminate selection; 60 healthy animals
in fighting trim would give better performance than if their
ranks had been swollen to 110 by the addition of 50 sickly
men. The unfit depressed the vigorous by the weariness and

31

uffering preceding actual breakdown. Those who were too young had little physical stamina, while criminals and cast-off social fragments fitted in poorly. By December, 1861, reported Olmsted, 58 per cent out of 200 regiments inspected made no pretense to thorough inspection of recruits, while thorough reinspection had taken place in only 9 per cent.

Few stopped to add up the costs of wages, rations, clothing, medicine, and transportation for each ineffective. For October, November, and December, 1861, the number discharged from the Army of the Potomac came to 3,939; of this figure 2,881 were dropped because of injuries incurred before enlistment. The "faithlessness" of doctors had cost the country not less than $200 for each of the disabled, making an approximate total of $200,000 a month. Had the handicapped collectively formed a regiment, this Gideon's army would have paraded to the hoots of nations. Dr. A. J. Phelps wrote: "Feeble boys, toothless old men, consumptives, asthmatics, one-eyed, one-armed men, men with different length of legs, club-footed and ruptured, and, in short, men with every variety of disability, and whose systems were replete with the elements of disease were accepted as recruits and started to the field only to become a tax upon the government, and to encumber the movements of its armies." [1]

Northern townships seemed intent on converting the army into a poor farm to relieve themselves of supporting the lame, the halt, and the blind. The War Department, in December, 1861, issued new directives, condemning the negligence of regimental surgeons and threatening derelict officers with fines for failure to obey earlier orders. Because of loose methods of recruiting the army never used its full strength; generally not more than 35 per cent of the muster roll strength of the Union armies appeared on the battlefield.

The army made no preparations to receive the civilian. He entered the "artificial state" little dreaming of responsibilities

[1] *Sanitary Memoirs of the War*, ed. Austin Flint (1867), pp. 43–44.

in hygiene and sanitation. At home women looked after the cooking and serving of his food; they made his bed, cleaned his room, and cared for his clothes. Understandably he found difficulty in adjusting to novel situations. Eastern recruits savored of the decadent and sybaritic, said the Rev. Dr. Bellows; Westerners, like Caesar's Belgians, made better soldiers because they lived far from the ways of trade. But most doctors spoke of Easterner and Westerner in one voice of praise. The volunteer's "intellectual enterprise" and daring set him beyond fatigue; his buoyant self-confidence—perhaps the product of national vanity and love of popularity—carried him through defeat.

Rarely had mass hygiene confronted Americans with such peculiar urgency. As essentials to good health, sanitarians stressed good food, cleanliness, dry ground, sunlight, and fresh air. Yet from the time he entered the army the volunteer received poorly cooked rations, which were served without cleanliness. The recruit spent the night in a crowded tent, where he experienced cold, dampness, and discomfort. Such an atmosphere, mistakenly thought some doctors, produced coated tongue, nausea, headache, nervousness, and tremors; it lowered resistance and left men the prey of fever. Water supply at inland depots rarely met physical requirements. Too often the soldier who wanted to bathe had no opportunity to do so; without example or instruction he saw no reason to keep clean. In time, feared sanitarians, the recruit would regard as permanent a condition he had at first considered temporary.

Apparently sanitarian convictions impressed few officers and men. The fetid warmth of herds gave little cause for squeamishness; soldiers seemed to feel no terrors about breathing "organic emanations" and "carbonic acid." A conscientious doctor could not bear "the slovenly, slipshod appearance of the clothing and accoutrements of the recruits, their filthy skins, uncombed hair, and matted beards." Officers rarely enforced the general order to wash feet, neck, and head, reported Olmsted in December, 1861. Soldiers washed clothes too infrequently; they never removed dirt entirely from woolen clothing. Volunteer regiments scarcely ever held a proper inspection. Laxity in appearance also characterized the officers. As careless of their coats as they were of *Army Regulations,* they left the one unbuttoned and opened while they kept the other shut. Each knapsack should be provided with clothesbrush, shoebrush, comb, and towel, advised Olmsted; each recruit should be held accountable for these articles in weekly inspections.

The cost of freedom from disease was eternal vigilance, noted Dr. Steiner; company officers must pay this price liberally, or everything would go awry. Generally the officer gave little heed to sanitary matters; like the private, he apparently believed these subjects took care of themselves. Either he knew not how to proceed or his mind was closed. Too many officers remained smugly ignorant, disregarding the soldier's dirty habits. If they did not ignore the surgeon, they might hinder him who set out to clean up a camp or improve a diet. Poor blankets, swampy locations for camps, heavy details for labor in the field, picket duty, and the citizen soldier's ignorance were the five primary causes of disease, said Tripler, medical director of the Army of the Potomac; but the greatest amount of sickness resulted from the laziness and stupidity of officers, for theirs was the power to check "bad cooking, bad police, bad ventilation of tents, inattention to personal cleanliness, and unnecessarily irregular habits."

- 2 -

Before the Civil War the medical profession thought proper diet included fat, protein, and carbohydrates as staminal principles. Protein was regarded as primarily essential to human growth, because blood and tissue were rich in it. Today we know that in any satisfactory dietary the indispensable or structural group of foods consists of a pint of milk for each adult together with vegetables and fruits; the whole supplies a necessary amount of amino acids, vitamins, minerals, and roughage. This group functions to maintain growth, and the metabolism of tissues. The supplementary group of food—cereals, legumes, meat, eggs, tubers, sugar, and vegetable oils—provide for the output of muscular work. To secure best results nutritional intake must be adequate for bodily energy requirements. Nutritional disturbances result from deficiencies in quality and quantity of food. Modern dietary has played an important role in preventive medicine, effectually reducing such diseases as scurvy, rickets, beriberi, and pellagra.[2]

The recruit in 1861 received all he wished to eat of whatever there was. One pound of biscuit—that is, hardtack, pilot bread, or crackers—or twenty-two ounces of bread or flour, one and one-quarter pounds of fresh or salt meat or three-fourths of a pound of bacon formed the basis of the ration; to it were added eight gallons of beans, ten pounds of rice or hominy, ten pounds of coffee, fifteen pounds of sugar, four gallons of vinegar, and two pounds of salt for each hundred men. By June, 1864, the ration was increased by six ounces of flour and four ounces of hard bread, in addition to three pounds of potatoes. This diet led to scurvy; among the causes of disease it proved the "most fruitful," thought one doctor. Veteranship did not bring immunity; the longer the term of service the more likely was the soldier to manifest some profound and marked state of constitutional upset.

At best the ration was monotonous. Prepared to withstand the hottest climate, salted beef was tough and liable to be tainted by the time it came to the soldier. Pork and bacon

[2] Wilson G. Smillie, *Public Health Administration in the United States* (1947), pp. 348–49.

frequently arrived rancid. The hardness of bread or hardtack did not keep out mold and maggots; regardless of its state, biscuit had to be soaked in order to be eaten. Soldiers ate too much fat, complained Sanitary inspectors, when they should have been profiting from onions, potatoes, and fresh beef. On the commission's recommendation the army slowly adopted the company fund, a means of introducing variety into the rations. Forty per cent of 200 regiments had these funds in November, 1861; the rest had none. The soldier used the company fund to purchase fresh vegetables, milk, butter, and pepper; it also helped him to buy cooking utensils, knives, forks, brushes, and blacking. The company fund, said Olmsted, promoted health, morale, and self-respect; but most volunteers, he admitted, were slow to understand this.

Volunteers without ways of commuting or selling their rations complained of the absence of fresh vegetables. In hard-fought campaigns soldiers often waited long before receiving them. When supply lines were interrupted and armies were short rationed, the Sanitary Commission called on farmers for vegetables and even helped plant gardens; but demands for fresh vegetables were invariably greater than could be supplied. The subsistence bureau found dried vegetables easy to handle; they could be transported in large amounts and with little deterioration. Today we know that this drying destroys vitamin C, the antiscorbutic property.

Armed with knife, fork, tin plate, and tin cup, the recruit sat down to eat; not until 1863 was he given a spoon. Some doctors spoke as though the careful preparation of food could improve the ration. Food poorly cooked, eaten without relish, and downed in haste, they feared, might result in indigestion, flatulence, and diarrhea. Dried beans, the worst offender, were eaten hard and partly cooked without a suggestion of flavoring to cheer their leaden descent. One doctor suggested paying greater attention to the Napoleonic maxim, "The soup makes the soldier."

Sanitary inspectors regarded poor cooking as destructive of morale. Dr. Aigner* of Cairo enjoyed many dinners prepared by soldiers; but their coffee was bad, and they persisted in using pork fat to fry cakes made of flour and water. Many officers and surgeons protested; they erroneously believed that fried foods brought on diarrhea and dysentry. Messing in squads invariably meant frying, said one Sanitary inspector; soldiers ignorant of ways to cook resorted to this simple method. Their tents became storehouses of uncooked food, which mingled with "unwholesome and disgusting accumulations of garbage and offal."

Early in the war the Sanitary Commission listed cooking as one of its major concerns. An address to the public read: " . . . the difference between well-cooked digestible food and ill-cooked indigestible food consumed by a regiment during three months of actual service in the field is equivalent to a difference of at least forty per cent in its available strength at the end of that period." Late in June, 1861, the commission sent a Mr. Sanderson to teach soldiers how to prepare soup, meat, rice, tea, and coffee. Sanderson did not reach all regiments east and west; and he did not seem sanguine . . . about the results of his instruction. In December, 1861, Olmsted told Secretary Cameron that soldiers did not like their own cooking, although it showed signs of improvement. Not until March, 1863, did Congress require cooking by companies; specially hired cooks helped soldiers detailed for that purpose. Surgeons and officers were held responsible for supervision and instruction. Cooking by companies was an improvement, but cooking by squads or by individuals did not die out.

- 3 -

The general tone of camps changed for the better after August 7, when General Mansfield ordered a cleanup around

Washington. In the same month Dr. Tripler ordered the vaccination of prisoners at the Capitol, a bath erected for their use, and outdoor exercise for their health; he directed a cleanup of the Pennsylvania cavalry camp on Seventh Street, and saw that troops left the flats near Arlington for higher ground beyond the "infected currents of air." Drill was turning excellent human material into admirable soldiers, said the Sanitary inspector in Missouri, but imperfect organization of camps in August made it impossible to report fully. Missourians in emergency had no camp police; their camps lacked a regular system of drainage or sanitary regulations of any kind. Dirty soldiers sported in good spirits. During a muddy autumn they lived on bad cooking without fresh vegetables, but managed fairly well for men accustomed to a rough Western life. They had sturdy clothes and shoes; blankets were just beginning to be distributed.

In December, 1861, Olmsted concluded that 5 per cent of the camps were in "admirable order," and 45 per cent fairly clean and well policed; 26 per cent were negligent and slovenly and 24 per cent were "decidedly bad, filthy, and dangerous." That the water was generally wholesome meant that it seemed clear and without offensive odor. Troops occupied a campsite for an average of twenty-one days. Western soil made good natural drainage in contrast to Eastern clay, and the result could be observed in fewer cases of rheumatism for the West than on the Atlantic seaboard. Artificial drainage showed improvement, but its imperfections helped create a long sick list. Soldiers pitched their tents too close together; they threw rubbish into the spaces between and left it to rot.

Eighty per cent of the privies were in good condition, properly arranged, kept in good order, and free from offensive odor. The remaining 20 per cent were a threat to good health. In 68 per cent of the camps men obeyed commands confining them to exclusive use of privies; in 32 per cent officers did not enforce the orders. That the men preferred to go off into the bushes was understandable. The sink was usually a pit surmounted by a rail; cleanliness meant throwing earth over the sink once a day and keeping its edges free of excrement. In 35 per cent officers allowed the men to urinate within camp limits at night. The British service provided one night bucket for each tent, but the Union armies apparently made no such provision. Soldiers disposed offal systematically in 77 per cent of the camps; they were very negligent in the remaining 23 per cent. Not infrequently stables were found within camp limits, a direct violation of *Army Regulations*. In general, camp police had improved since the summer of 1861. Many officers no longer treated certain faults as unworthy of attention, observed Olmsted; the names of camps that took pride in "an exact and severe camp police" were steadily growing.

Tents were of many types. Officers used wall tents, which were easily ventilated. Privates and noncommissioned officers used the wedge tent—an abomination to the sanitarian, because most regiments did not strictly observe the rule for striking tents in ventilation and cleaning. As it stood, the tent could not be ventilated. Five men crowded into an area of insufficient size. Soldiers frequently built a wedge tent; they leaned the rough boards against a ridgepole before nailing them. The government occasionally furnished lumber, and the men built shelters 20 by 50 feet, which housed one or two companies. Soldiers slept on two platforms, each about 12 feet in width; one was placed above the other.

During the winter of 1861 some regiments excavated pits and covered them with tents to increase comfort. Tripler condemned the practice as productive of disease, because it did not allow for effective airing and drying. He suggested sheds, rails, or palisades some three feet high, to be roofed over with tents. He later proposed the Chester hut, which permitted good roof ventilation and had seen satisfactory use at Balaklava in the Crimean War.

The Sibley tent was cone shaped. It was sixteen feet in diameter at the base, supported by a center pole with an iron tripod. The top of the pole carried an iron ring a foot in diameter over which was draped a conical cape; this could be raised for ventilation and letting out smoke. Housing sixteen men, the Sibley was comfortable in camp but unwieldly on campaigns. It made for effective camp police; soldiers could easily raise its skirts for airing and drying the floor. On campaigns the most convenient shelter was the pup tent, 4 feet wide by 6 feet long; one went to each man.

Soldiers built log cabins for winter. Contrasted with barracks, they appeared unmilitary but were more comfortable to live in. Round or split logs plastered with mud formed the walls; tenting or waterproof blankets made the roofs; board or rubber blankets served as doors. Some were so spacious that they could be divided into several compartments; others were large enough for two occupants in an area 6 feet square with walls 3 or 4 feet high. So economically did the occupants use this space that it was known to hold two beds, a table, a rack of arms, a clothes cache, and a fireplace. Log cabins expressed the soldier's individualism. German regiments near Fortress Monroe made shelters out of old boards, doors, and window frames which had been salvaged from the fire at Hampton. They arranged a portico to serve as dining or sitting room in the front of the tent. Lacking regularity of plan, the company streets took on a bewildering aspect. In Massachusetts regiments the men purchased lumber to build huts. Although without uniformity in plan, these furnished good and efficient protection. The project for building log barracks checked soldiers from setting up more huts.

- 4 -

Washington never squarely faced the difficulties of supply, treating them from the first as problems for the states to solve. Pressures in 1861 severely burdened the War Department. Scores of awkward situations tricked understaffed bureaus, as they worked without a definite war program. Secretary Cameron admitted that he could do nothing, so the loyal states furnished the volunteer with uniform and equipment. Out of indecision and confusion they did as well as possible. The dishonesty of contractors was scarcely their responsibility, but their frantic efforts to make up deficiencies gave the profiteer opportunity to line his pockets. States bidding against each other and the national government created scandals in food, shelter, and clothing. The War Department gradually remedied the worst abuses, as stricter regulations governed contracts. With closer inspection soldiers received proper articles more promptly, but shortages pursued the army with each increase of men.

The government was failing to dramatize the war, complained Olmsted in September, 1861. Soldiers fell ill, because they slept on the bare ground. Hay and straw were scarce; lumber was too expensive. Once informed of desperate shortages in men, arms, clothing, medicine, and food, the public would relieve the government "as a suffocating man is relieved by opening a window." Only let the need be shouted in the streets! But when Olmsted tried to raise his voice, McClellan said no; publicity might be harmful to morale. Olmsted worked hard to get blankets without letting the recruit learn of a serious deficiency; but his polite request appeared just when Quartermaster General Meigs tore the mask from all evasion by publishing his own call for blankets. Meigs's blunt style in no way dramatized the shortage; but his plea, Olmsted feared, might take precedence over that of the Sanitary Commission. Actually the quartermaster general had given directions to place the collected blankets in Sanitary storehouses.

Popular delusions about supply difficulties troubled the Sanitary Commission. People asked why Washington did not go into the home market for blankets and clothes. Was it necessary to beg from persons that private stores might be put to public use? Did the army absolutely have to send large orders abroad? The charge that Washington leaned over backwards to meet some arbitrary military standard was foolish, said the commission. At home the administration had bought blankets that were warm, strong, and durable; it stood ready to buy others, provided they were offered at reasonable prices. The United States had neither sufficient wool nor factory power to satisfy the call for blankets. Demand for domestic wool had jumped the price from 50 to 80 cents a pound. One firm boasted of clearing $100,000 profit. Many American mills were changing machinery in order to manufacture blankets. Why pay usurious rates at home, when imported wool cost 40 cents? Northern orders for wool meanwhile served as a magnet to European stocks, attracting 350,000 blankets toward our harbors. Military regulations specified that blankets should measure 84 by 36 inches and weigh 5 pounds. In December, Olmsted reported that in 75 per cent of 200 regiments the quartermaster had issued one good blanket to each man; he had provided two generally of inferior grade in 20 per cent; in 5 per cent not all the men had received even one blanket.

The War Department tried to meet the shortage by telling the recruit to bring his own. The soldier had good reason to be cynical. Government-purchased blankets were often but a third of regulation size, and frequently became so rotten that a man could push holes through them; their light and open weave gave no protection against cold or rain; many blankets fell to pieces without warning.

- 5 -

"Never, probably, was so large an army as well supplied at a similar period of a great war," reported Olmsted to the secretary of war in December. The army equipped about seven-eighths of the regiments fairly well with clothing, he estimated, while one-eighth were furnished indifferently and poorly.

Endless activity in October had not been sufficient to clothe all enlistments, the Sanitary Commission noted. Authorities bought anything that would hold together and hide nakedness, setting comfort before color. But certain firms were hoarding uniforms in hopes of profiting from distress. The cost of dye had gone up with the failure of India's indigo crop. Blue vats were scarce in the United States; fir wool, ordinarily selling at 5 cents, cost 75 cents in October. Competition among governors in hasty indiscriminate recruiting further increased prices. Not many American firms dealt in cloth; state agents, army tailors, and contractors were consequently obliged to deal with the same companies and outbid each other. Companies frequently set aside contracts made with Washington for much better terms from a governor; they commonly disregarded contracts with one state for greater advantages offered by another.

By October cloth had jumped from 75 cents a yard to $1.25. Home factories could not meet demand at this price, because they were unable to supply cloth in sufficient quantities to keep soldiers from suffering. Washington, wishing to protect domestic industries, had set their interests before that of the country. Too long had it put off ordering clothes from Europe, but in October the government had no other recourse than to call for 1,200,000 yards from abroad. Yet even so moderate a purchase roused protests from the greedy. The needs of the recruiting service were a minor reason for shortages. An unsuspecting gull was more willing to join the ranks, if he could picture himself in the deep-blue garment. The promise of a handsome uniform was the sugar that drew the flies; as a result, governors and recruiting officers kept more clothing at recruiting points than was necessary. Possibly authorities knew that men on parade and patrol were marching in underwear, but the proper appearance of fresh enlistments still received a disproportionate emphasis.

Soldiers seemed to have enough of other clothing. Flannel shirts they could buy. Stockings, though plentiful, were poor; they had a seam which ran all the way down the middle. The seamless stocking made by Potter's machine was the only machine stocking really suitable, but it could not be made fast enough to meet the demand. Woolen knit socks were a boon to the soldier. Women could knit these, suggested the Sanitary Commission, and its agents would distribute them after caring for the sick and wounded.

In December, Olmsted told Secretary Cameron that in 26 per cent of 200 regiments shirts were of poor quality. In 74 per cent they came up to regulations. Soldiers generally had two shirts. Shortages usually resulted from their sale or barter. Overcoats covered 82 per cent well; in 7 per cent men were indifferently supplied; 11 per cent had none, while 3 per cent wore coats of poor material. Sanitary inspectors found good cloth body coats in 75 per cent; flannel sack coats or cloth jackets supplied the remainder. The government provided soldiers in all 200 regiments with trousers; these were satisfactory in 175, fair in 8, and poor in 17. The authorities seemed to have made good other deficiencies, except when officers were culpable through ignorance, negligence, or knavery.

By the fall of 1862 the quartermaster corps improved its methods of distribution, its supplies equaling those in the best furnished European armies. Except for arms and ammunition, the total equipment of each soldier cost only $50.

Observers noted its excellence, and they also commented on its wastage. Soldiers often threw away clothes, blankets, overcoats, knapsacks, and other articles in battle and frequently lost them; until new stores arrived, they took up foraging. Lacking in foresight, they might discard winter clothing in summer before arrangements could be made for storage. Unchecked impulses to barter made troops dispose of unnecessary clothing and equipment; a soldier's love of whisky gave stimulus to trade. Yet in his defense let it be said that he was sometimes so overburdened that physical motion demanded the disposal of articles. In March, 1863, Congress acted to stop wasteful exchanges; any article not in the rightful owner's possession would be confiscated.

- 6 -

A visit from the paymaster improved fighting stamina, wrote a Sanitary inspector. In terms of American life in the 1860's soldier's pay was infinitesimal. The $11 a month that the private received at the beginning of the war was raised to $13 in August, 1861. Depreciated currency cut his wages, which Congress set at $16 by June, 1864. Actually after 1862 the soldier did not have so much as $8 a month. Payday supposedly took place every two months, but the volunteer often waited from four to eight months. That he grumbled and became anxious about family needs was not surprising.

Remittance of pay was a Sanitary concern from the first. Washington made no provision for transmitting funds to families. In the first days of official life the commission discussed with the secretary of war the feasibility of paying soldiers in gold and silver or by allotment. Could soldiers legally transfer a part by check, or would a special law be necessary? An allotment system meant boosting the soldier's morale, reasoned the commission; he would fight in confident knowledge that his family was living in hope and self-respect in the community.

The question of allotments agitated thoughtful men outside the Sanitary Commission. Failure to provide families with a monthly allowance might discredit the war in Northern cities and breed popular unrest. An allotment system was thought a simple solution, if each soldier signed a printed form authorizing his wife or some other person to draw his pay. But the government apparently objected to this plan, which would mean a staff increase in the paymaster's department. The economic betterment of the United States would more than make up for the few dollars spent on additional bookkeeping, thought Olmsted. He wanted the soldier paid a monthly bonus, which would be increased with each month of service. The volunteer would receive the full sum upon final discharge; but he ought also to set aside about ten cents from each payday for his family.

In July, Congress directed the secretary of war to introduce either the allotment system used in the navy or some other way by which a volunteer's dependents could draw a portion of his pay; but this did not settle the problem satisfactorily. The Woman's Central Association of Relief proposed that the commission serve as trustee; a Sanitary agent would follow the paymaster through the New York regiments and take the amounts on the spot; he would then deposit the sums in savings banks of different New York towns in the names of persons designated. To assume this position of trust might increase the commission's popularity; such an economy could plausibly give it a better hold on Congress. National expenditures would outrun estimates to an extent that called for caution; but legislators would appreciate the commission's practical value, if through its foresight large returns enriched the towns instead of the sutlers.

The commission heeded the proposals from the Central Association. It urged action on Secretary Cameron, who expressed distaste for allotments for fear of arousing newspaper criticism. The plan he adopted impressed the commissioners as another example of the careless and half-thought-through treatment of projects calling for intelligent application. Sums were to be transmitted to trustees, each to be selected by his military company; the trustee was responsible to his comrades, not to the government. Here was a grave error, thought the commission; government responsibility ended when the money reached the trustee's hands. A half million soldiers received $6,600,000 in wages. Half of this amount was $3,-300,000 spent on food, clothing, and hospitalization, while the remaining half needed safeguards against dishonesty to protect the welfare of Northerners. Who could tell whether the trustee would be faithful to his trust? He could not be forced to give bonds—in whose hands could he place them? To give them to soldiers or to the assignees was impracticable; and the government would not accept them without acknowledging the trustee as its agent.

Soldiers were meanwhile using the post office to send home money. To Washington came Theodore Roosevelt, nephew of Judge Roosevelt of New York, Morris Ketchum, and William E. Dodge, Jr., with recommendations from all Wall Street banks, and described as persons to whom the troops could entrust savings and allotments. Boston sent its Mayor Wrightman to treat the same subject. Philanthropists had permission to serve as trustees, if military companies gave consent. New York made use of existing machinery without incurring additional expense. Allotments once deposited, state treasurers distributed them for soldiers from the large cities, while county clerks performed the same service for volunteers from the interior counties.

By December, Olmsted reported to the secretary of war that in 57 per cent of 200 regiments the men sent home a large part of their pay, perhaps from one-half to three-quarters. Officers at Cairo were enthusiastic about the allotment system, said Dr. Aigner, but none put it into practice. Occasionally he had heard of the Adams Express Company's transmitting small sums, but acts of thoughtfulness generally came from the soldiers who loved their homes and families. The government ought to adopt a suitable allotment system without hesitation, Olmsted advised. Allotments keeping up family ties shielded the soldier from camp vices; they changed the fatalistic mercenary to the responsible citizen who was willingly bound to his community in peace and war. Volunteers ought to use money for replacements but nothing more, thought Olmsted. Allotments would cut down payday's drunken riot and its resulting sick list.

In so far as blankets and clothes concerned the soldier's health, they came into the Sanitary province. Otherwise the commission had little to do with the quartermaster corps. Whatever increased the volunteer's physical usefulness involved the Sanitary Commission. Prices, profits, and greed all affected the vigor of the ranks. What the recruit did with his pay became a part of the Sanitary sphere when he turned up sick from misdirected spending. The commission stressed anything that would strengthen the volunteer's morale; it was imbued with a "simple desire and resolute determination" to see that he secured what was the will and duty of the United States to give.

- 7 -

Army life was one to be endured and little to be enjoyed, thought Dr. Bellows. Army fare and sleeping in tents seemed enough to make a man homesick. In peace the soldier existed in idleness, dissipation, and temptation, while his life in war knew only labor, monotony, and danger. During the long waits between campaigns soldiers and officers did little more than drink and smoke "in horrible profuseness" and chew when they did not smoke.

Soldiers had various reasons for wanting to go home. For lack of training many fell out of rank from fatigue of marching, and were "packed off" in a "reckless," indiscriminate way. The sight of a man excused for homesickness tended to make a shirk of him who stayed with the army, noted Olmsted, while a surgeon might neglect precautions and provisions against sickness. Nothing compared with demoralized officers for sneaks and bullies. Some adopted disguises; others played the stowaway on boats and trains. Appeals to honor and threats of punishment met with contempt, for many officers were confident that political influence would remove any danger to them. Had the Medical Bureau full control of transportation, it supposedly could have checked the malingerers, who crowded among the sick and wounded and took the comfortable seats in railroad cars or else rode on the roofs. Malingerers brought "medical rule and discipline into contempt"; they put the Sanitary Commission in a suspicious light whenever it became the "innocent vehicle" for removing the seemingly sick.

CHAPTER III

The Army Hospitals, Surgeons, and Nurses, 1861

- 1 -

NO general hospitals existed in the army before the war. There were post hospitals; the largest, at Fort Leavenworth, held forty beds. The start of hostilities created problems of expansion, which the Medical Bureau seemed powerless to meet adequately. The quartermaster corps hesitated to build the structures it would have to furnish with a variety of expensive but essential appliances. Men needed guns, not beds, reasoned the quartermasters, who left little to that field where doctors were proper authorities. Threat of catastrophe might force the Medical Bureau to call for many new hospitals; but would the quartermasters sense this danger with the same conviction?

In June of 1861 Olmsted reported a diversity of opinions regarding the location of convalescent hospitals. Cameron wanted to use the Naval Academy at Annapolis; New York was too far from the war zone to permit sending patients to an institution there. Colonel Cullum, Major Shiras, and Dr. Wood preferred the Northern city; Olmsted himself thought there was good reason to send away the sick rather than the wounded. He advocated a series of hospitals; the convalescent might move from one to another, depending on his stage of recovery.

Old buildings—menaces to life and property in the opinion of the Sanitary Commission—served as general hospitals in the Washington area. The commission found them overcrowded, although not filled to capacity, while foul smells and poor ventilation pervaded the structures. Windows were too small and too few, even though pleasant weather permitted their being raised for long periods. The quartermaster corps had neither installed artificial ventilation and fans nor set up steam engines in the cellars. Wards were not large enough; they did not allow each patient his necessary air space. They were crowded five in a room, and the beds and bedsteads were generally poor. The commissioners objected to the halls as "narrow, tortuous, and abrupt, and in many instances with carpets still unremoved from their floors, and walls covered with paper." They found bathing provisions and water closets either defective or nonexistent. In one instance, patients abused a water closet by choking the pipes with clothes, stockings, spoons, or anything they wanted to throw away. These makeshift hospitals had no mortuaries; corpses lay in a lower room. Cellars generally remained damp and undrained.

Old buildings showed evidence of wood decay, and formed "storehouses for morbid emanations"; artificial ventilation made them "comparatively safe," but the procedure was complicated and expensive. If the army was to continue using unsuitable structures, the commission urged correction of certain architectural defects to warrant the name of hospitals. Water should be entered on each floor, and mortuaries built apart. Ventilation properly functioning ought to draw off foul air and fumes; and buildings must be constructed to retain warmth in winter. But an immediate increase in a better kind of hospital was the "grand want" of the army.

Governed by a few rules, general hospitals lacked system. With the help of assistant surgeons the senior surgeon in charge visited the sick, and tried to see that the hospital was clean, well ventilated, and not crowded. Responsible to the surgeon general and the general commanding the district,

the surgeon did not know whom to obey when orders con-
flicted; he was likely to be a law unto himself, checked solely
by reports from Sanitary inspectors and army medical inspectors.

The "grandest" of wants was an efficient surgeon general,
said the commissioners. To give patients adequate care
called for a strengthened medical corps. Doctors and nurses
could not be blamed for lack of foresight in the Medical
Bureau; they were overworked and had only their good intentions to guide them. For every woman put in, a man was
taken out of service. Patient care suffered whenever one of
the overtaxed medical cadets fell ill. Medical officers then
enlisted convalescents to carry water, scrub, and perform
those menial tasks which drained strength from the strong.
Several doctors complained of the medicines as poor and
weak. To get the better of an inefficient surgeon general and
a slow medical purveyor, the shrewd physician made out
requisitions far in advance of shortages. Hoarding might
solve his difficulties for a time, but it generally resulted in
less for other surgeons. The Kalorama was the most deficient
of Washington hospitals, thought the Sanitary Commission; it
lacked cups, plates, blankets, and everything essential. Two
women divided the patients, the one taking 61 and the other
45. Surgeon and patients generally appreciated women
nurses and considered them indispensable; only at the
Georgetown and Union hospitals did the commissioners hear
them criticized.

During October the Sanitary inspector in Missouri found
hospitals worse than he had expected. In Jefferson the army
crammed 500 sick into an old seminary, two taverns, and a
private house. These had formerly sheltered Southern chiv-
alry, who in retreat left filth and ruin in small, close, and dirty
rooms with broken windows. Some Union men lay on "cots
without beds"; others lay on "beds without cots," while the
rest stretched out on the floor. No one had cleaned or emp-

tied the stinking spittoons and chamber pots. Uninhibited, the men turned the grounds into a privy, and it was with difficulty that they realized the importance of cleanliness. At Sedalia the ill lay in an old store and an empty private house. The army supplied sick soldiers in Missouri with beds manufactured at state prisons; but a general had taken fifty hospital beds for himself and his staff, leaving the incapacitated to find comfort on the floor. Floors, bedding, and men needed "scraping." Patients at breakfast ate dry bread and drank black coffee. Doctors felt helpless for want of nurses; the sick were left to the care of the sick.

On his second visit, however, the inspector discovered signs of gradual improvement. Proper food and better cooks were being introduced. Sisters of Mercy took over the tasks of nursing, while new beds were arriving. Women had been found to do the washing.

By September, 1861, there were in Maryland and on the Potomac about 2,700 beds in general hospitals. In mid-August 48 regiments had reported that 916 were sick in hospitals, while 1,546 were confined to quarters. Tripler did not know the aggregate strength of the regiments, but guessed at about 38,400. In case of Union advance, 5 per cent of the troops would require hospitalization. If numerical strength reached 200,000, the army would need at least 10,000 beds, said Tripler; it would be wise to anticipate a heavy action and have 60,000 beds ready; but in case he had to compromise, Tripler estimated that accommodation for 20,000 would be reasonable. Philadelphia consequently made ready to receive the incapacitated, should Washington hospitals become filled. Total accommodation came to 6,000 beds—a wholly inadequate number—when the Army of the Potomac set out for the peninsula.

In July, 1861, the Sanitary Commission had proposed wooden pavilions as sanitary and economical. Built at government expense, these would be shanties with a difference.

Drs. Agnew and Van Buren suggested that they be "fully provided with water for bathing, washing, and water closets, and simple arrangements for ventilation and for securing warmth in winter . . ." Each ward formed one of a series of detached buildings, and housed 40 or 50 patients. Each pavilion was theoretically placed at a specified distance from the other to avoid contamination; it allowed for easy distribution of cases into proper classes and was more convenient for patient and attendant.

The commission wanted enough pavilions to shelter 15,000. McClellan and Tripler feared this large building program opened the door to dishonest contractors; they reduced 15,000 to 5,000 and five buildings to two. Tripler, said Strong, confessed that he did not have medical officers enough to take care of more than two. Meigs, Cameron, and Lincoln fortunately approved Sanitary plans before further abbreviation. To the commission this was a significant victory. The year 1861 saw the beginnings of two pavilion hospitals in Washington; the one was put up on Judiciary Square, while the other was built on Stone Farm. Under Dr. W. A. Hammond's direction the extensive hospital building program took place after the reorganization of the Medical Bureau in 1862.

- 2 -

The doctor drawn from civilian life directed regimental hospitals in the volunteer army. Their success depended on his alertness and native intelligence. Generally made up of three hospital tents, each regimental hospital held an average of 40 patients; it also used certain supplies specified by the Medical Bureau. A steward was generally one of the personnel. Regimental hospitals started with almost nothing, and were soon overcrowded. Patients had to stay in them longer than desirable in spite of scarcities of medicines and aids to quick recovery. The sick on Federal Hill, Baltimore, were piled solidly into one hospital tent. Overworked, the surgeon let medical stores stand in the open air without protection. With the approval of General Dix the Sanitary Commission engaged a large suite of rooms to supplement the hospital.

The responsibility of caring for regimental hospitals weighed heavily on Olmsted. No obligation bound the Sanitary Commission to furnish them, but ineffectiveness in the Medical Bureau was starving certain establishments, so the commission must provide for sick German soldiers in Blenker's division. Miles from its regiment, the hospital of the 19th Indiana had some 250 patients; because the purveyor supplied them inadequately, they relied "largely and systematically" on charity. If the public learned of this condition, Olmsted feared, a scandal might result, which would lessen the confidence of the army in the government's ability to care for the sick.

In December, Olmsted reported that out of 200 regimental hospitals 105 were good, 52 indifferent or tolerable, and 26 bad. Fourteen regiments had no hospitals; 4 were without report. About half the regimental hospitals were defective regarding tents or buildings, ventilation, the supply of medicines, and the quality of instruments. Olmsted found surgical instruments especially poor and frequently useless. According to a common charge, the sick did not easily recover in field hospitals. The diet was limited and poor; army doctors generally gave surgical cases first consideration. Nursing was bad; attendants were negligent, and nurses were not employed for night duty.

Tripler preferred the regimental hospital. He considered general hospitals a necessary evil for receiving the sick when the army set out on the march. The soldier best preserved his qualities, said Dr. Jonathan Letterman,* when he stayed in camp with his comrades; he also gave his surgeon the opportunity to trace the issue of "professional labors upon the field." Convalescents in general hospitals ought to return to camp, thought the Sanitary Commission; but the success of this measure depended on the captain's agreement not to put them on duty at once.

Relations between regimental and general hospitals were vague and undefined, and resulted in haphazard cooperation and innumerable clashes. Olmsted asked the secretary of war to clarify their functions. Absence of even simple rule-of-thumb guidance had given rise to unpleasant debate between Finley and Tripler. How sick, they argued, should a sick man be before his transference from regimental to general hospital? The ill commonly stayed so long in camp that they infected the healthy; the regimental surgeon took a chance in sending them to a base hospital, where the surgeon in charge would possibly refuse a patient either because of a mistake in the signing of papers or a lack of extra beds. Perhaps the rejected sick soldier spent the night in an ambulance at the hospital door; he was possibly returned to camp sicker than ever or dead. Western surgeons took up the practice of sending only the dying from camps to base hospitals, which soon won the name of charnel houses; as mortality rates for general hospitals showed a rise, their patients expressed apprehension. Soldiers at a Washington hospital stayed out of doors as long as possible; they became sicker from exposure, and suffered on being moved. In case of a general advance, base hospitals might be overwhelmed when regimental hospitals sent away their cases.

Surgeons at general hospitals were certainly not heartless. But what were they to do when without warning patients arrived at the crowded hospital in small numbers or in large groups? Malingerers often found their way in during admissions and deprived real sufferers of beds. The situation gradually improved, however. Until they were assured of available bed space at base hospitals, field surgeons kept the dangerously ill in regimental hospitals. Medical directors in the field gave better attention to hospitals under their control. In June, 1862, the surgeon general's consent became necessary if medical directors wanted to transfer patients outside their own department.

Let time-honored conformities yield to present needs, said the Sanitary Commission, for the soldier's health took precedence over forms. Make discharge orders more explicit. Volunteer surgeons usually knew little about the exact forms for sending men to the hospital or discharging them from service on medical grounds. A patient's record rarely accompanied him to the hospital. Convalescents awaiting discharge sometimes died before receiving their papers. Medical and Quartermaster bureaus too frequently seized on trifling errors as grounds for holding up requisitions. A slight sacrifice of official precision would enable the surgeon to take proper action; but he would do well to learn the rules and fit into the military scheme with the least possible friction. The practices of the regimental hospitals, Olmsted noted, "must vary according to the mobility of the regiment, the season, the locality, the prevalent diseases, the proximity to available base hospitals." The army, advised the commission, ought to publish an official paper, giving information and the fullest explanation of orders. Let surgeons have discretionary power to achieve that end which all Union men desired—an effective hospital system.

The status of brigade hospitals at first perplexed Tripler. Lacking specific authorization to set them up, he nevertheless admitted that his was the power to do. They would have certain advantages, such as relieving crowded hospital tents, keeping men in the vicinity of camps, and making it easy for convalescents to return to camp. But Tripler worried: once brigade hospitals were created, would not rules and regulations tie his hands? Would he be able to provide the necessary kind of help? Brigade surgeons urged taking a chance— do what was not likely to be questioned. Boldly this son of strict construction took up his courage, and furnished brigade hospitals with the necessary detail from the regiment. Brigade hospitals should be regarded and conducted as aggregations of regimental hospitals, he ordered, and called for the mustering of stewards from regimental rolls.

Never good by modern standards, hospital fare was starchy and inadequate in fruit and vegetables. Olmsted recommended wider use of the hospital fund; rations not needed in the hospital were resold to the government for money value. Volunteers relied on this fund "for hospital bedding and clothing, and for all extra delicacies and medical and other appliances which the sick and convalescent require." By December, 1861, not one-third of the regimental hospitals had such funds. Regimental commissaries, said Tripler, strongly opposed them, although hospital funds had been ordered for the Army of the Potomac in September, 1861; four or five months passed before the system succeeded in establishing itself.

- 3 -

Nineteenth-century Europe took giant strides in medicine. Here were the great hospitals, clinics, and doctors, who shelved or discredited the traditional arts of healing and removed fruitless speculative elements from basic research. The French coordinated the clinical and pathological systematically by relating symptoms to their lesions. Seizing on statistics, they classified diseases with an exactitude hitherto unattainable. Using the new achromatic microscope, German scientists established the cell as the structural and physiological unit of living organism; they treated tissue cells in their structural, functional, and developmental relationships, while their investigations of diseased tissues elevated pathology to a science. Enlisting mathematics, physics, and chemistry, the Germans pushed ahead to make medicine a science of healing. From the United States came occasional contributions of significance in pathology, anesthesia, surgery, dentistry, and biochemistry. America had educators of note, but its thinking was provincial; its foremost medical centers did well merely to reflect European developments.

With the second quarter of the nineteenth century the proprietary medical schools in America grew like weeds. The expanding republic needed more doctors than the better schools could provide. Proprietary medical schools combined an apprenticeship system with public lectures. Enrollments showed a steady increase, helped on by few requirements, irregular attendance, and easy graduation. Teaching more nearly resembled a trade than a profession. Most school equipment did not include the stethoscope, clinical thermometer, hypodermic syringe and needle, microscope, ophthalmoscope, and ophthalmometer. Relatively few American doctors had any acquaintance with these instruments. Classes in anatomy long went without sufficient suitable material because of public prejudice against dissection of cadavers. Few institutions could support clinics. Teachers in rural areas emphasized lecturing and neglected clinical instruction. Most young men entered private practice in their apprenticeship.

Military medical difficulties were greater than the Medical Bureau. The public mistakenly believed that a good doctor in civilian life would also do well in the army. The officer of the line shared the ignorance of the public. The government was improvising a medical corps without considering its quality. Who but the soldier was the inevitable sufferer? The medical standards of the army had scarcely improved on those of the Middle Ages, thought one surgeon; so in all fairness "the purely military portion of the service" ought not to grumble should it fall into the hands of operators little better than "barbers, farriers, and sow-gelders." To Dr. Jonathan Letterman the duties of an army doctor were more than medical; he must also be a kind of medical strategist—one who kept the army vigorous and "efficient for enduring fatigue and privation, and for fighting." A doctor like Letterman put his knowledge and experience at the disposal of the army; as an administrator he must be quick to perceive, sound in judgment, and prompt in action. The surgeon assumed an increasing number of responsibilities, but because of the "absence of progressive promotion and of pay" he apparently thought himself unappreciated. Surgeons eager to advance their branch of the service believed the standard of the medical profession was a "gauge" of a country's civilization and "the measure of the real advancement of an age or people." But most Americans judged their country by other axioms; their leadership in medicine was yet to come.

A board appointed by the surgeon general examined applicants who wished to become surgeons in the regular army. Approved candidates became assistant surgeons, and by merit rose to fill vacancies. According to Olmsted, past examinations had been thorough, bringing in men of more than average ability. With encouragement army doctors could have won renown; but stationed at a remote frontier post, they let ambition flag. So little happened to tax their ingenuity that they were largely "unfitted for professional responsibility of a wider range." Not many doctors had sufficient drive to follow advanced practices and study new methods. To keep up with medical progress called for stimulation from active minds. The surgeon on duty ought to be supplied with excellent reports, said Olmsted; investigations, records of cases, and scientific reflections should be written so well that they would attract both civilian and military doctors. But as it was, the "pure spirits" who loved sweetness and light were rare among the regular surgeons.

In May, 1861, Congress authorized a surgeon and assistant surgeon for each regiment of volunteers. Governors appointed them after examining boards had passed on candidates. The secretary of war reserved the right to approve or reject appointments. Difficulties in enforcement at once appeared. Colonels of independent regiments frequently asserted that the order applied exclusively to the states, and did not bind them; they consequently excluded surgeons who failed to win their approval. All Western states except Missouri had medical boards. Some tests were rigid, others careless. These Western states allowed surgeons to enter the army without examination, complained the medical director of the Army of the Tennessee late in the war. Most Western doctors had practiced in the locality from which the regiment was recruited. They made no pretense to thorough education, unusual qualifications, or broad experience; but at home they attended the recruits in sickness or in health. Washington was wise to employ them in the field, said one Sanitary inspector, because the national emergency did not call for "the absolute standard of true science."

But ignorance cast disgrace on the profession, answered intelligent surgeons, and harmed the entire medical corps. In September, 1861, Olmsted appealed in vain to governors to established uniform examinations; that appointments without examination had been given 10 surgeons from 57 regiments was reason enough for calling a central board to weed out incompetents. Tripler subsequently discharged the medical officers. Olmsted complained because the board had no power of removal. Court-martial was the only way of removing the unfit from the army, and an incompetent could easily avoid trial. But seven-eighths of the surgeons were fairly well qualified, the commission decided. Results were better than had been expected, although two candidates confessed never having seen an amputating knife; one had been trained in a barbershop, while another knew only enough to prescribe ipecac and Epsom salts.

Owing to want of military experience, obstinacy was an-

other besetting sin of volunteer surgeons. Tripler spoke of
having to force them to make requisitions for cots which
their hospitals badly needed. Some seemed at a loss as to
how to make proper observations; others were too lazy to
record them. By withholding vital information a surgeon
delayed Tripler's reports and crippled his action; their helplessness produced difficulties in identifying diseases and
learning ways to prevent them. A volunteer surgeon should
have used foresight, complained Tripler, who had to teach
him the rudiments of procedure and buck his fixed ideas.
At the seat of the difficulty was the surgeon general, said
the Sanitary Commission. He neglected the "thousand" surgeons and assistant surgeons of the volunteers. As 1861 drew
to a close, Finley had not bothered to send them "one line
of special instructions, or advice and sympathy."

Volunteer surgeons had their virtues. The army accepted
their services; then it left them to sink or swim. In 1861 the
doctor reached his regiment, where at the cost of delay and
vexation he received three hospital tents, medicines, and
furniture. There was little written authority to consult. The
regular surgeons seemed to bow before *Army Regulations*
like medieval scientists before Aristotle; apparently their
contempt for the volunteer arm of the service was no secret.
Time and large-scale battles showed up the inadequacies of
the Medical Bureau's rules. Conforming to procedures did
not always mean that the surgeon received what he wanted.
The bureau would not allow the use of medicines not listed
on the supply table, even though the surgeon thought them
indispensable; substitutes were often insufficient in quantity;
instruments were liable to be poor in quality and too few in
number. If regimental quartermaster and brigade commissary
refused to countenance the hospital fund, they deprived the
sick of more varied diet. So numerous were the drawbacks
of a regimental hospital that frequently the surgeon gave little more than first aid.

Had volunteer surgeons been unwilling to learn, the medical corps would have made no progress. At the end of the war many volunteers felt damned with faint praise; their abilities, accomplishments, and sacrifices had received few rewards, for these went mainly to the regulars. The Medical Bureau was the old sow that ate her farrow, one surgeon complained; it took without thanks and gave nothing in return. Volunteer surgeons as a class had been misjudged and misrepresented, said the Sanitary Commission. What other military group could equal their devotion to self-denying labor? Many doctors had died in performance of their duties, martyrs to their faithfulness; or else they returned home broken in health.

The law of July, 1861, provided each brigade with a surgeon, but made no allowance for personnel and equipment. Proper care of the sick called for well-equipped staffs as well as supplies that could be brought into the field. The Medical Bureau issued no instructions on the duties of the brigade surgeons, earnest medical officers complained, but commissioned "improper and unfit persons." The imperfectly defined authority of the brigade surgeon puzzled the regimental surgeon, creating conflict and confusion. To cure evils and gain greater efficiency Tripler tried to bring brigade surgeons into active participation. Since they were superior to the regimentals, he would use them as instructors . . . and inspectors, who kept Tripler informed of conditions in the Army of the Potomac. Not until June, 1862, did the brigade surgeon serve in his proper sphere, when he became surgeon of the volunteers with rank of major and eligible to all the privileges of officers in the regular corps.

To bring about medical reform the service needed a medical inspector with rank above major. The army stood to profit from his extensive and varied knowledge. More important than generals supposed, the inspector was the best judge of the soldiers' physical condition; to learn whether the army could sustain a forced march or where was the best camp-site one must consult this officer. Without him surgeons carried the burden of special reports in addition to their regular duties. Military health would have improved more rapidly, said Tripler, had he had competent medical inspectors at his command from the first. Three regular surgeons subsequently served in this capacity. Such was their usefulness, said Tripler, that he was able to correct errors in hygiene, improve discipline, and get the army in readiness to advance.

The Sanitary Commission proposed creating the post of inspector general, one of "increased assimilated rank." His duties would include inspection of all camps, hospitals, barracks, and supplies; and he would keep the surgeon general informed. Every European army had recognized the need of such an officer. Only thorough inspection could stimulate efficiency, remedy neglect, and remove abuses. Medical directors in 1861 served as inspectors general. Congress took no action on the inspector-generalship until the passage of the bill reforming the Medical Bureau in April, 1862.

Working under immense handicaps, surgeons did without most of the instruments and appliances we judge essential. Operations on the field—especially at night—must have been extremely difficult. There was no such thing as sterile procedure. Helping the overworked surgeons at Antietam, Dr. L. H. Steiner managed to sharpen his knife on a window sill before cutting a cortical ball from a man's arm. Great battles brought added assistance from civilian surgeons, but the army had to learn to use them to advantage. These pestilential nuisances clamored for tents, horses, forage, and stable space, said Olmsted. Medical officers thought their surgery "reckless." Civilian surgeons often suggested cormorants in their pursuit of the wounded; their neglect of the sick seemed unjustifiable. Sanitary inspectors reported seeing doctors at Antietam who insisted on operating but refused to dress wounds. During the Peninsular campaign Tripler had nothing but praise for six doctors sent by the governor of Massachusetts; using the same supplies as the army surgeons, they managed to set up a model field hospital.

- 4 -

One of the first women to offer her services to the national government was Miss Dorothea Lynde Dix, who had already won a reputation for reforms in the care of the insane. Miss Dix, arriving in Washington in April, 1861, immediately called on Dr. Bellows to provide special outlays for volunteers. Appointed superintendent of nurses, she asked aid societies to set aside small amounts to care for sick soldiers.

A wide range of opinion has been attached to her name. Once she had beauty; now her thin-lipped smile set off a lean face. Her voice had its music. She moved noiselessly, a graceful and slender figure. Precise in manner, she could be winning at times. Doctors found her a mixed blessing, one nurse dismissing her as "a self-sealing can of horror tied up in red tape." Essentially a lonely person, Miss Dix worked zealously on her own. She bothered over distributing supplies and paying surprise visits to hospitals—details that subordinates should have carried out. An angel of mercy in her generation, she often answered the caustic description of a "do-gooder" in the twentieth century.

Beauty in Miss Dix had not made her tolerant of it in applicants for nursing. She stressed the need for strong hearts and willing spirits who would take orders from surgeons. They should give their services at any time, meet either part or all expenses, travel in pairs, be prepared for duty at a moment's notice. Suffering, said Miss Dix, called for sobriety, self-sacrifice, and earnestness in candidates. They ought to breathe and exhale self-control; unmarried and matronly, they must communicate the sense of secure repose to patients through calm and steadfast habits. Too often her policy resulted in the appointment of women who were Mrs. Sairey Gamp's spiritual heirs but who lacked the geniality of that night nurse.

As with so many divisions in the War Department, the Bureau of Nursing needed greater definition of powers; too much of Miss Dix's work had no clear purpose. She worked without plan but according to her ideas of what was right and fitting. Never empowered to enforce obedience, Miss Dix watched many of her efforts grow meaningless. This want of system produced a general order in October, 1863, which placed the assignment and employment of women nurses under the exclusive direction of medical officers and limited Miss Dix's power to the approving of candidates. The general order secured the muster and pay of those in service and maintained discipline. No longer did Miss Dix's canons of taste and usefulness block candidates for nursing. Surgeons were now free to choose their own helpers.

Though the Sanitary Commission gave aid to nurses, it interfered as little as possible in Miss Dix's realm. The problem of supplying nurses to government was a new departure in July, 1861, calling for much clarification. It was understood that nurses would be needed, and that they should be trained; but who was going to pay them? The Women's Central Association of Relief said it could not possibly assume the obligation of financing so expensive an undertaking; selection and training of candidates, yes, but paying them, never. Surgeon General Finley had no idea whether the government would pay nurses. Early in September, 1861, Congress set their wages at 40 cents a day plus rations.

How the army would accept them was the big question. They were to be substituted for soldiers in general hospitals, when either the surgeon general or the surgeon in charge thought their presence expedient. By November, 1861, the Woman's Central Association of Relief had sent thirty-two women to military hospitals. Their reception was not all that could have been desired. Medical officers gave them the unpleasant treatment usually accorded innovators, patronizing and snubbing the women who comforted the sick and performed hard manual labor. The best of surgeons were noted for roughness, complained the association, but the gentleness of women nurses appealed to the incapacitated.

Many of the women were unable to bear the hardships. Katherine Prescott Wormeley* urged the appointment of the refined and educated, because these women gave tone and won the respect of officers. Less sanguine, Alfred J. Bloor* had watched the enthusiasm of educated women dwindle under the hard, wearing life; those who had lasted for any length of time seemed scarcely young and delicate. But they could bear fardels with greater ease than man's ingratitude. Slander dogged women nurses wherever they went. Not even Miss Dix, nun of the seven cardinal virtues, escaped suspicion and innuendo. In the West the army proved so intractable about accepting help from women that Dr. Newberry despaired of making headway against prejudice. No one could fully appreciate their usefulness in general hospitals, while officers spurned aid from women nurses. Women worked successfully in hospitals at St. Louis, said William Greenleaf Eliot of the Western Sanitary Commission; he disregarded criticism, because it was generally the evil communication of indolent males. Immoral women there were among nurses, but in Eliot's experience the doctors and stewards had brought them in; thus the corruption of a few placed good and useful helpers in a doubtful position.

Army doctors had their argument. Prima donnas of self-righteousness came to nursing with little or no training; they took matters into their own hands and disregarded orders, at times going so far as to give their own diets and administer homemade remedies in place of what was specified. Imbued with Victorianism, the proper lady was full of what was her due. She demanded extra considerations, but she was not always generous toward her colleagues. Women nurses made no effort to hide envy, reported a Sanitary agent. To get what they wanted they resorted to bullying. If one nurse received something unusual from the commission, the others demanded the same or even better. Each woman distributed delicacies and extra comforts to enhance her own prestige.

Rivalry sprang up between Protestant nurses and Catholic sisters. Complaints reached the Sanitary Commission that army officers preferred nuns, docile and obedient workers, who took no notice of the evils which the Protestants denounced. Critics accused the sisters of showing partiality to Catholic soldiers and withholding the consolation of the Bible from men of other faiths. Lacking warmth, they exercised formal discipline and turned a hospital into a house of reform. Champion of Catholic nurses, the non-Catholic Surgeon General Hammond said they were numerous in army hospitals because they were good nurses. What Protestant nurses could compare with the Sisters of Charity in efficiency and faithfulness? He deplored any attempt to discharge loyal servants on the basis of religious difference, but he agreed to increase the number of Protestant women.

Masculine jealousy throttled many able women in 1861. Dr. Elizabeth Blackwell, for instance, trained nurses for the Woman's Association. In spite of her quiet but considerable influence, she found herself hampered by traditional prejudices. Under Sanitary auspices a limited number of women received instruction for a period of weeks before turning to help the army. Dislike of this assistance was reportedly more pronounced in the medical corps of the East than in the West. That women nurses were not fully appreciated was the fault of the Medical Bureau, said the commission. In the Peninsular campaign the commission used them with unquestioned success, but in October, 1862, it had ceased to furnish them; this did not mean that the commission declined the services of nurses, but its branches no longer trained them.

In the opinion of the Sanitary Commission, the army should be provided with a specially trained hospital corps.

An estimated total of 3,200 women nurses labored against a changing background. The strength of Civil War nursing lay in the unselfishness and dedication of the women it called on. These pioneers were intent on meeting a national crisis. A job had to be done; it called for native skill and practicality. Necessity taught them; the stronger the devotion the better the discipline. Civil War nursing was amateurish and lacked organization. But out of it there came positive results; a nursing bureau was set up in Washington, while the experiences of influential citizens on the Sanitary Commission later resulted in demands for improvements of hospitals. Insistence on betterment brought about schools for nurses, which were established about the same time in the big cities of the Atlantic coast.

CHAPTER IV

Ambulance Corps, General Supplies, and Medicines, 1861

- 1 -

THE Sanitary Commission fought a pestilence that walked in darkness more than destruction that wasted at noon. The Commissioners believed that pure air safeguarded good health. But war meant overcrowding of soldiers. Army regulations permitted the crowding of regimental camps at the rate of 86,000 men to a square mile. Commissioner Elisha Harris wrote: " . . . in hospitals and transports the natural evacuations and bodily excretions, the suppurating wounds, the gangrenous parts, and uncleansed persons and clothing of vast numbers of soldiers in an unhealthy condition, are combined to vitiate the local atmosphere." [1] Given these circumstances, Harris feared the "worst of endemic infections."

Theoretically the medical officer could control, anticipate, and prevent disease if he took proper precautions. By repeated physical examinations he could help rid the army of weaklings; by revaccination of troops he could minimize the threat of smallpox. In reality a conscientious surgeon might go to the trouble of setting various receptacles in boiling water, fumigating his patients' uniforms, washing their underwear, ventilating his hospital, and separating his patients; then, as though in defiance of his efforts, he frequently watched the symptoms of epidemic disease develop in the

[1] Elisha Harris, *Hints for the Control and Prevention of Infectious Diseases in Camps, Transports, and Hospitals* (1863), p. 14.

patients he was trying to protect. Science had yet to subdue the "general epidemic influences." The commissioners would have to admit that fact: but until the day the world discovered the "primary cause" of disease the commission would take for its guide the old sanitary theory in addition to the latest findings of science.

In the Civil War five men died from disease for every two who met death from wounds; out of 359,528 deaths nearly 249,468 died of disease. Many soldiers suffered from typhoid in the summer of 1861, Olmsted noted. December brought fewer cases, but the rate of pulmonary infections rose. The amount of typhoid among an estimated 130,000 men was negligible, said Dr. Tripler; in October and November fevers of all sorts totaled 7,932. Of this number about one thousand were reported suffering from typhoid. Here, thought Tripler, was a record to be proud of!

The commission could point to success in treating malaria with quinine. It distributed 220 gallons to regiments having special use for it. Reports indicated improvement in health and a reduction of the sick list under this treatment. Tripler urged the surgeon general to supply the army with quinine. Since Finley delayed coming to a decision, Tripler asked the commission to meet urgent cases. It spent $500 for quinine. When at last the surgeon general gave his opinion, he directed limited use of the medicine as an experiment. To the Sanitary Commission this timidity only pointed up Finley's unfitness.

Smallpox had been present in the Army of the Potomac ever since its formation. Tripler ordered the vaccination of all unprotected soldiers before setting out from places of rendezvous and immediately upon arrival at camp. To help prevent a smallpox epidemic Dr. W. H. Van Buren prepared a monograph, advising Sanitary inspectors to combat the "loose ideas" of those in authority, for he heard reports of constant neglect of vaccination. Official channels made such few provisions that surgeons drew on the commission for vaccine virus. In December, 1861, arrangements had begun "for a more systematic and enlarged action." Scarcity of vaccine in January, 1862, obliged the commission to call on its branches for an additional supply. Tripler seemed to think the Sanitary Commission needlessly alarmist. By immunizing 3,500 unprotected soldiers the brigade surgeons had saved the army from the ravages of smallpox. Statistics for seven months disclosed 168 cases, most of which had been detected before they arrived in Washington.

Treatment of epidemic disease at the Kalorama Hospital revealed the confusion of thought prior to the great bacteriological discoveries. According to reports, doctors made no effort to separate patients, letting smallpox mingle with measles. Convalescents discharged as cured of the one had been known to return suffering from the other. The commission knew of six regiments in which as few as one and as many as nine had been prey to measles and smallpox. The hospital director did not deny these accusations, but perhaps he qualified the charges to make them sound farfetched. Infection of convalescents had been infrequent, although he admitted that nine from the Wisconsin regiment had been sick with measles and smallpox due to a change of ambulances. New doctors brought new theories, and introduced a novel system of management. Under the supposition that smallpox would be modified by its indefinite extension and circulation throughout the building, the administration threw open every avenue connecting wards of smallpox with those of measles. Immunity was supposed to result from exposure.

The Medical Bureau ignored Sanitary protests as the cries of men in petticoats. The commission would not be put aside, but asked General McClellan to admit none but smallpox patients to Kalorama. Commissioners proposed the granting of discharges only when all possibility of infecting others had definitely passed. As a precaution they suggested placing contaminated clothing in ovens and subjecting it to high temperatures; they further asked that smallpox ambulances be painted yellow and used exclusively for victims of this disease; they proposed that McClellan place a guard about the hospital to prevent "improper access" and requested that no encampment be set up within a quarter of a mile of the Kalorama.

Measles increased the rate of sickness. Tripler knew no way of stopping it. Many recruits brought measles with them from home. This disease was no respecter of persons; but it infected some regiments more than others. Tripler rarely found it in the regular army, where soldiers were more strict about sanitary matters.

Tripler thought health in the Army of the Potomac satisfactory from July, 1861, to January, 1862, when 6.18 per cent out of 181,082 were ill. Olmsted did not share Tripler's lightness of heart. December, 1861, found volunteers on the Potomac in slightly better health; but the average for the entire force east and west had been inferior to that of the regulars. Absence due to illness meant needless waste of money and military efficiency. The average length of time lost from active duty came to a little more than five days for each man. In some specially stricken regiments the number of sick varied from 33 to 49 per cent. Patients in general hospitals stayed on an average of twenty-four days. The aggregate of cases treated in Washington, Georgetown, and Alexandria hospitals totaled 2,078 for September and 1,963 for October.

Armies in West Virginia, Illinois, and Missouri, reported Olmsted, had been subject to privations and exposures. From the sanitarian's point of view most sickness took place where men from Northern and highland areas were removed to lowland, river, and seaboard sections. Troops from Minnesota, Maine, Vermont, and the ridge counties of New York were more subject to illness, mental depression, and demoralization than any others in the Army of the Potomac. New Hampshire, Massachusetts, Rhode Island, and New Jersey, states with seaboards, sent the healthiest troops. The average constant number of indisposed or sick for every thousand men came to 63 for the Army of the Potomac, 162 for the department of West Virginia, and 116 for the Mississippi Valley. In both East and West from August to October the constant average amounted to 77 for every thousand.

According to these averages, the army could not advantageously use a large part of available manpower, raised at great expense. To secure a force of 300,000, said Olmsted, the United States would have to support an army of 325,000. Wasted effort resulted in aimlessness; many soldiers expressed their restlessness in head colds, excessive fatigue, and indigestion. The same persons might behave differently before combat, when every man on the sick list reported himself well and took his place in line of battle.

The important point, said the Sanitary Commission, was the fact that disease could largely be prevented. Intelligent application of *Army Regulations* and common sense would do much to forestall epidemics. It was nothing new to medical experience that smallpox could be checked by vaccination and malaria by quinine. However mistaken, Olmsted was expressing current opinion when he proposed that typhus could be arrested through systematic attention to cleanliness and ventilation. Enforcement of rules would materially diminish waste of efficiency by disease and the resulting costs of war; to bring about this enforcement became the duty of government. Experience had strengthened Sanitary conviction that the best precautionary system was the most economical. The Medical Bureau neglected its proper functions, the commission charged. Cure of disease had become the first concern of the medical corps; prevention was now a subordinate duty, if it could be recognized at all as part of the bureau's obligations.

The war began with almost no ambulances. They had played no part in the Mexican War and later Indian campaigns. In 1859 a medical board experimented with one having four wheels, which was sent with an expedition to New Mexico; the medical officer in charge turned in a favorable report. The army never really tested the two-wheeled ambulance, but it became the basis of the ambulance system. The quartermaster corps built as many as possible, when the war broke out. For every one with four wheels, five with two wheels were constructed. The proportion proved unfortunate. The two-wheelers, or Finley model, become unfit for the strains of service. Out of 228, no fewer than 119 disappeared in the three months beginning July 1, 1861. Tripler deplored its use; but there it was—a matter of regulations.

On Tripler fell the duty of seeing that McClellan's troops had ambulances. He found that Finley models were being used for anything but their original purpose; officers and men used them for cab service from camp to Washington, until the ambulances broke down. Tripler stopped this misuse; he allowed each regiment one two-wheeler for exclusive use of the sick and wounded, and the rest he turned back to the quartermaster. By October, 1861, the regiments were using 109 two-wheeled ambulances to 12 of the four-wheeled. The quartermaster defended the proportion on the ground that two-wheelers were easier to handle; he did not take into account structural weaknesses. The number of four-wheelers was never high. The army entered the Peninsular campaign with only 177; of this number 74 ultimately returned to Fortress Monroe.

The quartermaster failed to supply the Army of the Potomac a full allotment of ambulances. When the army set out on the Centreville-Manassas expedition, the wretched roads destroyed a number of ambulances and hindered medical activities considerably. Tripler's preparations went awry. The ambulances he asked for in early March, 1862, did not reach him until May.

Ambulances must be placed under the control of the Medical Bureau, said the Sanitary Commission, as it denounced two-wheeled ambulances as having every abominable quality but scarcely one excellence. The springs were so light that the jerking and bumping over rough roads made travel a martyrdom. Curtains served no use; they tore at the loopholes, where they should have fastened down. The horses were too light; bad care made them give out too quickly. Drivers, careless and unskilled boys, could not be relied on in times of difficulty and danger. The Sanitary Commission advocated using four-wheelers, horse litters, and pack mules. Transportation by railroad was little better than by two-wheeled ambulances. Wrapped in blankets, patients lay on the floor. The male nurse generally could do little more than keep their canteens filled with water; he was lucky if he found them any food. Swaying and jolting intensified discomfort; a delay of hours on a siding to let another train pass prolonged suffering. Patients had to bear unseasonable heat or else drafts and freezing temperatures. Small wonder that some arrived at their destination sicker and others dead.

Not until Jonathan Letterman became McClellan's medical director in July, 1862, did the Union Army set the foundations for an effective ambulance corps. Up to that time many suggestions had been worked out, but nothing came of them. In September, 1861, the surgeon general of Pennsylvania had offered a complete ambulance company, consisting of two officers, sixty-seven men, and forty-five ambulances to serve with the Pennsylvania Reserves. Tripler approved the offer, but the secretary of war ignored it. In March, 1862, a Mr. Pfersching submitted a more complex plan. Two lieutenants and a noncommissioned officer in each regiment would command 100 men; they were to follow the army into battle, carrying the wounded back to ambulances. The proposal came to nothing because it met the disapproval of Tripler and Finley.

A general order stipulated that hospital attendants and members of the band should make up the regimental ambulance corps. Medical officers were to drill it daily, except Sunday. Tripler reported satisfactory progress whenever this order was obeyed. Olmsted believed that Tripler did not want an ambulance corps. Medical officers had no military authority; were such a corps formed, its members would no longer be under his command. Complacent about his preparations, Tripler cited their success at Ball's Bluff, where fifty-nine two-wheelers and seven four-wheelers, besides seven transport carts, moved with speed and safety. They came as close to the field as possible, but circumstances forbade crossing the Potomac River. A different account reached the Sanitary Commission. Everything was wrong about the ambulance system at Ball's Bluff, said its informant. Conveyances were too few; removals were made by board and blankets, stretchers not being available. Regimental bands might as well have been playing marches and quick-steps, for as an ambulance corps they were nowhere seen. Panic-stricken soldiers helped back the wounded to the northern shore of the Potomac, but did not return to aid other casualities, who were removed with slowness and difficulty. A general ambulance corps would have overcome difficulties in a shorter time; there would have been none of that strange inhumanity wherein a regiment of one state refused to help the fallen from another regiment or state, because a general ambulance corps would rescue the wounded without regard to these distinctions.

Cairo, Illinois, gave meager evidence of an ambulance system. By November, 1861, the entire force there had two ambulances and an average of two stretchers for each regiment; ambulance drill had not yet begun in any regiment or brigade.

A general belief continued well after Bull Run that wounded soldiers generally managed to creep back to their lines. Few appreciated the support that a vigorous ambulance corps could give to morale; without it the able-bodied left the battlefield pretending to help the wounded; they betrayed their cause, when many soldiers ran away to help one straggling battle casualty. Few people seemed to think that if a man gave his life in national defense he was entitled to humane consideration from the government. Yet battlefield misery served its purpose in eventually creating a satisfactory system of relief.

- 2 -

Secretary Cameron and Surgeon General Finley seemed engulfed in ignorance and paralysis, thought Olmsted. He spent the first week of July, 1861, in search for "definite and certain knowledge" through a confusion resembling primeval night. Assurance glazed the shell of uncertainty; contradiction was the language of officials unfamiliar with their duties. Of this, however, they felt sure: government would give whatever was essential for the soldier's health on field and in hospital, and to this end it would grant powers to certain officers; but no one could agree on what was essential. The medical purveyor issued drugs and other supplies at stated intervals; a regiment was either oversupplied or starved of common necessities. Olmsted felt certain that the medical purveyor could not supply much that the soldier needed.

Shortages begot disorder. Snags in procedure created critical demands. Patriotic citizens wasted time producing the useless, because some person in authority guessed that soldiers might want a certain article. Typical was the havelock fever. The Sanitary Commission steered clear of this rage to protect the ears and nape of the military neck. Miss Dix appealed to the Woman's Central Association of Relief for 20,000 havelocks against strong sunlight; these were made of thick, coarse white linen and flannel. W. H. Russell of the London *Times* had never seen them in India or in Europe, reported Olmsted; Russell had known nothing about them until his recent arrival in the United States. Havelocks kept necks too warm in summer humidity, so soldiers discarded them.

Olmsted felt sure that hospitals would not have sufficient clothing for patients. After Bull Run the Sanitary Commission publicly appealed for donations of ice, wine, spirits, sheets, flannel, toweling, and mosquito netting. Branches of the Central Association and aid societies at once gave shirts and sheets, in addition to such delicacies as currant jelly. The commission provided pens, paper, and writers for patients who could not use their arms; for their increased comfort and better appearance it furnished a barber. By August the Commission had supplied everything but dressing gowns, slippers, and "some irreligious reading." A surgeon in Alexandria advised Olmsted to send literature of a light nature; Thackeray's *Vanity Fair* he considered "too heady."

The Medical Bureau in 1861 neither furnished the hospitalized with clothing nor made an effort to supply the need. According to Dr. W. A. Hammond,* the bureau had never given his hospital at Wheeling, West Virginia, "a single article of bedding." Hammond had to call on the Sanitary Commission for this necessity. Olmsted urged the branches to build up a backlog of supplies, for epidemics and battles would quickly drain Sanitary resources. By close observation the Sanitary Commission worked out its procedures, quickly learning to distinguish between what was necessary and what the soldiers wanted. What was not available in its storehouses the commission purchased in the market. It came to the aid of surgeons at the General Hospital of Alexandria, who lived a precarious existence along with their patients.

They asked for no luxuries but found themselves cut off from necessities. The market was open two days a week, when only enough produce was brought in to supply the limited wants of remaining civilians.

The hospitalized required certain basic things, so the commission made a point of having them on hand. Hospitals continually called for bed sacks. These were filled with straw for field hospitals. The best kind measured seven feet by two feet ten inches, and were left open at one end. Olmsted called on the branches to keep on hand liberal supplies of bandages and body bands, quilts, pillow cases, bed spreads, drawers, dressing gowns, slippers, and hospital furniture. From the Woman's Central Association of Relief came water beds, successful devices for healing bedsores and amputated stumps. The Commission passed on washing machines and beds; it condemned the iron bed for tending to fracture and twist out of shape in transportation, but advocated a collapsible cot of wood and canvas as firm, durable, and portable.

Warm clothing was in steady demand. The commission tried to have large stocks of woolen underclothing in winter, while accumulating canton flannel clothing for the summer; yet it never succeeded in getting "a quarter" of the flannel shirts and drawers and woolen socks it asked for, said Bellows in November, 1862. Miss Dix had early provided aid societies with a pattern for drawers; but the shape of the male torso apparently failed to impress her. Bellows wrote: "Most of our ladies . . . have so magnified our soldiers in their hearts that the shirts and drawers they send us would fit the Anakims, and when found in future ages . . . the people will say, 'There were giants in those days.'" Start with your husband, Bellows counseled a friend; he is your pattern. "Let the majority [of your shirts and drawers] be a medium size, a quarter part a little larger, none smaller." [2]

[2] Bellows MSS. H. W. Bellows to Mrs. R. Swain, Nov. 13, 1862, New York.

Soldiers aid societies sent jellies in large quantities to the several depots. The commission learned from the inconvenience of broken jars that dried fruit was safer. Dried fruit spared trouble in preparation, exorbitant rates, and disappointment on receiving a ruined consignment. Dried apples, peaches, and pears were a few of the items it gave to hospital kitchens. Lemon and blackberry syrup added to the variety of menus. Pickles, cabbages, onions, sauerkraut, horseradish, and codfish gave nutritive value and flavor to the diets of the bedridden. Surgeons were by no means agreed about "delicacies"; they did not always have time to see to their distribution or proper preparation. Patients were often too sick to eat them.

Now and then a branch would send presents which it hoped would prove useful. The "inconsistent and unstable statements" of newspapers about lint had so confused contributors that a "Babel of tongues" was heard in the land. The kind of lint depended on a surgeon's preference. Bellows said: "As to quantity—there was a scarcity, but a call from the Surgeon General flooded him! It rained lint for the space of forty days till the Surgeon General was barely visible above the deluge." [3]

Military hospitals at Frederick, Maryland, were short of stores, but surgeons had little use for the gift of mutton tallow; they preferred water dressings to greasy applications, applying tallow only in case of blistering. Dr. Lewis Henry Steiner ruled out specially prepared washes for wounds in favor of water and castile soap. The imagination had its needs, he said, and women could provide its satisfactions; books of travel histories, biographies, allegories, and pocket editions of the New Testament eased the tedium of convalescence. Games such as backgammon and dominoes Steiner encouraged, but cards he ruled out as signposts along

[3] Bellows MSS. H. W. Bellows to Mrs. R. Swain, Nov. 13, 1862, New York.

the primrose path; a taste for cards implied that the soldier would fritter away his wages and everything else. The Sanitary Commission refused civilian clothes for soldiers without uniforms; gifts of this kind led to desertion and other bad practices.

The Sanitary Commission understandably found difficulty in creating a reservoir. The rate of accumulation was slow, but cotton drawers, flannel shirts, and bed and pillow sacks quickly drained away to places pleading loudest. Up to November, 1861, Washington headquarters took from the Central Association almost eight thousand shirts of all kinds and about two thousand sheets; the total number was sufficient to keep hospitals moderately stocked. East of the Appalachians general hospitals housed approximately three thousand patients. The Sanitary Commission gave no less than four sheets, two towels, two handkerchiefs, and two pairs of socks to each case demanding frequent changes. But so acute were cries for help that storehouses had little to spare and nothing to waste. The situation began to take on alarming proportions. Olmsted asked American women to make the commission the object of their generosity. If they sent hospital stores to camps, soldiers either did not use them with intelligence or else sold what they could for whisky.

New England rescued the Sanitary Commission. In the middle of December came such large contributions from Boston that Olmsted had to admit an upset in calculations. In one month Boston had sent four times as much as the Central Association of New York in six months. This accumulation would relieve the pressure of demand. From Washington alone the commission distributed 34,081 articles of clothing to 116 regimental hospitals and 20 general and "irregular" hospitals; the average number supplied each was a little more than 200. Among the contributions were many unenumerated articles, such as 1,000 books and pamphlets. Total gratuitous contributions for relief in November amounted to at least

$11,000. Active and energetic auxiliaries in Ohio, Michigan, Illinois, Iowa, and Wisconsin had offered goods worth over $30,000.

The year 1862 found the Sanitary Commission drawing more supplies from branches and soldiers' aid societies, as great battles threatened to wipe out all reserves. Olmsted consulted with each commanding general in the East before the spring campaigns, and saw to it that regimental surgeons received the stores they wanted.

What motives prompted people to give? Was it patriotism or pity? Patriotism seemed to move most contributors, said Olmsted. They expressed devotion to the Union, and closely associated it with emancipation. Olmsted thought that the rate of contributing supplies provided an index to the popular temper. Early in the war people made large shipments of old shirts and sheets, but householders soon found themselves in Old Mother Hubbard's position and their contributions became small. "Jolting periods of sentimental enthusiasm" were followed by a "fall." As prices went up and the discouragements of war increased, contributors took hold with a stronger mood, giving more generously and more thoughtfully. On January 31, 1863, Olmsted noted:

. . . household contributions . . . have never been as large as at present; the volume is ever slowly and steadily increasing. Its value is not far from $3000 a day, which, recollect, is wholly a free-will offering of households, about two-thirds of it being a money expenditure of the fathers of families, the remainder of it being the labor of women and children.[4]

- 3 -

The Medical Bureau could not immediately satisfy demands for medicines, bandages, medical appliances, and

[4] Olmsted MSS. Private Letter Book, p. 226. F. L. Olmsted to S. A. Hurlbut, Jan. 31, 1863, Washington, D.C.

other necessities. Had it been a model of efficiency, the bureau would have been driven hard the first year of the Civil War. Supplying vast bodies of men placed strains on the purveyor, Dr. Lamb. He refused all help from Tripler, until events demanded quicker transaction of business. Since transportation of hospital stores was secondary to the provision of weapons, medical officers were obliged to carry their own supplies to camp.

Tripler furnished each regiment with three hospital tents. Since canvas was scarce, officers frequently used these shelters for storage rather than for the sick. Tripler did his best to rectify errors, demanding complete inventories from regimental surgeons and filing requisitions in proved deficiencies; but he could scarcely be expected to inspect every regiment. Each surgeon had stores sufficient for three months, he felt certain. Of course, there were always improvident surgeons with the army, and at the start of the Peninsular campaign a few turned up begging for tents; but the Army of the Potomac was in motion, and Tripler would not unpack his stores to satisfy the negligent and indifferent.

Fortunately the surgeons were more effective than the Medical Bureau. Consider the days of August and September, 1861, when a battle was daily expected. Washington had neither a reserve of hospital stores nor unoccupied beds for 300 additional patients. In event of conflict, as many as 10,000 men would need immediate shelter and treatment; a general cry would go up for medical supplies. Authorities admitted all this, but it had never been the bureau's custom to collect large stocks. Supplies would come from New York if necessary, while workmen could be employed to hammer beds together. In September a trifling skirmish took place at Lewinsville; the Medical Bureau, unable to care for minor casualties, appealed to the commission for lint and bandages. Vigorous surgeons came to the Sanitary Commission with complaints. According to Dr. Hammond, he submitted his requisitions to the bureau and then waited two months. In the interval he bought whatever was necessary from an apothecary. The bureau delayed for over a month in sending stores to Baltimore hospitals. Medical supplies for Burnside's expedition did not arrive until it was about to leave for North Carolina. Among Sherman's troops ready to leave for South Carolina there were cases of smallpox; the medical director could not obtain vaccine from the Medical Bureau but relied on sources in New York. Delays and mismanagement could be avoided, said Hammond, if the bureau would establish supply depots in the larger cities instead of going into the market to fill a requisition.

The medical supply table gave rise to many complaints. The Medical Bureau did not furnish several essential medicines, said some doctors; but Olmsted doubted the validity of this criticism. In the past its framers had carefully prepared the supply table, setting down what they thought important for curing diseases. Here was a snag, for one doctor's panacea seemed another's poison. The Germans generally complained of the absence of many medicines, although American surgeons did not find the same want. Keeping on hand a large and varied drug supply presented difficulties. Tripler apparently did his best to give the surgeons whatever they asked, even though their demands frequently sounded farfetched. How to get around the rigidity of the supply table was his biggest problem. Shackled by regulations, the medical purveyor refused to recognize the priority of Tripler's orders and referred them to the surgeon general. Finley granted no special favors; he forbade issuance of unlisted stores, insisting that anything extra must have his sanction.

Nearly all volunteer surgeons agreed that the quantity of medicines was not sufficient to meet their needs; they also protested against receiving defective stores. Repeated Sanitary protests had little effect on the Medical Bureau. The remedy, thought the commission, must come with an entire change in organization and direction of the bureau. Olmsted recommended that the secretary of war appoint an examining board for the revision of schedules; standards should be the findings of the latest and most enlightened medical science.

Some surgeons had asked why the Sanitary Commission did not take over the distribution of medicines. In extreme cases it had done this on a limited scale, buying what was wanted from a Washington apothecary. Now the commission frowned on making a temporary expedient a fixed policy. It tried to keep its own sphere separate from the government. In theory the administration aimed to supply all the sick with medicines but not food and clothing. Each man would supply his own clothing, it assumed, and every surgeon would give his patient the proper diet by exchanging whatever a sick man could not consume of his rations. In practice responsibility for finding food and clothing rested with the soldier, although he generally received help from the surgeon. And the commission made up what neither government nor soldier could eke out.

In theory the shortage of a medicine arose from one of two sources: either the directing surgeon had not bothered to ask for it or a surgeon of higher rank did not believe the occasion warranted its use. In practice ranking medical officers often made capricious judgments; not infrequently they withheld necessary medications, working on the assumption that the volunteer surgeon was ignorant and excessively demanding. From their point of view it was unwarranted impertinence for the commission to make rough places plain by correcting abuses and doing those things which officers had not done. Theory allowed the ranking officer to take a mother-may-I go-out-to-swim attitude; medicines could never be wanting where the regimental surgeon had been provident about making his requisitions, except when a superior medical officer had said they were not wanted.

Neither systematic nor desultory provision of needed medicines by the commission would solve the difficulty. Responsibilities would have been greater than it could meet; they would call for the employment of a staff of apothecaries at each depot and a doubling of expenditures. A task of this magnitude called for a minimum backing of $100,000; to spend less would do more harm than good. The problem was one for the surgeons to solve.

The commission ought to supply surgeons by issuing through the medical directors, proposed Dr. Hammond, because giving freely to medical officers begot waste and dependence on irregular sources of supply. But, countered the commission, the mismanagement of a few could not offset the benefit thousands received from a generous distribution of its stores. One surgeon could not hold all the regimental stores in his pocket; one ambulance could not carry those of a brigade; one field hospital could not contain everything that a marching army cried out for—but it was possible for the commission to give what the moment demanded.

To remedy specific abuses the Sanitary Commission asked the War Department to encourage a more liberal interpretation of regulations in Medical and Quartermaster bureaus. Rigid rules left the commission no choice; it must furnish more than inquiry and advice. Failure to answer urgent calls would have alienated public support. In a strict sense the commission had overstepped its duty; its stated functions did not include employment of hospital dressers, washing patients' clothing, hospital bedding, bandages, and towels. Time and events had compelled departures from the executive order of June 13, 1861. The commission considered itself an economical and efficient distributor; it paid freight charges, although the principal lines had reduced their rates.

Sanitary duty, said Olmsted, lay in preventing "as far as possible the sacrifice of human life to matters of form and consideration of accuracy of accounts." Methods in distribution were as efficient as could be maintained consistently with this obligation. The business of supply had steadily increased and demanded more clerical help. From every regiment and hospital came vouchers for every article that the branches of the Sanitary Commission had issued.

A small-scale emergency like Ball's Bluff found the commission's reserves so reduced that it was obliged to purchase from shops in Washington. Had the battle been of first magnitude, thousands would have died for want of medical stores; big cities on the Atlantic seaboard could not have responded fast enough; heavy rail traffic would have delayed the flow of stores; Washington, the seat of national power, could not have satisfied one-quarter of the needs, especially if great numbers of Confederate wounded had fallen into Union hands. The Sanitary Commission protested against unpreparedness. Skirmish or battle, these struggles spread a horror, sometimes catching officials and citizens unawares. Few people seemed to know the meaning of suffering. Bull Run taught no effective lesson. Since the retreating army had left most of the badly wounded on that field, not many serious cases reached Northern hospitals. If the experience of foreign countries had any meaning for United States, said Olmsted, the North must prepare to give relief to about thirty thousand.

The idea that the commission was running a charity was repugnant to its members. The government paid Union soldiers better than soldiers were paid in Europe; their wages ought to cover the cost of clothes. The commission decried costly gifts as unfavorable to the development of "true military spirits." Olmsted wanted his group to do less, if Washington would meet supply squarely and take on the burden of the problem. Until that time the Sanitary Commission would carry a heavy load. Minor critics chirped like crickets; the commission, they said, did not supply regiments and hospitals scattered around the country. Olmsted referred detractors to the itemized accounts in his books.

The question of waste was difficult to determine. That Sanitary workers never wasted stores would be impossible to maintain; but rarely were those devoted to the commission's cause willfully careless and improvident. Katherine Prescott Wormeley knew of no deliberate waste of materials. Understandably the commission received much that was never returned; its employees practiced economy but not so as to interfere with the work. The Sanitary inspector at Beaufort, South Carolina, heard no criticisms; the commission's name gave better protection than "a guard in New York City." A Quaker nurse told her mother to send supplies through the Sanitary Commission, because it did "the business right."

Give the soldier hospital stores, underclothes, shirts, sheets, and warm blankets; let the government and the women of America pour out their liberality on some 500,000 in camp and field; but men—poor, naked, forked creatures—would still know days of wet, shivering, and sickness. This was in the nature of war. Because those who stayed at home set out to allay suffering, the commission made the collection and distribution of supplies a growing feature of its work. It never calculated the value of its stores exactly, but they approximated $15,000,000. This was not the great Sanitary accomplishment, thought Olmsted, for furnishing hospitals was incidental to its work. Sanitary activities were many-sided, he said; in their totality they made the army stronger by many brigades.

- 4 -

The Sanitary Commission met Bull Run with almost $11,000 in its treasury. Defeat threw a shadow over the financial prospects, for any check to patriotic exuberance meant a lessening of income. The $7,423 of August mounted to $13,630.03 on September 1. In autumn the Sanitary Commission wanted all the money it could get. With an increase in the number of inspectors expenses started to rise rapidly. The press praised the commission for standing on its own legs without government support. Commendation was sweet, but a growing body could not feed on a chameleon's diet. Bull Run proved a financial drain. Without publicity and mass support the commission could not organize large-scale relief.

Funds came slowly—$1,212.04 was scarcely enough for a November bank balance. Through David A. Wells's efforts the city of Troy, New York, sent in $900 early that month, while a few weeks later he fired the city to give $1,200 plus supplies. The ledger held the gift of tongues; columns of figures arrayed in black and red won converts where argument failed. During the fall about five hundred soldiers had been known to die from malaria. The commission believed it could have saved two-thirds of these wasted lives, had its resources allowed the introduction and carrying out of certain prophylactic measures in the army. Its services at $5,000 a month could scarcely be called superfluous, but they were expensive to provide.

People would always need a representative to express their personal wishes. An efficient Medical Bureau would still leave duties for the commission to perform. The commission did not claim all improvements as its own victories over ignorance; but it had done enough to prove its value as a good investment. It had awakened many to the need for health precautions and possibly lessened the threat of epidemic disease.

The commission paid each of its fifteen inspectors about $1,200 a year. The printing of medical monographs for surgeons cost money. There was the expense of paying for hospital stores, comforts, medical appliances, vaccines, nurses, dressers, bedding, water beds, stimulants, besides freight costs on these and a host of special objects called for from time to time. Big freight bills accompanied generous gifts of medical stores. To increase functions meant meeting all demands and obligations; to cut expenditures threatened efficiency and usefulness. The commission had funds enough to last a few weeks, although it felt the need for more inspectors. Up to November 25 most of the $28,107.95 had come from New York; the Boston branch sent in $10,000 by the end of December, the Pacific Mail Steamship Company giving $1,500, and Philadelphia offering $2,000. Commissioners sported in the showers of money that renewed and refreshed dry hope; they planned to spend $4,500 monthly if the war did not last longer than January 1, 1863.

There were men generous with pleasing words who held fast to their purses; beggars could not be choosers, they said, and the commission was no exception. Let it present its facts and figures to be worthy of charity. There were those who were stingy, and damned the commission for wantonness and folly. There were always the shrewd, self-confessed of ignorance. James Buchanan, formerly president of the United States, would not give a cent to men who usurped the duties of government; but at last he agreed to match whatever the citizens of Lancaster, Pennsylvania, paid out. Lancaster gave next to nothing to the commission, because local efforts went to the care of its own in the army.

As the war progressed, large shipments filled Sanitary storehouses in fits of sentimental enthusiasm. New York City gave less proportionately than rural areas. Peace Democrats blocked generosity in scattered villages, and malingerers back from the front spread slanderous tales about the commission. Besides high prices, rising transportation costs checked country people from contributing; expense kept the commission from furnishing aid societies with material to be made up. Railroads offered liberal terms, but the commission hoped its stores would soon travel free. Speakers visited remote districts to make the Sanitary cause more popular. One described as "very plain" but "good for the many" carried his "wisdom and simplicity" with firm conviction to the hesitating heart.

A good canvasser satisfied the general love of oratory; audiences delighted in hearing an expert put his critics to flight. Horace Howard Furness, the Shakespearean scholar, covered Connecticut and New York for the Sanitary Commission. When he returned to Philadelphia, Furness reported to Olmsted by letter:

It's now some nine months since I surrendered myself to you, body and soul. I have worked in season and out of season. . . . I have addressed large bodies and little bodies, and nobodies and somebodies. I have spoken in Town Halls, in Concert Halls and in Court Rooms, in Presbyterian, Methodist, Baptist, Lutheran and Episcopalian Churches, from pulpits and from judicial benches, before communion tables and baptismal fonts. I have seen before me eyes glistening with interest and eyes drowsy with sleep. I have heard stentorian yawns and rapturous applause, and . . . when I am for the last time . . . pulling off my seven league boots . . . I would . . . believe . . . that the autumn will again see me . . . working . . . for my sick and wounded countrymen.[5]

[5] Olmsted MSS. H. H. Furness to F. L. Olmsted, June 8, 1863, Philadelphia, Pa.

CHAPTER V

Winds of Controversy

-1-

THE Sanitary Commission and the Medical Bureau could do nothing but clash. Their ideas were at variance regarding hospital buildings, adequate supply, the needs and comfort of patients, promptness in answering requisitions, and an adequate medical force to care for a given number of men. They had no common standards for furnishing a military expedition and its probable future needs. Their views differed about vaccine, virus, and quinine. The commission opposed the bureau's views on organization, forming "a very unfavorable and even anxious and indignant conception of its wisdom and humanity." Some twentieth-century critics have expressed little patience with the inadequate hospitals and transportation, the faulty organization of communication lines, and the unsystematic, inefficient, crude, and wasteful methods of handling supplies in the Medical Bureau; they deplored the stupidity of appointing medical directors but depriving them of personnel, equipment, and the means with which to start work.

But the plight of the bureau was not wholly of its own making. It was not its own master but leaned on other administrative units. The exclusive right of building and equipping hospitals as well as transporting the sick and wounded belonged to the quartermaster corps. The Subsistence Corps alone provided food. In peacetime this dependence caused no embarrassment; in wartime it made the Medical Bureau feeble. The bureau could neither form policies concerning care of the sick nor take a stand on disease prevention. Without its own general hospitals it had to accept the quartermaster's ill-adapted makeshifts. The medical division was helpless without inspectors, the right to build its own hospitals, and furnish its own food.

To be partly paralyzed was bad enough, but to accept that fate as right and natural was worse. Before the war the Medical Bureau had the reputation of clinging to hard-shelled ways. It did nothing wicked and nothing wise. Enlightened American doctors knew of European progress in caring for the sick and wounded; yet the bureau disdained these developments as inapplicable. It stressed its own unruffled etiquette. Other divisions of the War Department were learning to meet the new and strange without protests, petitions, newspaper wars, and investigations. Able men headed these sections; appointed without a strait-jacketed regard to seniority, they cut red tape when necessary.

Here was the broad setting in the fight for reorganization. Community interests were at stake. Military considerations necessitated the sacrifice of sick and wounded; but foresight, wisdom, industry, and boldness must lighten suffering. These were the qualities of surgeon-generalship. Making inspection and prevention duties of the bureau, a forceful and intelligent surgeon general would see that a good law produced good results. The commission wanted relief from "painful and thankless functions." To correct one fault apparently entailed righting a myriad errors. Surgeons must be given the chance to work effectively, insisted the Sanitary Commission, and merit, not seniority, must be the basis for advancement. The commission proposed sending home the incurably diseased from military hospitals; it called for well-stocked army medical storehouses; it advocated a large general ambulance corps under the bureau's direct control; it urged building general hospitals which would benefit from intelligent application of European experience. All these things could come to pass after Finley had been removed and his successor appointed by act of Congress.

- 2 -

Work had piled high on the Sanitary agenda for September. There was more to do than an extralegal body of inquiry and advice should have undertaken. Commissioners attended to problems rightly belonging to the bureau. Complaints to Lincoln, Cameron, and Scott produced no effect. Either the commissioners continued to work with the War Department and Medical Bureau or they denounced their inefficiency. Bache, Wood, Shiras, and Cullum objected to any disturbance that would create hard feelings; but, answered their colleagues, there was little good and less honesty in hushing the outrageous simply to appease the bureau.

Suppose the commission ousted "ossified and useless" Finley. Who would take his place? Dr. Wood had long been bobbing for the apple of leadership. His teeth had a distressing way of sliding over the peel, with the apple slipping away; and all he ever got was a snoutful of water and the thankless sense of having done his duty. Wood was "warmhearted" but "blind and fanatical" in loyalty to Finley. Dr. Tripler, another possibility, was energetic and active. Though spasmodic and crotchety, he was better than the "present wooden head." But no fitting candidate seemed at hand.

In September the commissioners turned to McClellan, asking that all medical directors be given discretionary powers with regard to hospital accommodation and supplies. These important officers should be released from the "stringency of regulations adapted only to a smaller and less exigent state of affairs." Age and seniority scarcely qualified the present medical heads, who were as fit to assume great responsibilities as country apothecaries. Tripler and Wood deserved more consideration because of merit and services. Commissioners also asked McClellan to form his own ambulance corps. They hoped he would treat their remarks with confidence. Their program must be made clear to the government; but action must seem to result from official decision. Being humble practitioners, they showed no disposition to arouse public discussion by opposition, for they made it their "loyal study" never to embarrass the administration.

Commissioners also sent certain demands to Simon Cameron. Finley should be retired or given an indefinite leave of absence. McClellan must have an independent ambulance corps. The hospitals ought to employ men and women nurses more extensively. Since relations with the bureau called for confidence and cooperation, the surgeon general should be compelled to grant or deny Sanitary requests in writing. Sanitary inspectors ought to have administrative powers to enforce orders. According to the commissioners, they made these requests for the public good and at McClellan's suggestion, because he wished their organization to exercise a stronger influence on the military machine.

No one knew why Cameron turned this letter over to the surgeon general. Was it part of official routine? Did Dr. Finley read the communication or merely pass on what had been set before him? It scarcely mattered. In his eyes everything Sanitary seemed to carry the mark of the beast. Finley was now glaring "horribly" at A. D. Bache, who bent over backwards to be pleasant to everyone. The surgeon general apparently returned the letter to Cameron, who referred it to McClellan to carry out whatever he approved. The general sent a letter to the commissioners rejecting what he had previously accepted. They had misunderstood him, said McClellan. In the interests of discipline he refused to grant inspectors the power to enforce orders. The recommendation to shelve Finley he ignored; this was understandable, if no available candidate fitted the surgeon-generalcy. McClellan approved the remaining suggestions, ultimately agreeing to put them into effect in the Army of the Potomac.

The curtain rang down on the unresolved confusion of a political comedy with a grim backdrop. Olmsted stormed. Must dying soldiers be offered in daily sacrifice to the moloch of the bureau? Unskilled in political manipulation, the commissioners put an end to solving difficulties in detail. With reformation of the Medical Bureau all other difficulties would fall into line. The commission was too well entrenched in public favor for enemies to attack it openly. The extralegal body was too radical, insinuated critics, and foolish sentimentalists dominated its counsels. With or without government help the commissioners would have to oust Finley; but that they must stoop to conquer was now clear.

- 3 -

A wind had meanwhile blown out of the West threatening Sanitary unity. The Western Sanitary Commission, an independent organization, had been set up in St. Louis. No one could deny the bitterness of war in Missouri. General Frémont proclaimed martial law; the seriousness of this action disturbed thoughtful Northerners, when Lincoln was trying to hold the Border states. A declaration confiscating the property of all rebels acting behind Union lines and granting freedom to their slaves deepened the gravity of the conflict.

Why did Missouri need a separate sanitary association? Easterners wondered. Early in the war Bellows had set up a society in St. Louis subordinate to his organization. Never did the philanthropists founding the Western Sanitary Commission explain their motives clearly. The Rev. William Greenleaf Eliot dilated upon the peculiar difficulties of Missouri, when Confederate invaders and guerrilla bands devasted the lands, destroying trade and sowing dissension. The sympathy of wealthy elements were generally with the

South, while the abrupt transition from slavery to freedom changed all social and industrial relations; the resources of St. Louis were nearly all cut off, as it faced problems of extraordinary magnitude.

Little was in readiness when the wounded poured into St. Louis after the battle near Springfield. They lay in the same clothes for three or four weeks without attention. Help came through the Western Sanitary Commission, created by General Frémont at Dr. Eliot's suggestion on September 5, 1861, and composed of businessmen and philanthropists from St. Louis. In six weeks it established four large general hospitals with over two thousand beds. James E. Yeatman,* Dr. J. B. Johnson, C. S. Greeley, George Partridge, and W. G. Eliot were men of stature in St. Louis. New England, New York, and Washington thought highly of Yeatman and Eliot. Greeley was treasurer of the St. Louis group, Partridge a wealthy tradesman and philanthropist, and Johnson a distinguished physician.

During the greater part of the war the Western Sanitary Commission had exclusive direction of relief for armies west of the Mississippi. In the first year it claimed almost a monopoly of fitting out and supplying hospital steamers and of furnishing medical supplies to Mississippi gunboats. At every important front in the Western Department it maintained agents and hospital stores; it set up numerous soldiers' homes, each of which could boast caring for six hundred men a day; it built and supplied hospitals; it selected and assigned to duty all women nurses in the Western Department; it cared for Union refugees from rebel states and fugitive contrabands. This work duplicated that of the larger national organization, but the Western Sanitary Commission did not play second fiddle; its distribution and expenditures amounted from one-fifth to one-fourth of the amount done by the older group and all its branches.

Without auxiliary societies and collecting agents the Western Sanitary Commission enjoyed "a spontaneous stream of money and supplies" for four years. Now and then large gifts from New England and California filled its treasury. Bostonians organized collections which netted $50,000 by January, 1863. This commission distributed 4,218,922 articles, whose value approximated $3,500,000. Cash gifts came to $770,-998.55, making a total of $4,270,898.55 in donations. When the St. Louis group finished its work, there was a surplus of $59,193.80 to be applied to charity. Like its rival, the Western Sanitary Commission dispensed its blessings with a national view.

Broad and general as the enveloping air, the Sanitary Commission had intended to represent all Americans; hereafter it would be known as the United States Sanitary Commission. Its representative at St. Louis was Dr. William Buel of New York. Just why Frémont and the local philanthropy had decided to ignore his organization was a mystery to Buel. Prior to September 5 the general had welcomed him with assurances of "cordial cooperation." To support his words he gave the doctor letters of introduction to various commanders in Missouri.

Repeated efforts to see Frémont again ended in failure. Buel was not the right man to tackle the unusual. He followed explicit instructions well, but without them he let I-dare-not wait upon I-would. The Western Sanitary Commission ought to have a free hand, he thought; any interference from the United States Sanitary Commission would be unwise and ungenerous. Buel had no stomach for his cause; indecision caught him when he was sick and without a friend. Dr. Newberry, secretary for the Western Department, failed to answer his letters. Listless and self-depreciating, Buel set down as useless his inspections at St. Louis, Jefferson City, Benton Barracks, and Irenton. He wanted his family and better pay; he wanted to resign. Buel spent days in lamentation, when the United States Sanitary Commission might have seized the initiative. The way was open for the Western Sanitary Commission, as it charted an independent course.

- 4 -

"Impetuous in modo, perhaps, conservative in re," Olmsted set out to discover a strong candidate for the surgeongeneralcy. The Sanitary voice in the wilderness called out for "a big humane heart" at the head of the Medical Bureau. No time should be lost; the commission had reached a "zenith," but failure to act would beach it in "another ebb of the tide." The shoe latchets Olmsted felt himself unworthy to unloose belonged to Surgeon William Alexander Hammond, then thirty-four years old, of "superb physique and fine presence," six feet two inches tall, and about 260 pounds in weight. A remarkable flow of language enlivened his powerful voice and pleasing delivery, making him a popular speaker. Apparently unknown to McClellan, he was acquainted with the general's brother, Dr. J. H. McClellan, his aide, Major Williams, and Assistant Secretary of War Scott. Medical leaders in New York and Philadelphia were backing him to head the bureau; scientists like "Loyal John" Le Conte praised him without qualification.

At a secret meeting the commissioners discussed the next move in the ousting of Finley. Hammond's name had a prominent place in their discussions. Bellows, Strong, and Olmsted visited Cameron. Scott, the assistant secretary, wanted Finley removed, but Cameron feared newspaper comment more than the bureaucratic imbecility. Scott supported Hammond, but Cameron would have none of him; he counted the Hammond family among his political enemies in Pennsylvania. In a two-hour interview with Lincoln in October, Sanitary leaders presented their case against Finley and demanded his removal. Commissioners wanted to run the show, said Lincoln; but this they refuted to their own satisfaction.

- 5 -

The United States Sanitary Commission was concerned with medical service, and at first gave little thought to the possibility of a rival. What little information it gleaned was false. Strong, for instance, blamed Miss Dix for the schism, because commissioners failed to say yea and amen to all her suggestions. Bellows and Olmsted regarded the Western Sanitary Commission with gravity. Other states were following Missouri, now virtually removed from the general scheme. Iowa, a frontier state, was forming its own society and contributing to St. Louis. Indiana was setting up its own sanitary gods; Chicago's behavior seemed to smack of independence. While Wisconsin accepted the national plan, Michigan took time before taking Eastern direction. The United States Sanitary Commission could rely on New England, on the central and Border states, except Missouri, and on Ohio and Illinois. Californians gave it more generous support than they sent to the Western Sanitary Commission. Bellows ordered Dr. Newberry to St. Louis. Here the doctor learned that people who walked in darkness liked it; but the Western Commission agreed to keep to its side of the Mississippi and not cross over into areas which had no agents from the national commission.

Writing late in September to Secretary Cameron, Bellows deplored unfavorable reports from Missouri. An efficient officer must replace the present decrepit medical officer, Dr. De Camp; St. Louis must be compelled to enter the national sanitary body. Bellows next wrote to Eliot. What relation did the new organization bear to the Sanitary establishment? General Frémont's action passed comprehension. Could Miss Dix have urged him to act against the government's authorities? Could she have counseled this separatism? No sanitary commission was an island unto itself. The charity of the national body was catholic. It would continue sending stores to the city but only through appointed authorities; calls from an officially unknown group would not be answered, "even when signed by the honored name of Dr. Eliot." The secretary of war had been notified of these complaints; and he had ordered Frémont to dissolve the local commission and accept that of the national government.

But St. Louis stood proud and stiff. If cast off from the army, its philanthropy would go on serving in local hospitals. If the piece must have a devil, Eliot accepted the role. He, not Miss Dix, had founded the body, and Frémont had carried out his suggestions. Eliot refused communion in one sanitary church; the two commissions held common aims, and that was enough. Bellows' letter to the secretary of war was one more of those misunderstandings which so often interfere with good works; but hostile acts would rebound on the perpetrator.

Frémont, continued Eliot, maintained an official character, at once reasonable and cooperative. He allowed the Western Sanitary Commission to undertake anything necessary and essential. To accuse the United States Sanitary Commission of indifference had never been Frémont's intent when he took the nearest way to overcome a great and urgent task. General Frémont, ever the Pathfinder, had squarely met the crisis. To organize under the national commission would have consumed precious time, when St. Louis stood ready to furnish 2,000 beds at once. Here the patriotic citizen treated the sick and wounded more promptly and provided for them better than anywhere else in the country. The Western Sanitary Commission was less than a month old; it was without money, and paid neither officers nor agents, but cooperated with the army. Nothing as a legal body, the Western Commission could make no contracts and do no independent work; but its members found their cue and motive in the Christian virtues.

Exact information might have spared Bellows some embarrassment. At Washington headquarters Miss Dix said she had no part in creating the Western Sanitary Commission. Correction and rebuke came from Dr. De Camp. Eliot had shown him the letter from Bellows. Dr. De Camp rejected all charges with defiance, calling for an investigation of his official record. Bellows was at fault only with reference to civilian-managed hospitals in the city; he had grounds for criticizing the state military hospitals. The quartermaster had furnished Benton Barracks, for instance, with utensils and cooking ranges; but the convalescent home lacked beds and blankets, and a constant fire burned in the stove to keep over a thousand patients warm. They understandably complained of an unvaried diet of meat and bread. Buel thought the medical director lacking in intelligence and efficiency. Rivalry and confusion resulted from different emphases. Eliot and Dr. De Camp stressed St. Louis hospitals; Bellows referred to Missouri's hospitals, and consequently found the medical director wanting.

Dr. Eliot went to Washington on invitation from the United States Sanitary Commission. Bellows, a Sanitary Hildebrand, hoped to hear recantation from one not ready for Canossa. An evening's discussion saw "many wry faces." According to Bellows, the "firmness and union" of the commissioners surprised Eliot, who acted with bad grace and threatened to abandon the entire venture. They based their argument on the authority derived from the secretary of war and the plea for national unity. Eliot was fluent, plausible, illogical, and tenacious. He and Bellows, Strong noted, "clawed each other in an urbane, velvety, brotherly professional Christian way." But Bellows kept his temper. Shortly after midnight the meeting came to an end. Eliot said he would recommend that his association yield. Shattered and angry, he went off to bed.

But his rivals won no victory; to Eliot went the infirm glory. Cameron and Lincoln told him that St. Louis could be as independent as it liked. Hopes for reconciliation and unity now died. The United States Sanitary Commission could not officially deny the existence of a competitor. The Western Sanitary Commission no longer doubted its own place, but it never reached the stature of the older organization. The two commissions agreed to cooperate, but their relations were rarely free from jealousy and suspicion.

Replacing Dr. Buel, Dr. J. H. Douglas and Dr. Warriner of the national commission followed a policy of cooperation with St. Louis. Cautiously Douglas felt his way. In hospitals outside the city he did his best to help the sick, supply the wants of surgeons, and make officers feel that aid was always at hand. He rented a storehouse, but saw little chance of making headway against localism. The Western Sanitary Commission reserved 125 beds at the St. Louis Hospital, while at the Sisters' Hospital it made a similar agreement for 250. The city quarantine grounds took in the sick, as did the convalescent home at Benton Barracks. Three large general hospitals had a bed capacity of about six hundred each. Men nurses were paid $15 a month and daily rations. Women nurses numbered sixty, inclined Sisters of Mercy, Charity, and Holy Cross. Most women offered to work for nothing, but the Western Sanitary Commission preferred hiring them at 40 cents and one ration, the rate set by Congress. Some hospitals provided special service for washing clothes. The Western Sanitary Commission saw that the hospitalized received underclothes, and provided special food for the very sick. Largely through the efforts of the Western Sanitary Commission, St. Louis had become a military medical center by the close of 1861, but not until its rival started to work in the Missouri army hospitals did the Western Commission go out among the regiments.

As the United States Sanitary Commission had to contend with Surgeon General Finley, so did the Western Sanitary

Commission with Medical Director Wright. When General Nathaniel Lyon was in the field, regimental hospitals alone cared for the sick and wounded; by the time he died only one post hospital was open, at Jefferson Barracks. The army needed no hospitals outside St. Louis, until Frémont started to move. So great was the rush that many men gave out. The quartermaster corps consequently built hospitals along the Pacific Railroad to Sedalia and Rolla, but because of overcrowding, patients had to be transferred to St. Louis, and much suffering resulted. From a hospital at the Pacific Railroad station with 125 beds, the army distributed patients to three general hospitals; it also set aside a special establishment for measles, and improvised a post hospital at Benton Barracks. But exclusive emphasis on large general hospitals in St. Louis deprived those at the front of proper bedding and other comforts.

Dr. Wright succeeded Dr. De Camp as medical director. He reversed his predecessor's policy by building hospitals along the routes and near the camps. Ignoring the Western Sanitary Commission, he retained only those general hospitals that he thought necessary. Small wonder that a quarrel broke out between them in November, 1861. According to Eliot, Wright turned general hospitals into death wards for the relief of post and regimentals. Eliot attacked him in the papers. Benton Barracks was overcrowded, he charged. Regimental hospitals looked like sties, where men lay in unchanged clothes without sheets and pillow cases and sometimes without beds, while at the Fourth Street Hospital 250 beds stood empty. Eliot turned to the United States Sanitary Commission, pleading for help in the return of Dr. De Camp. He also sent McClellan a letter through Dr. Bellows. The general apparently checked Wright's operations, for Eliot thanked Bellows for his "cordial and effective interference."

The medical director stayed in office, but relations between him and the Western Sanitary Commission continued
chilly. Wright was not wholly in error, thought Dr. Douglas.
He had to encounter military and medical ignorance in addition to Eliot's hatred. His emphasis on post and regimental
hospitals was correct. Douglas cultivated Wright's acquaintance and even shielded him from further attacks; but efforts
to play peacemaker came to naught. Douglas also admired
the Western Sanitary Commission. Yeatman, a man of "simple habits and unpretending manners," labored "every minute of the day." Eliot, an uncomfortable factor, was "wily"
and "obstinate."

- 6 -

It might have been in November that Bellows presented
McClellan with a long list of grievances against the Medical
Bureau. In the general's presence he drafted a bill of reformation, striking at "the venerable do-nothings and senile obstruc-
tives" who would throttle "no-matter-what-amount-of-skill,
knowledge, reputation and fitness at forty." From the bottom
of the list McClellan picked Hammond's name. Of the entire
medical corps he alone had a just conception of the duties of
leadership and sufficient energy to perform them.

In December, Bellows went to the White House. Here he
"formed a fourth in a quartette of which President Lincoln,
General McClellan and Mr. Prentiss of the Louisville *Courier*
(the great wit who is said to have saved Kentucky to the
Union) formed the other three parts." [1] They sat in the cabinet room, chatting pleasantly and profitably for half an hour.
Perhaps it was on this occasion that Lincoln approved the
reform legislation. Bellows told the president that promotion
by seniority suggested "the man who, on receiving a barrel
of apples, eat every day only those on the point of spoiling,

[1] Bellows MSS. H. W. Bellows to R. Bellows, Dec. 15, 1861, New York.

and so at the end of the experiment found that he had devoured a whole barrel of rotten apples."[2]

Secretary Cameron was absent from the War Department, but Assistant Secretary Scott endorsed the measure. In December, Senator Wilson introduced the bill (S. 99) which was referred to the Committee on Military Affairs.

The Sanitary Commission wanted a director general, with the rank, pay, and emoluments of a brigadier general, to take the place of the surgeon general. An inspector general, with rank of colonel of cavalry, was to supervise the sanitary condition of quarters and camps and the efficient functioning of the field and general hospitals. Eight inspectors, each ranking as lieutenant colonel of cavalry, would inspect quarters, camps, and field and general hospitals; their additional duties called for written reports on the skill, efficiency, and conduct of medical attendants in the corps. Forty-one first-class surgeons, all with the rank of major of cavalry, would be assigned to staff, bureaus, and hospital duties. Fifty second-class surgeons, ranking as cavalry captains, would be assigned to regimental hospitals. Examining boards were to examine one hundred medical cadets between the ages of eighteen and twenty-three in special fields. Three years of good service plus good character references would fit them for promotion after examination. Their rank was to be that of the highest grade of noncommissioned officer. Hospital stewards with the rank of sergeant were to be employed as the situation demanded.

Immediately on passage of the bill the president was to select suitable persons for surgeon general, inspector general, and inspectors from the medical corps. Merit would dictate their appointments; seniority would determine the advancement of all others up to and inclusive of first-class surgeons. Assistant surgeons would be drawn from civil life, their ad-

[2] John Murray Forbes, *Letters and Recollections of John Murray Forbes* (2 vols., 1899), edited by Sarah Hugh Forbes, Vol. I, p. 267.

vancement depending on examination. Retirement was set at sixty-five. Such was the kind of Medical Bureau the commission wished to see. Its strength and thoroughness would depend on able administrators. The bill had been written with a view to applicability and practicality.

McClellan notified Hammond, giving him assurances of ultimate success. The general promised to demand his appointment on passage of the legislation. Hammond looked forward to the progress and expansion of the bureau; he wanted to establish an army medical school in New York under Dr. Van Buren's direction and organize a corps of pathologists. Honored by Sanitary backing, Hammond expressed pride in his record for organizing hospitals at Chamberstown, Hagerstown, Frederick, Baltimore, and Wheeling. He suspected that Surgeon General Finley had sent him to West Virginia to get rid of opposition. Senators Lane and Pomeroy promised to support the bill, but Finley and his cohorts would attack it. Blair of the House Military Committee had supposedly agreed to give Finley his backing if the law allowed the president to retain a surgeon general who had passed sixty-five. Sly tricks scarcely justified reorganization, protested Hammond, and might ruin his chances of appointment.

Only a newspaper battle could make a public spectacle of "rigor mortis" in the Medical Bureau, thought the commissioners. They knew that the surgeon general was anything but supine. After forty-three years of meritorious service he would give no quarter to keep his office. The alignment of forces was not without irony. Republican commissioners acquiesced in the Copperhead leadership of Manton Marble of the *World*. Protecting Finley was the Republican editor, Henry J. Raymond of the *Times*. His enmity stirred up mischief for the commission, spreading "a vast amount of misconception, ignorance, and positive lying."

There was no evidence that Finley took an active part in the battle of print. A Miss Powell came to his defense. Little was known of her; before the war she had worked in a New York woman's library. Miss Powell apparently divided humanity into blackest fiends and dazzling seraphs who behaved in the style of Dion Boucicault. Most fallen in nature was the arrogant Mr. "Olmstead," lord of the Sanitary Commission. This Svengali was bent on destroying the surgeon general. The commission screened Olmsted and his accomplice, Hammond, in a conspiracy to sink "their arms up to their elbows" in government funds. Olmsted used the names of prominent persons who had signed as commission members, but kept all plans to himself. Hammond, a stranger to things military, suffered a gull's fate. The army ultimately "degraded and sentenced" him to ten years in prison for cheating and robbery.

Miss Powell had known Olmsted personally. Once they conversed together about supplies. She discerned his Mephistophelian fascination—"the man of consummate abilities" who worshiped power "and the handling of millions"—but she had not forgotten her moral sense. As "voluntary superintendent of nurses in a military hospital" Miss Powell met Surgeon General Finley on his visits to her patients. On one occasion he saved a patient "in the last stage of typhoid fever" with a dose of quinine. None of the six resident doctors had had courage enough to take this step. Finley was so solicitous about comforts for the patients that Miss Powell opposed any plan to oust him. Since she had mastered the facts to her own satisfaction, she donned the armor of righteousness. Raymond heard her revelations of Olmsted's plans to rob the United States Treasury.

She said: "I shall not begin the attack unless the *Times* will help me, for I would be useless. You know Mr. Olmstead better than I do . . . '"

He answered: " 'You are fighting a mean and flagrant injustice. Go ahead and do not doubt my help.' " [3]

The war started about the same time that Wilson presented the reorganization bill to the Senate. In an article written by Dr. Agnew, the *World* accused the bureau of doing nothing. The American people on the eve of Thanksgiving could bless the good weather that had saved the army. The volunteer surgeons would benefit from new leadership. Their present surgeon general bound them in red tape, made no effort to clarify their duties, and heeded nothing about the latest developments in hospital construction. The Sanitary Commission, answered the *Times,* would do well to pluck the beam from its own eye. Its workers let the sick lie in camps until beyond recovery; 60 per cent of the deaths in Washington's general hospitals had come from camps under Sanitary care. The commission, retorted the *World*, was the government's "right arm." It could point to results. Sanitary inspectors had distributed smallpox vaccine for five thousand men, but Finley provided nothing with which to meet the threat of epidemic.

Miss Powell, arrayed as "Truth," now indulged in operatic pyrotechnics, accusing the commissioners of a maximum expenditure for a minumum of results. They set up expensive model hospitals in Washington, which would be useless when the army set out on its march. Their bed capacities were too small. Why build two hospitals to house two hundred, when some eighteen old buildings would meet military needs? To whom was the Sanitary Commission indispensable? Who felt the charms of this chimera? The public deserved a report; it wanted to know how its money had been spent on improving camps and distributing supplies.

In December a letter from Olmsted appeared in the *Times,* assuring Raymond that the commission was pursuing pre-

---

[3] Miss Powell to Adolph Ochs, Feb. 15, 1901. By courtesy of A. H. Sulzberger.

scribed duties. Findings from 300 inspections had been sent
to the War Department. Each day Sanitary distributions came
to $1,000 in value. If "Truth" would visit Olmsted's office,
she could read properly signed vouchers for more than
20,000 articles furnished hospitals in November. The New
York *Tribune* charged Finley with laboring to defeat reorganization. His adverse report on the bill confused age with
merit. The surgeon general attacked proposals which would
empower Lincoln to make his own selection and retire surgeons at the age of sixty-five. He opposed giving brigade
surgeons an equal chance of promotion with regular army
doctors. To save the face of united opposition, continued
the *Tribune*, Finley was quietly sending to distant posts
those surgeons who favored the measure.

The *Times* published Dr. Eliot's report on the Western
Sanitary Commission. Perhaps Raymond thought that in St.
Louis the public had a model of generosity, sacrifice, and
pride unmarred by ambition. But Eliot was no catspaw. Years
of peace had dulled the edge of the Medical Bureau, he admitted, but it had cooperated with St. Louis in creating "the
most complete and best managed" hospital system in the
United States. Support from the Western Sanitary Commission could have been greater in urging reformation. By an al-
liance of commissions the bill might have been pushed
through Congress, reported Dr. Douglas, but the Western
Commission understandably felt "a little shy." Eliot supported
the measure in so far as it would help him get rid of Wright.

In the middle of December the Sanitary financial statement drew Raymond's fire. Out of $28,000, about $18,000
had been spent in salaries and traveling expenses, printing,
and hospital supplies; the last-named item included nurses
and amounted to $2,596. That operating expenses should
average about $5,000 sounded suspicious. Why were fifteen
civilian inspectors hired, when they knew nothing of military life? The *Times* demanded a report on military health

and the work of Sanitary inspectors. The commission had failed to supply every regiment with vaccine. Its attack on Finley had been covert and insinuating until the introduction of its bill, a blind to place the commissioners in the saddle. These geese of Juno would hiss Dr. Finley out of office, because they had failed "to substantiate any charge involving inefficiency or dereliction of duty in any respect."

Olmsted gave Raymond the lie in a chance encounter. The fifteen inspectors were improving with systematic inspections; the commission hoped to add three more. The *Tribune* held up the *Times* to scorn, reminding readers that the commission lacked the immense sums necessary to vaccinate the whole army; it had no authority to touch a single soldier. Why should an extralegal body perform the bureau's specified duty? Did the *Times* really believe a commission of inquiry, and advice, could supplant this division of government? Was this the reason for hindering the commission? If so, Raymond had pinnacled himself on the inane. His reason was "not only preposterous but criminal." The Medical Bureau was in a position to know what every army needed, but from all sides came reports of its sins of omission. Since it had not kept up with other sections in the War Department, reorganization would clearly serve a good purpose. Seniority was good, but energy and talent were better.

Union troops sailed to Port Royal, South Carolina, without proper hospital and medical equipment, charged the *World*. One-third of General Sherman's army was on the sick list. He ordered a hospital built, but the surgeon general put his foot down: winter was too pleasant in South Carolina to warrant this expense. But tents failed to keep out the cold. That four convalescents froze to death did not change Finley's mind. Smallpox was "unusually fatal." The commission sent 130 boxes of hospital stores, including vaccine and 1,200 blankets.

As Miss Powell surveyed the field, she noted how the forces

of evil were winning the battle. According to her report, Olmsted saw to it that Mrs. Raymond was brought on the scene. Now the full wrath of this lady made Raymond act "like a whipped hound." Olmsted saw to it that Mrs. Raymond heard about the "undue influence" which a girl in Washington was exercising on the editor of the *Times*. Gossips told Mrs. Raymond that this Morgan Le Fay was out to wreck the commission. Miss Powell admitted:

When I heard of this thru' Raymond my wonder was that he hadn't tried it long before, for certainly this was the effective thing to do. Raymond appealed to me to release him from his promise for the sake of "escaping hell" within his own doors.

Miss Powell denounced his cowardice, and sent no more letters to the *Times*. Once she met the Raymonds at a musicale. Mrs. Raymond lost all self-control and insulted Miss Powell, who, though she "took no notice of the offense," carried off the honors of the evening. She wrote:

I left . . . in a few moments, saying to the white faced Raymond, as I left the parlour, 'Mr. Raymond, I shall send an article to the *Times* in a day or two, and in common justice to the Army officers in the Medical Department I shall expect your aid in having it published.'
'Ah, that was wicked,' said the Colonel [her host] as he and his wife escorted me to the door, 'but it was like a woman.' [4]

Miss Powell had only herself to think about, but the Sanitary Commission was obliged to stand on its record before the country. Reform the bureau by mobilizing public opinion, advised J. M. Forbes of Boston, but remember that citizens would want overwhelming proof before they were willing to interfere with the military. A precise and factual report would win them over; it would add force to moral weight, and enlist men of influence to fight the Sanitary battle. Forbes wrote:

[4] Miss Powell to Adolph Ochs, Feb. 15, 1901.

The President is notoriously tender hearted about removing anybody. It is his weak point. To get him to do it you must make out a strong case to him and bring all possible influence besides.[5]

Early in December, Strong spent about five days in Washington. Not in years had he worked that hard, outlining the subject and leaving "a great pile" of notes for Olmsted "to polish into shape and comeliness." Olmsted enjoyed working under pressure, sleeping one night out of seven and drinking pale ale as a "prophylactic" against nervous exhaustion. He and the printer bent all efforts toward publication; and when at last the *Report to the Secretary of War* appeared in public, it sang "God rest ye merry, gentlemen" to the contending parties.

Olmsted's *Report to the Secretary of War* answered all questions about the commission; it synthesized reports covering campsites, drainage, water, food, ventilation, tents, diseases, surgeons, hospital administration, organizational expenses, and many other items. The *Report* won applause at home and admiration abroad, because Olmsted refused to palliate evils or compromise his exacting standards. He presented "the most exhaustive and authoritative *exposé* of the various causes which affect the true efficiency of an army that has ever been made public."

Nowhere did Olmsted descend into the arena. Not once did he mention Raymond and the battle with Finley. The *Report* brought new points of view to bear on difficulties in the Union Army; it substantiated existing criticisms with statistical evidence, and summarized the commission's experience for five or six months. He advocated increasing the rank of the army medical staff; its relations with all ranks and departments called for greater intimacy, confidence, and influence. Any obstructions to greater medical efficiency would meet Sanitary opposition. Those impugning the commission's motives were deluded, making personal a problem of human-

[5] Box 639. J. M. Forbes to H. W. Bellows, Dec. 13, 1861, Boston, Mass.

ity. The volunteer's welfare was the Sanitary end; preservation of his right to proper care was its basic duty. Pointless criticism objected to improvements, for many citizens, more volatile than thoughtful, feared the entrenchment of militarism in American life. The army must be one with the citizens—that was the central truth of American life. All the Sanitary Commission asked was the "invigoration of proper departments" that they might truly function and relieve the extralegal body—"an artery of the people's love to the people's army."

The *Times* slowly and unobstrusively started its retreat. The purpose, methods, and results of the commission showed that it had done more than quarrel with army doctors, admitted Raymond. The *Report* was a picture of "humanity ministering to wants and sufferings that would become horrors but for such merciful ministrations." Yes, it was Happy New Year for the commission. The *Herald*, that political weathercock, and the *Post* now joined the *World* and *Tribune* in paying compliments. If the bureau reformed itself, the public could thank the commission; otherwise, reorganization would be one of the benefits the Sanitary Commission was about to confer on the nation.

Months later Raymond and Miss Powell ended their "silly platonic friendship." Presumably the scene was acted in high manner. According to report, the curtain came down with the entrance of the police, and the lady was forced to quit Mr. Raymond's premises.

CHAPTER VI

Mixed Blessings

- 1 -

ITS machinery worked steadily as the commission grew in prestige. The uninformed feared and hated it; those who understood its operations showed increasing respect. But the Sanitary prospect was one of drift. President, Congress, and the people, thought Olmsted, still failed to grasp the commission's importance. *World, Tribune,* and *Post* clamored for medical reorganization. They reminded readers that since June, 1861, disease had disabled thirty for every one man incapacitated by violence or accident; at least fifteen of these had sickened as the result of neglect. An efficient surgeon general was becoming as imperative as an able commanding general.

Olmsted, anything but hopeful, was prepared for "entire indifference" in Congress. Senator Dixon, knowing nothing of the bill, thought he might support it. An obstinate opposition was making Senator Wilson wish he had never proposed reorganization. Threatening was the turn of affairs in the House of Representatives. As an act of friendship, Frank P. Blair, Jr., chairman of the House Military Committee, presented a bill drawn up by Dr. Wood, heir apparent by seniority. It received the backing of a strong lobby, whose operations had been limited and retarded by hatred of the Sanitary Commission. The House would act when Blair chose to push the measure vigorously. The commissioners themselves were not of one mind. In distress Dr. Wood had called

116

on A. D. Bache and played on his sympathies. That Wood was Finley's henchman was no secret to Bache, but he gave assurances that the commission had no bill and was responsible for none. Olmsted expected a clash at the next board meeting. Howe, Bache, and the Western members showed a disposition to act with Wood, while Harris would compromise. To meet this disturbance Olmsted succeeded in putting off the session until Congress had begun to act on the bill.

Cameron—that cross between Reynard the Fox and "some large chilly batrachian reptile"—was out of office in January, 1862. It was not altogether easy to see him go, said Bellows, because Cameron had taken pride in the commission as one of his own creation. His successor, Edwin M. Stanton,* was "bold, prompt, incisive," said Olmsted, and worked well with McClellan. The commissioners formed a pressure group along with representatives from life insurance companies and relatives of volunteers from Boston, New York, and Philadelphia; they would visit Stanton to demand Finley's retirement and Hammond's appointment. But how could visitors make the unwilling willing? pondered Olmsted. Wilson, pushed to present the bill, would do so with little relish. Had his committee passed the measure, the Senate would have enacted it without difficulty. Legislators forced to act would decide against their inclinations. According to Olmsted, Wilson refused an interview with the visiting committee. The Senate would not pass the Sanitary measure because his colleagues thought it not of primary importance.

That Washington knew little about the Medical Bureau surprised the pressure group. The newspaper battle had as much bearing on the lives of public servants as Mr. Pickwick's Theory of Tittlebats. On January 23, 1862, McClellan and Stanton visited Sanitary Commission headquarters. Having just recovered from a long illness, the general showed signs of wear and tear, while the features of the "rather pig-faced" Stanton shone with a virtue resplendent. The secretary doubted whether anything could be done until Congress acted, but he supported reform. The commissioners could ask for nothing more. Bellows exchanged confidences with Stanton, parting from him like a brother. All friendliness, Senator Wilson forgot his decision not to see the committee. Visitors and congressmen worked over for two days the details of proposed legislation and presented "a highly concentrated bill embodying the minimum of revolution." They visited the White House, where Bellows asked to be heard before appointments were made to the surgeon-generalcy. This was impudence but necessary, thought George Templeton Strong. "Puzzled and confounded," Lincoln replied, "Well, gentlemen, I guess there is nothing wrong in promising that anybody shall be 'heerd' before anything's done." Strong watched him with something of the condescension of Major Pendennis, but admitted that Lincoln was the best president since Andrew Jackson.

On a visit to St. Louis, Finley loudly defied the United States Sanitary Commission. He confined his visit to city hospitals, noted Douglas, but stayed away from struggling post and regimental hospitals. Finley's resignation now seemed more than a possibility. Only Miss Powell defended him. The Senate Military Committee received nothing but complaints about the Medical Bureau. Convalescents in Alexandria were reported as resorting to swill tubs for food, while the surgeon general fought all attempts for reform. Signs of desertion mounted in his own corps, as staff members conceded his cause lost. The Senate started an investigation of army hospitals.

- 2 -

Malaria, privations, and exposure in the West sniped better than the enemy. Surgeons numbered too few for regiments at maximum strength. Nowhere did they have at hand the conveniences of large general hospitals; drugs, medicines, and hospital stores were secured with difficulty, partly because of the quartermaster's irregularities at Cairo, Illinois. Medical supplies were generally below the quota set by regulation. In battle an orderly carried them in a knapsack. Each regiment had two or three stretchers. Two-wheeled ambulances soon broke down, while those with four wheels withstood harsh treatment better. Not more than one hospital tent was given to a regiment. In cold damp February, Dr. Henry S. Hewit,* medical director under General Grant, commanded surgeons to carry from fifteen to twenty extra blankets. A funnel-shaped stove, open at the bottom and placed on the ground, kept the sick and wounded warm; it heated smaller tents better than the larger. Western armies moved over uncultivated vastness, through comparatively few towns and villages. Along rough roads and across miry fields they campaigned miles from their bases. To make practical arrangements ahead of time was extremely difficult in wilderness campaigns. Though the bureau slept, its surgeons expanded the bed capacity of Mound City, Illinois, from 1,000 to 1,700, while they tried to build up another bed reserve at Paducah.

Fort Henry capitulated to General Grant on February 7. Encouraging also was the news that General Burnside had captured Roanoke Island, taking the Confederate force and its gunboats. In the West, Union gunboats met pro-Union sentiment along the Tennessee River in northern Alabama. Untried volunteers largely fought the battle around Fort Donelson, where General Grant scored a victory on February 16. To Dr. Hewit went the honor of organizing ambulance corps and field hospitals after the manner used in more advanced European countries. Under trying circumstances, and on a shoestring, surgeons worked as efficiently as possible. Each regiment went into battle with one medical officer, who stayed with the fighting unit regardless of its fortunes. He treated severe injuries on the spot, even though surgeon and patient were under fire. If the injured could walk, he was ordered some three hundred yards to a rear depot, generally a ravine out of Confederate fire. Here he met an ambulance train, which took him over a winding route with little danger of exposure. Three log huts, outbuildings, and a tent made up the hospitals; other buildings were later added. Experience showed the unsuitability of log huts and stables; more preferable were crude shelters of canvas that covered hay strewn on the earth, where the wounded rested and were fed. They stayed four or five days before steamers took them down the Cumberland to the general hospitals.

Medical equipment was the same as that used at Bull Run, but planning made the difference. Sanitary inspectors thought Hewit fussy and of few abilities; apparently they were mistaken. Where Tripler was fearful, Hewit proved resourceful. Hewit organized the ambulance service by brigade, not by regiment; he used the ambulance train wherever needs were most urgent. He seemed to have been the first to use tent hospitals. Hewit's organization of field hospitals and dressing stations in the rear contained "the germ of our whole modern system of service at the front."

It was impossible for the Medical Bureau to care for all casualties. In winter weather hundreds lay beneath the sky. Hospitals in Western cities were overtaxed; supplies vanished in a short time; the work was greater than limited facilities could undertake. Such Western branches of the Sanitary Commission as Chicago, Cleveland, and Cincinnati had made elaborate preparations. Cincinnati fitted up the *Allen Collier,* a river transport, and sent it to Fort Donelson. Dr. Hewit accepted everything that Cincinnati gave, but roundly abused the delegation of doctors and nurses as "interlopers."

Grant opened up the South to Union arms. Confederate troops withdrew from Bowling Green, Kentucky, and Nash-

ville, Tennessee. By March 1, Union gunboats had moved up
the Tennessee as far as Pittsburg Landing, where Grant followed. There on the west side of the river he remained
for one month without fortifying his position. Drs. Read and
Prentice, agents of the commission, set up headquarters at
Nashville and there received large Sanitary shipments from
Cincinnati and Cleveland. Near the end of March, Newberry
opened a station at Louisville, one of the most important
branches. From Fort Donelson to Shiloh the Union troops
fought sickness. The Sanitary Commission gave everything
it could muster to check its spread. The sick lacked proper
shelter, while surgeons ran short of drugs and comforts.
Savannah, Tennessee, became a hospital, all houses containing invalids. Government boats were inadequate; except for
City of Memphis, they were not fitted to carry the sick. The
one steamer did what it could, until a hospital fleet from St.
Louis brought some relief.

Misery in the Army of the Cumberland apparently left the
Medical Bureau unmoved. Early in February, General Lander's division was scattered over the hills in all directions for
forty miles. Mrs. Lander told the commission that a thousand
were in the hospital, but others lay without tents; nearly all
were "starving" and "wanted everything." No one in authority had warned Tripler: that troops were stationed in Cumberland was news to him. His investigator found the abandoned men in want of discipline, system, and funds for the
commissary. They were crowded into dirty quarters and ate
badly cooked food, while sick men staggered through the
streets in search of shelter and medical attendance. That the
sick received proper hospitalization and attention was largely
due to Surgeon George Suckley. His labors almost immediately reduced the number of deaths. The bureau sent him
some help, but he complained that it was not enough. Suckley felt justifiably proud of his record, as he examined his
1,314 patients and looked after 200 attendants.

- 3 -

The commissioners could depend on Senator Wilson for
sly tricks. After Congress had passed the medical bill, he
said, the lawmakers would vote on another measure to in-
stall Hammond. The deception was plain, thought Olmsted;
Wilson would arrange to make another man surgeon general. McClellan seemed indifferent about pushing reorganization. Finley was gunning for Hammond with charges of
physical unfitness. Olmsted worked to round up senatorial
support for the young doctor. Senator Pomeroy swore by
Hammond, who "in the very darkest hour" long ago had
stood by Pomeroy when others failed.

On February 7, Wilson introduced bill S. 188, a compromise that had received Stanton's approval. It lacked "definite-
ness upon the all important principle of selection and the
removal of the present incumbent." The commission objected
to choosing the surgeon general from the senior surgeons of
the regular army exclusively. Everything looked as though
the bill would preserve the status quo. But the printer had
made an error; as the bill read, it failed to accord with the
committee's decision. Wilson corrected the mistake; the surgeon general was to be chosen from the whole medical staff.

So different in scope and extent were Wilson's small-scale
alterations that the commission's proposed legislation assumed a drastic character. His bill would add ten surgeons,
ten assistant surgeons, and twenty medical cadets to the
Medical Bureau. It would allow the surgeon general to appoint as many hospital stewards as he thought necessary for
the service. It conferred on him the rank of brigadier general,
and made colonels of both assistant surgeons and inspector
generals. The bill directed the inspector general to supervise
everything relating to "the sanitary condition of the army,
whether in transports, quarters, or camps, and of the hygiene,
police, discipline, and efficiency of field and general hospi-

tals . . ." Eight medical inspectors were to hold the rank of
lieutenant colonels. The bill charged them with inspecting
transports, quarters, and camps, and field and general hospitals. Their reports to the inspector general would relate to all
circumstances concerning the skill, efficiency, and good conduct of medical officers and attendants.

Senators debated Section 4, providing for appointment of
the higher officers by the president with the advice and consent of the Senate. Higher officers were to be chosen from
army surgeons without regard to their rank. Section 5 concerned the office and duty of medical purveyor. Section 6
dealt with examination of medical officers.

The act was restricted to the medical corps of the regular
army, said Senator Wilson. Senator Foster of Connecticut
could see no justice in this. The standard was merit; let
worthy surgeons be appointed to posts of command. But
claims of the regulars preceded those of the volunteers, answered Senator Rice. Government was under contract with
medical officers; their claims to promotion were prior to the
volunteers', who had entered the army at the bottom of the
scale. Volunteers accepted an "implied contract" that they
would take promotions whenever vacancies should occur.
But only ten new officers were being created, protested Senator Grimes of Iowa. The president must be free to appoint
a man "who stands head and shoulders among his fellows, a
perfect Saul among the prophets."

Higher positions ought to be open to assistant surgeons,
Wilson noted. In many instances they were the equals if not
the superiors of senior surgeons. Now he was chary of placing
brigade surgeons on a par with the regulars. Brigade surgeons
did not want to share the benefits of the proposed legislation,
said Wilson; their patriotism did not compel them to enter
the army permanently. Selfish careerists might take unfair
advantage of generous prospects for advancement. The regular corps formed a broad enough basis for selection. Yes,

agreed Senator Nesmith of Oregon, the rights of faithful servants must be defended from "empirics, quacks, politicians." If the bill included volunteer surgeons, congressmen would make the Medical Bureau a political football; Esculapius and Galen would have to resort to political influence were they to apply for surgeoncies.

But, countered Grimes, the majority of soldiers were volunteers. Surely they had the right to choose their own doctors. They disliked the treatment of regular surgeons, preferring to be "physicked and dosed by their own neighbors and friends, men whose reputations they knew at home." Obviously the ablest should fill the important positions, said Senator Fessenden of Maine. That men should bleed and sicken just for esprit de corps was singular indeed. The army chose good officers from the civilians. What was to prevent it from using eminent doctors? To attract talent, enlarge the circle of choice.

But Senator Nesmith liked to see men working up from the bottom. Why should the citizen soldier express his medical preferences when the bureau was the heir of all the ages? Its surgeons were better than many an individual might choose for himself. The Sanitary Commission favored selection from the regular army, said Wilson. Coveting places for supporters and friends was not its forte; it simply demanded the appointment of the fittest. The Senate majority decided to expand the basis of selection, including volunteers as well as the regular medical corps. Senator Hale of New Hampshire proposed that the president be allowed to draw at large on the country's skill; this motion was defeated. Senator Grimes added an amendment restricting the act to the rebellion.

That government was best which cost least, thought Senator Sherman of Ohio, who reasoned not the need. The present surgeon general had made no complaints about receiving $2,740 a year. The bill proposed to give him $4,760. New officers would receive about $500 more than Surgeon General Finley's annual stipend. Why these large increases? Sherman would have none of the bill, unless surgeons' pay continued without alteration. But the measure would save more than it spent, said Wilson. Nine qualified surgeons would spare health and cut down on hospital expenditures by "tens of thousands of dollars annually." What difference did it make whether an inspector was general or colonel? asked Fessenden. The rank of lieutenant colonel was vital, if you wanted to enforce decisions, answered Wilson. Inspectors could work as simply as surgeons, insisted Sherman. They had no responsibility other than making inspections and submitting reports. Wilson answered that as colonels they could give orders.

Sherman was not impressed. Officials acting in an advisory capacity did not need high rank. He succeeded in demoting the surgeon general to a colonel, and reducing his salary from $4,760 to $2,740 a year; he stripped the assistant surgeon general and inspector general of their colonelcies, and specified that they must be surgeons of ten years' service; he took from the eight medical inspectors their rank as lieutenant colonel, requiring them to be assistant surgeons of ten years' service; he lumped ordinary surgeons together with inspectors, making no allowance for experience, ability, or length of service. Wilson pointed out that a doctor who had the rank of major and had served for fifteen years could not become inspector unless he accepted reduction in rank and pay. Inspectors could make money on mileage, answered Sherman. Rates were 10 cents a mile.

Nesmith digressed on homeopathy. The military committee had suffered many trials in the hearings on this bill. A spiritualist "proposed to use clairvoyance in treating disease." If everyone had had his way, "clairvoyances, spiritual rappers, homeopathists, and practices of all other systems of medicine" would be flooding the army. Did the bill exclude homeopaths? asked Wilson. It said nothing about other modes of practice. How would an examining board know if its candidate was a "pill doctor"? The difference between conservative doctors and homeopaths was in "the size of the dose." Grimes contradicted him, saying that the two systems employed totally different medicines. Conservative doctors controlled examining boards, added Wilson; they were jealous of their ways and would guard against novelty. This had the advantage of conferring uniformity upon army medical practice.

- 4 -

The Senate announced to the House of Representatives on February 28 that it had passed a bill to reorganize the Medical Bureau. Finley's official life was sinking, but the newspapers showed no respect for the dying. The Cincinnati *Times* demanded that the War Department overhaul its backward division. The time for fighting was drawing near, cried the *World*. What decent provisions had been made for casualties? Army surgeons were fighting the Wilson Bill in the House military committee, reported the *Tribune*.

In March, Finley struck at the Sanitary Commission. He denied it the use of the bureau's files, and banned inspectors from army hospitals. "Irresponsible and ignorant pretenders," they published distortions as evidence of Finley's incapacity. The commission had continually embarrassed and weakened the bureau's control. The surgeon general, however, was suspended early in April. Here was the triumph of their cause, thought the commissioners, but apparently they had little to do with his immediate removal.

Finley had chosen Dr. John Neill of Philadelphia to prepare a number of hospitals in that city. Neill had an enemy, a physician in Pittsburgh, who sent Stanton a letter of praise. Certainly, he said, the secretary of war deserved the presidency; but as though in afterthought the writer asked how such an incompetent as Dr. Neill came to be superintendent of hospitals in Philadelphia. Stanton sent this letter to Finley demanding an explanation.

Finley endorsed it. According to his original intention, he would return it to the secretary of war; he would also ask to be permitted to send Neill the letter to answer. But the surgeon general changed his mind. Copying an extract, he sent it to Neill, who at once brought suit against the "defamer." Finley now felt "the weight of Mr. Stanton's displeasure." In an interview the secretary charged the surgeon general with "violating the confidence of the Department as Head of a Bureau." Finley asked for a court-martial, but Stanton replied, "I have a shorter way of dealing with you than by Court Martial—I can strike you off the rolls." Finley appealed to Lincoln for protection against "official injustice." Stanton called the Medical Bureau inefficient, but the secretary "was more open to that charge," wrote Finley; blame Stanton for the delays that had taken place in the Medical Bureau.[1]

On being ordered to Boston the surgeon general appealed to his friend Senator McDougal for an investigation, but Stanton's friends quashed this move. Finley asked for retirement, a favor that was granted. For forty-four years of active service he received the brevet of brigadier general.

Dr. Elisha Harris was perhaps alone of the commissioners in believing that Finley had been tormented needlessly. Most army surgeons accepted merit as the basis of selection, he noted, but they did not like Hammond. Dr. Wood again became acting surgeon general. The commission immediately offered cooperation, while he lifted the ban excluding Sanitary inspectors from general hospitals.

The Senate referred Bill No. 188 to the House Military Committee on March 11. The next day Frank P. Blair reported

[1] Robert Todd Lincoln collection. C. A. Finley to A. Lincoln, April 11, 1862.

back a substitute. The House postponed debate until March 18. The Sanitary Commission had more to say about the House bill, for it sought elimination of paralyzing amendments in S. 188. Bellows spoke effectively to the House committee, while Blair openly supported the commission. Blair introduced the following significant change before the House of Representatives: " . . . the surgeon general, the assistant surgeon general, medical inspector general and medical inspectors shall immediately after the passage of this act be appointed by the President, by and with the advice and consent of the Senate, by selection from the regular medical corps of the Army without regard to their rank when so selected but with sole regard to qualifications." The bill specifically provided for the appointment of the surgeon general. Holding him down to colonelcy was mistaken, said Blair, when other bureau heads were brigadier generals. He thought the addition of ten surgeons and ten assistant surgeons inadequate. Wounded soldiers at Fort Donelson had lain a week without surgery or medical care; they needed immediate attention, not treatment a week later. Had there been enough surgeons, tragedy might have been averted. As it was, the army had to send for civilian doctors from St. Louis, Cincinnati, and parts of Indiana.

McPherson of Pennsylvania wanted Wilson's bill as amended. The surgeon general would be paid more than the size of his corps warranted if he rose from colonel to brigadier general. Other bureaus would begin to demand special attentions. Now was the time to retrench. The surgeon general had no need for a thousand-dollar raise. Let reforms wait until the end of the war, when calm and objectivity had returned. A large bureau was needless in peacetime. To rule that higher medical officers must be drawn from the regular army set limits to the presidential power of appointment. What if Lincoln wanted an able volunteer as leader? Such a restriction interfered with efficiency. Blair's bill permanently

changed the bureau, protested McPherson. He suspected interested motives, suggesting that this legislation was of a
pork barrel nature—favorites had to be placed and old debts
paid.

Nothing had excited more anxiety than the care of Union
troops, answered Blair. The Sanitary Commission was a response to the public demand that civilians be helpful in time
of crisis. The military acknowledged its "great service." The
commission had its critics, he owned, but none could deny
its accomplishments. Blair's committee was scarcely rushing
through the change pressed for by the commission. Difficulties surrounded reform; interests had to be studied and accommodated. The Wilson bill inaugurated "promotion backwards"; surgeons promoted to inspectors really accepted
lower rank. Real progress meant that inspectors must have
the rank of lieutenant colonel, said Blair. The expense was
trivial. The difference in pay for these ten surgeons and ten
assistant surgeons would not be more than $2,000 a year
above the present establishment.

A majority of representatives agreed to the need of change.
How reform was to be brought about became the point of
discussion. The role of Congress, observed Blair, was to
create conditions attractive to medical talent. Proper administration of the bureau called for a leader familiar with both
military and medical worlds. Leadership itself did not give
bedside care; its duties related to direction and control of the
machine. Blair had no objection to widening the basis of
selection, but the regular army provided the necessary ability. Its staff corps officers directed regulars and volunteers
alike, and benefited the general service.

- 5 -

Reorganization of the Medical Bureau was necessary for
the commission itself. Funds had sunk so low that Sanitary

doors were in danger of closing. The insurance companies would have to write out another big check or the government must make it part of the military machine. The branches and the Lincoln administration must decide whether the commission was expendable. It might retire with honor when the bureau could provide for inspection, hygienic precautions, and improved supply.

The Sanitary treasury received $19,682.95 in December, 1861, and $910.75 in January, 1862. People gave generously but never enough. In February, $7,200.62 was paid out, leaving a balance of $7,249.39 by March. The executive committee agreed to follow a policy of contracting operations and eventually stop work. The army placed greater demands on its machinery, as calls grew more insistent for expansion. People would give supplies but not money; little did they think of the costs involved in distributing the things they gave. While the government ignored the commission, it leaned increasingly on Sanitary methods and efficiency; good results only brought more work into its limited sphere.

Before extended military operations the administration seemed powerless to help itself. McClellan and Stanton proved faithless to the commission. Lincoln seemed little better. For the commission to ask citizens for money merely screened Washington "from the consequences of its own misconduct and neglect." Only popular anger could frighten men in high places. The commission decided to reduce expenditures by giving up the inspector system. Dr. Newberry had the job of cutting down services in the West. He set up a system of local agencies in West Virginia and Kentucky. Chicago took over the soldiers' home at Cairo. Louisville and Nashville worked through agencies. Dr. Douglas regretted this move. The Sanitary Commission had just succeeded in winning widespread recognition on the Mississippi, while every Western army needed its inspectors.

The United States Sanitary Commission, said Douglas, had

driven the Western Sanitary Commission to improving army
hospitals outside St. Louis. Yeatman the "gentleman" and
Eliot the "sharper" had worked like "beavers." They "managed" General Halleck, and had won contributions from
New England. Steadily and constantly they cut in on their
rivals, bombarding the New England Women's Auxiliary
Association in Boston with appeals to send all it had. Here
was a source of embarrassment. Commissioners explained to
Boston that Yeatman and Eliot had chosen to reign in St.
Louis rather than work in Sanitary federation. "A hearty
fellowship" was not possible, since St. Louis had dropped its
local mask and appealed abroad for support. Its very title,
Western Sanitary Commission, was localism self-puffed to
national proportions. St. Louis would like to compromise
the reputation of the United States Sanitary Commission,
confining its rival to the Atlantic seaboard in public thinking. It pirated money and supplies in an attempt to make
people believe the whole West dependent on the East.
Competition involved both organizations in a mad scramble
to see which one would reach the battlefield first. The
United States Sanitary Commission pledged itself to follow
the troops. The obstinacy of St. Louis had caused "scandalous confusion," a waste of energy, and loss of supplies in transportation. But the commissioners doubted the
wisdom of public exposure. Accusations of scandal would
scarcely win men who clung to local pride; controversy
would divert public attention from matters of graver importance. Now, St. Louis might have problems that the commissioners did not understand; but since theirs took precedence
as a national organization, the commissioners believed their
needs should receive first consideration from the branches.

What would keep the St. Louis cow out of the Eastern
clover? Olmsted wondered. He accused Yeatman of pursuing
a course objectionable to "benevolence." Eliot and Yeatman
answered that gifts for Sanitary Commission purposes be-

longed to the nation at large; storehouses should remain open to both commissions. His rival was a dog in the manger, wrote Yeatman to the *Times* in May; it did not give cheerfully from its well-stocked storehouses, but required "intervention and circumlocution of red tape." Called to account, Eliot explained the letter as part of a private correspondence with Mr. James Roosevelt and not intended for publication. He corrected the article, but expressed mortification at the necessity.

- 6 -

Bitter victory went to the Union at Shiloh (April 6–7). Confederate troops caught Grant off guard. They held the key positions and might have smashed Union lines on the night of April 6. But General Albert Sidney Johnston of the Confederacy was killed, Union gunboats continually shelled enemy lines, while reinforcements hurried to the scene; and after ten hours of stubborn fighting on April 7 the Union still held the field. The Union lost 13,000 out of 63,000 soldiers; out of 40,000 the Confederates lost 11,000

Grant's soldiers were not in promising condition before battle. Many had long been suffering from diarrhea, and when weak and fatigued they had to face attack. The Confederates swept through Union camps, capturing stretchers, ambulances, stores, instruments, and even doctors in post hospitals. Too few doctors remained to attend the avalanche of Union wounded. How to provide on nothing at all taxed Surgeon Hewit's ingenuity, for the wilderness around Pittsburg Landing offered neither depot nor sizable town. He improvised hospitals with a few tents and a log house. The wounded were brought in under great difficulties; those who managed to receive treatment dragged themselves to the rear. Hay scattered on the earth served as a bed for the seri-

ously hurt, unless there was place in the hospitals. Invoking
the Muses of epic and medicine, one surgeon exhorted the
reader to imagine thousands of wounded and lacerated lying
in every conceivable manner on the ground under a pelting
rain without shelter, without bedding, without straw, and
with little food. Shot fell freely among these "writhing
masses," whose further removal or protection was impossible.
Tides of the panic-stricken rushed through the hospitals in
search of safety; they could not concentrate long enough to
serve as nurses, cooks, or attendants. Toward the end of the
day the *City of Memphis*, the hospital transport, began removing casualties to Savannah, seven miles down the Tennessee River. As the second day brought Union advance and
Confederate retreat, greater numbers of injured from both
sides descended on the field authority. All tents that could
be found were pitched at once, and an operating staff was
detailed. Arks, not hospitals, would have to be built if the
rain kept up much longer. Mud was knee deep. No one
would carry hay for mattresses into the tents. Doctors had to
spend time seeing that others did the innumerable chores.
Dead men lay unburied in and outside the hospitals.

The Army of the Ohio came to Grant's rescue when the
battle was half over. Bad roads and want of time prevented
Dr. Robert Murray, its medical director, from sending tents,
bedding, ambulances, and stores. His major accomplishment
was seeing that government transports were equipped to
ferry the fallen to base hospitals; but the government lacked
sufficient vessels. Both Western and United States sanitary
commissions worked on a national basis, but state and local
groups kept up a false distinction. One state refused to receive the injured of another. State emphasis encouraged
desertions of the slightly wounded on a large scale. Special
agents carried away their own citizens without military de-
tection; they placed the severely wounded in private houses,

thus creating extra expense for the national government. All differences, commanded Murray, must bend before equal care of the helpless, Union or Confederate.

After the battle the United States Army covered the hills for miles around. Closely packed steamers lined the west bank of the Tennessee River, discharging forage, provisions, clothing, artillery, army wagons, and ambulances upon a steep muddy bank. Humanity poured onto the shore in a "noisy, turbulent, chaotic flood." Soldiers hurried to and fro in the interweaving crowd; army wagons floundered through the mud, some interlocking and upsetting their loads; ambulances and litters carried the wounded to the boats; the dead lay on the wet ground, while squads of gravediggers rapidly consigned them to shallow trenches.

The Sanitary Commission was well represented. Cincinnati had fitted out steamers better than those of most relief societies. Nurses, doctors, and stores had arrived on April 7 and started work before the battle was over. Irregular results betrayed weaknesses in the local charitable impulse. Drs. Newberry and Douglas tried to harmonize discordant elements, but the commission's decision to curtail operations hampered their efforts. Without paid help they could neither systematize the removal of the dead and wounded nor distribute supplies equitably. They had no large body of field workers to collect supplies in Northern villages; they needed their own regiment of agents to dominate and direct local efforts on the battlefield. Western branches refused to turn over for distribution their abundance to the machine they helped create; each wished to do the work of the whole. Inexperience meant waste, and jealous duplication of effort discredited the work of relief.

According to Dr. Newberry, army officers had ample warning of an approaching battle. General Halleck declined Cincinnati's offers just when Grant's medical purveyor was making large requisitions on Sanitary branches at Chicago,

Cincinnati, and Cleveland. Never had the Medical Bureau been so wanting as on this "bloody field." Its failure to rush supplies immediately accentuated suffering. Dr. Wood telegraphed the medical purveyor at Cincinnati to send doctors and stores; but that was two days after he had heard of the battle, when much had already been sent from Cincinnati. The bureau had had ample time to build up a backlog of supplies. Dr. Hammond did not blame Grant's medical staff. Dr. Hewit's many requisitions went unanswered. He ought to have had no trouble in procuring nurses. Once the fighting started, no time remained to organize an ambulance corps; the firing lines could not spare men for extra duties. At Shiloh the old bureau, Mosaic in harshness, reached its nadir.

-7-

April 9 brought back debate on the medical bill in the House of Representatives. Representative Stevens of Pennsylvania questioned its desirability, for Secretary Stanton did not believe it necessary. But the secretary had not referred to that measure, replied Blair. Stanton had written that "he thought some reorganization of the medical department was necessary." The secretary of war, answered Stevens, discouraged "in some degree" the passage of this bill; he was apparently more dissatisfied with the personnel of the bureau than with its system. But Stanton himself had not indicated any preference, said Blair. This bill would satisfy all interests as well as any measure could.

Representative Wright grieved for those untimely and unjustly removed from office. He pleaded for Finley, seemingly unaware of his exile to Boston. "Sound sense and judgment" supported seniority as an axiom of government. Who but the Sanitary Commission was responsible for the bureau's unhappy plight? It had brought on the conflict by assuming to direct the army's medical affairs. The bill did not apply to volunteers, said McPherson. It provided too many new surgeons and assistant surgeons for the regular army. The correction of abuses called for more regimental and brigade surgeons. What folly to increase the surgeon general's rank! added McPherson. How modish to be a brigadier general! Everyone aspired to that rank. Why not give Lincoln the power to remove a man over sixty-two if he had been in the service for forty years and was inefficient?

The proposed legislation was to serve the entire army, answered Blair. The inspector general would give "his personal attendance to sending medical supplies to the army in transports, in temporary hospitals and upon the march." Brigade and regimental surgeons applied to him for medicine when they were active in the field. Restoration of peace would reduce the army to 50,000 for the maintenance of order; medical enlargement was obviously necessary for the days of conflict and their aftermath. As for the the surgeon general's rank, other countries betrayed no impulse toward discrimination; its equivalent in France was major general. McPherson's penny pinching meant niggardly policy, protested Blair. He who carried such heavy responsibilities should not be denied a brigadier-generalcy. The House passed an amendment to include volunteer surgeons for higher offices.

Military committees from both Houses sat in joint session on April 15. The Senate concurred in legislative changes. Hospital stewards were to be paid $30 a month, and medical cadets given a daily ration in addition to pay. On expiration of the act all officers promoted from the medical staff would retain their respective ranks, besides any promotions they may have won. Both Houses concurred in these alterations. On April 16 the bill to reorganize the Medical Bureau and increase its efficiency was passed.

Patiently, the Sanitary Commission had suffered misrepresentations, snubbings, and repulses. Hope deferred had filled its members with disgust and despair, just as the bill slipped through Congress. But reorganization was Sanitary work, except in so far as it caused the regulars to lose face and made the volunteer brigade surgeons eligible to the newly created office of inspector. These results were "revolutionary," thought Strong. His colleagues had resisted their enactment before both Congressional committees. The regulars could now see the commission in a more friendly light if they had eyes. "Obstinacy and stupid bigotry" had almost ruined the bureau. According to Olmsted, Lincoln and Stanton admitted that the commission had been right; they regretted that the work of reform had not been undertaken sooner.

- 8 -

To win the surgeon-generalcy Dr. William A. Hammond had to overcome the opposition of Dr. Robert C. Wood and the secretary of war. Stanton apparently preferred a Dr. Chaffee from California. Wood prophesied that Hammond once in power would prove lifeless. Stanton asked Dr. Van Buren to suggest candidates for the higher offices, but the doctor refused to act independently of the commission. As one of its members, he presented Hammond's name for surgeon general; for the other offices he proposed Drs. Vollum and Edwards of the regular corps and Drs. Lyman and Clymer of the volunteers.

Bellows visited the president, who was being shaved. Lincoln seemed impressed by his visitor's fluent and energetic talk. Later the same day Bellows returned to the White House. The president sat at a desk piled high with documents. He nodded to his guest. Bellows sang the praises of Hammond to the accompaniment of Lincoln's eyes that scanned pages, the dipping of his pen, and the writing of his signature. This went on for fifteen minutes. Bellows nearly ran out of breath, but Lincoln showed no signs of eye strain or writer's cramp. At last the president spoke:

"Shouldn't wonder if Hammond was at this moment Surgeon General, and had been for some time."

"You don't mean to say, Mr. President, that the appointment has been made?"

Looking up for the first time, Lincoln answered: "I may say to you that it *has*; only you needn't tell it just yet." [2]

The Senate Military Committee was not ready to acclaim Hammond in hosannas of unanimity. Dr. Wood had been at work among its members. Senators King and Rice were against Hammond. Wilson seemed unsure the Senate would follow his committee's recommendation. Bellows had no sooner returned to New York than Olmsted wired him to press the committee and demand the proper appointment. Olmsted himself wrote Wilson that no other man had Hammond's record for hospital administration. On April 25 came news of Hammond's unanimous confirmation by the Senate. His elevation threw surgeons of the regular army into angry excitement; but an old friend of Hammond's, Dr. Lewis Henry Steiner, remembered the days of the Baltimore riots, when the new surgeon general had been his assistant.

- 9 -

"Mea culpa, mea maxima culpa!" Lamentations rent the air. To the Commissioners came Dr. Richard Satterlee, one of their bitterest castigators in the days of Finley. Now he appeared "hearty and earnest in counsel" with offers to honor all requisitions. "The enlightenment of this dark old official" proved that the age of miracles had not passed, said George Strong. Henry Raymond's confession of error was the other

[2] Carl Sandburg, *Abraham Lincoln: The War Years* (1940), Vol. III, pp. 434–35.

marvel. Along with his check came expressions of regret for attacks and misrepresentations.

Commission and bureau now worked with "one heart and will." Hammond needed capable subordinates. Commissioners wanted either Dr. Lewis A. Edwards of the District of Columbia or Dr. R. H. Coolidge of New York as assistant surgeon general. Dr. George H. Lyman would make an excellent inspector general. The following were Sanitary candidates for inspectors: Dr. Andrew K. Smith of Connecticut, Dr. Jonathan Letterman of Pennsylvania, Dr. Robert Bartholow of Maryland, Dr. E. P. Vollum of New York, Dr. John Moore of Indiana, Dr. J. K. Cuyler of Georgia, Dr. Warren Webster of Massachusetts, Dr. Meredith Clymer of Virginia, and Dr. George F. Suckley of New York. Perhaps Satterlee of Michigan was named for medical purveyor because of his profession of Sanitary faith.

What was to be done to the old barnacles clinging to the bottom of the Medical Bureau? Younger and more capable surgeons made conspicuous Tripler's regulation brain and red-tape circulation. Dr. Wood moved to keep his job of assistant surgeon general. To Stanton's amazement he secured Hammond's approval, causing the secretary to set down the surgeon general as weak. So Wood, the "fogiest of fogies," stayed in office. Possibly by the end of May Hammond realized his mistake, for Wood seemed to forget who was boss. The commission protested the confirmation of his nomination. Wood would be the surgeon general's withered arm, while Tripler would complete the paralysis. Cameron had specifically authorized Tripler to act without Finley's supervision; now the Peninsular campaign was spelling out the medical director's inefficiency. Only the Sanitary hospital transports were shielding him from public anger.

No sooner was Hammond in office than he clashed with Secretary Stanton. The surgeon general refused to fawn and flatter, but demanded respectful treatment. Stanton took his time about nominating Dr. Letterman as inspector general and Drs. Cuyler and Keeney as inspectors. The cabinet, he said, must first be consulted. Who could move mountains without cooperation? Hammond himself lacked sufficient power to make permanent changes, so he placed the burden of reorganization on Stanton's shoulders. Political advantage was going to govern new appointments, Hammond feared. To oblige Senator Trumbull the secretary was willing to nominate Dr. Allen, a brigade surgeon. Before the war lawyer Stanton used to appear in Judge Grier's court, so now he would nominate Grier's son-in-law, Professor John Le Conte of Philadelphia, a graduate from a medical school but not a physician "in the spirit of the bill." Commissioners opposed the political stimulus that made Le Conte a choice; his appointment would bring the proposed reform into contempt. The purpose of the act was meeting defeat.

On May 1, at Yorktown, 5,000 lay sick and wounded, while in the West 10,000 men were incapacitated. Growing casualties threatened disaster if the army lacked inspectors. In vain did Dr. Van Buren ask Stanton for an interview. Bellows now dreaded the secretary of war, "that inscrutable fellow." Stanton returned to Washington about noon on May 12. General Hitchcock had placed Van Buren's letter where human eyes could not fail to see it. The secretary ignored it. He was reported ill and unable to go to his office. Bellows best described what happened the next day:

General Hitchcock recommended me to come early this morning—between nine and ten o'clock. I did so—after waiting fifteen minutes, and being then on the point of going away I met Mr. Stanton on the stairs. He knew me and stopped to ask a civil question, and I said,

"Can you see me a minute?"

"Yes, walk in."

I followed him into a room, where a dozen people of greater or lesser magnitude were waiting to see him, and at the door of which twenty others, were glaring in, as at a wild beast at a show. He took position, at his desk standing.

"Well, Doctor. I'm glad to see you looking so well."

"Thank you, Sir. I am sorry to see you *not* as well as myself."

"I am *perfectly well,* Sir, never better in my life," he said with the nervous petulance of a man who fears that others are fancying him *not* well and who wants to hide it from himself.

"I see you have a blind over one eye," I replied, excusing my mistake in referring to his health.

"Yes, a little cold in the eye."

"Well, Mr. Stanton, have you read Dr. Van Buren's communication in forwarding our medical reform bill?"

"What communication, Sir?"

"One he left here in the office after waiting several days to see you."

"No, Sir. What was it about?"

"Why, Mr. Secretary, to tell the truth, we have been feeling very anxious to see the reform, so slowly and painfully prepared for, in our legislation carried out in practice. Nearly a month has elapsed since the law requiring the Government *immediately* to fill up the great offices in the new Medical organization was passed, and yet, the Surgeon-General, appointed to carry out this work, is left without arms and legs. He cannot but feel baffled and we are distressed at what seems needless delay. Pray, Mr. Secretary, is the hesitation unavoidable? Are there practical difficulties in making the appointments?"

Mr. Secretary turned very pale and looked angry. He replied, "Doctor, I can't be catechized this way! The Government will act when it gets ready."

"Mr. Stanton," I said, with a very formal politeness, drawing myself up to all the height I had! "I certainly intended no undue liberty in asking these questions, which I supposed to be authorized by our relations, and by a certain responsibility we have had in bringing this Medical Reform to a point. But as I see that you are dissatisfied, I beg leave to withdraw and shall trouble you no further, except by written communication!" I presume I looked indignant and determined, as I uttered these words, and bowing formally, turned to leave.

"Doctor, I am ready to hear you now, if you have any advice or counsel to offer me in this matter—but I cannot allow myself to be interrogated upon matters that belong wholly to the Department."

"Mr. Stanton, I have no advice to offer, except to urge the importance of dropping all personal or partizan considerations and sticking by the letter and the spirit of the law in making these medical appointments. *We know* who the proper men are, and have presented them in the letter Dr. Van Buren has left with you. There may be other men as good—but we do not feel that there are. The service is suffering immensely for prompt action in this matter—and we cannot feel easy while this action is delayed, nor can we willingly see it take a wrong direction."

"I don't see what responsibility you have in the matter that you should allow it to disturb you, Doctor."

"Is that frank, Mr. Stanton?" I said. "Have we not carried this Bill through the Congress? Are we not identified with this reform? And have we not a moral, if no legal responsibility in the matter? At any rate," I added, "we cannot throw it off without thus remonstrating over the delay at this critical moment."

"Well, Doctor, the Government will act, as I told you, as soon as it sees its way clear. I thank you for your advice—and shall always be glad to see you."

"Good morning, Sir," I said shaking hands and leaving the room —with a feeling that Stanton was ashamed of his petulance—that he felt that he had mistaken his man, and was angry with himself and with me, for being the cause of his petty violence but also with a conviction that I had planted a thorn which would prick him into action of some sort with promptness.

I am sorry to say, that the impression of Stanton left on my own mind is that of a man with a brain in a very dangerous state of irritability, and one who in the use of his vast power forgets the rights and the position of his peers who chance to be in private life. A man who presumes on the helplessness of a clergyman—to assume a tone of voice and manner he would not use to a layman of station, is a poltroon. I never allow it to pass. I think Stanton is honest *and suspicious* that other men are not so, and that his self-confidence and position have with his intensity of labor and his bad physical habits, lack of exercise, I mean, induced in him, a manner and, I fear, an internal temper and cerebral condition which will come to some disagreeable end, if it continues to increase.[3]

Sanitary influence at the War Department lay dead. Stanton warned Hammond to beware of the commission; its backing had been the chief obstacle to the surgeon general's success. By summer solstice Stanton's detestation of the extralegal crew burned for all the world to see. On May 21 he promised Hammond to send Lincoln a list of nominees. They included Wood for assistant surgeon general and Tripler for inspector general; Cuyler, Coolidge, Keeney, Vollum, James R. Smith, Bartholow, Le Conte, and Lyman were candidates for inspectors. The secretary said he would honestly recommend this selection, but the president might want to make "one or two variations." These were "enough to make a saint swear," especially St. Olmsted. He hated "that canting, small politician, the Secretary of War," a greater fool than knave but still "a big knave."

[3] Files of the United States Sanitary Commission, Box 638, and Bellows MSS. H. W. Bellows to W. Van Buren, May 13, 1862, Washington, D.C.

CHAPTER VII

The Melancholy Battles

- 1 -

JANUARY 1, 1862, and no Union advance, but continued operations. McClellan intended a series of attacks on different parts of the South. This meant creating a general plan; it called for readiness and precise timing. East and West, he, the creator of armies, must breathe into them the breath of life. Preparations had to be complete before McClellan would take risks. The Army of the Potomac was far from ready, thought Olmsted. He deplored the "scandalous quality" of army clothing, the waste of excess rations, and the starvation of horses. The soldiers needed years of training, because their officers seemed incapable of discipline and instruction. Let slowness, tedium, and patience, said Olmsted, supplant melodramatic and extravagant demands for a "grand coup."

People understood delay in the fall of 1861, but uneasy questioning grew with the new year. Radical Republicans censured McClellan's inaction. Certain newspapers tried to goad him into action, although winter roads made a forward move impossible. Delay paved the way to distrust of his leadership. War had run up a debt of $600,000,000 by March 1, 1862, and many demanded results commensurate with the magnitude of costs.

One gusty morning in March the Army of the Potomac marched out of Washington. The enemy withdrew, leaving worthless fortifications at Manassas and Centreville. McClellan could have taken them in December, bayed critics. The general then ordered his 50,000 troops aboard transports at Alexandria on March 17, as the Peninsular campaign started in low gear. This campaign brought to a breaking point the rift between him and the administration. McClellan's failure to make explicit arrangements with the Navy Department about joint operations in Virginia, his neglecting to settle with Lincoln on the protection of Washington, his overestimation of opposing forces and ignorance of their preparations—these were but a few of McClellan's sins of omission. He kept his own counsel, consulting a few officers; he gave friendship to those unsympathetic with the administration and alienated men who might have helped in evil days. Foes in Congress and the cabinet seized on his weaknesses. McClellan's attraction to Southern ways and dislike of abolition made him suspect. Secretary Chase did not hide his hatred, and Stanton seemed ready to kill any chance of McClellan's success.

Ships bound for the peninsula moved across the water like "floating cities." Sounds of bands and singing men died away as colored lights on riggings grew indistinct. Bugle calls and drumbeats punctuated the evening; occasionally the boom of cannon quieted all other noises. Campfires along the southern horizon turned the sky red. By April 2 the Army of the Potomac had reached Fortress Monroe. The army set up headquarters in a large meadow. Ordnance and forage barges crowded the shore, where men were unloading big guns and making piles of shot and shell. Over the crowded ground moved orderlies holding horses, sentries, black and white helpers of the quartermaster, and wagons. Fatigue parties worked in relays with dirty, lounging soldiers. The crash of falling trees roared through the swamp forest. Shouts from teamsters trying to direct their wagons alternated with the calls of pioneers making corduroy roads. Horses sank in the mud and sometimes smothered. A blue column in the sunlight marched into the shadow, the bayonets shining far into the woods.

The Confederates evacuated Yorktown on May 4, after delaying McClellan's advance one month. On May 5, Williamsburg fell but not without a hard fight. A two-day rain complicated the suffering of those who lay shelterless and starving. Many straggled back to base hospitals without reports, nurses, or food. On May 15, McClellan set up headquarters on the Pamunkey River. Large trees shaded the brown cottage called White House, once owned by Martha Custis Washington. Lawn sloped down to the river; roses blossomed in the garden.

The freshest green outlined the banks of Virginia's creeks and rivers. Locust, oak, and weeping elm seemed to lean toward the passing boats, and overhanging boughs almost swept the smokestacks. Knotted roots formed paling, while behind them bloomed magnolia, catalpa, and fringe trees. Beyond stretched fields of wheat, "tall and fresh . . . taking the sunshine for miles." The Pamunkey River followed its own will, "returning upon itself every half mile or so." Often the boats seemed to glide over "a little wooded lake without inlet or outlet." At sunset sky and water gleamed alike, while all the trees looked black. In the dark only cranes broke the silence. During the outbursts of battle and bloodshed river views brought inner peace—a rainbow in the stormy sunset or a lunar rainbow at night.

Tripler had equipped surgeons with stores and the means of transporting them; yet a flood of requisitions greeted his arrival on the peninsula. Doctors had left tents and medicines behind. The purveyor, they believed, could easily replenish their losses. Storms held up shipments, while those that arrived were either too few or too late. Scattered in the holds of various ships, hospital stores took time to locate and hours to unload. The Sanitary Commission also suffered from the army's lack of system. Military authorities never thought of assigning the Sanitary inspector to certain quarters. He had to ride around the country until he found an abandoned store. For more than a week he did everything himself, because military authorities would accept none of his helpers as representatives of the Sanitary Commission. The inspector spent a day hunting for his supplies, finally finding them on a steamer and a barge in the outer bay.

Old guard surgeons in key positions created confusion and impaired efficiency. Tripler was calling for supplies, while Dr. Wood kept assuring the commission that "everything that heart could desire" was awaiting requisition at Fortress Monroe and Yorktown. Tripler, chary of further issuance, was saving for the evil days of battle. Many surgeons took to begging from each other. In one instance a doctor dug for medicinal roots which he might substitute for drugs. One thousand more men might have stood in readiness, reported a Sanitary inspector, had quinine not been weeks late. About 6 per cent of the army was invalided every ten days, he believed. Recruits pushed suddenly into campaigning broke down; men who left the ranks did not come back. Troops were known to sweep the sick along with their advance. The sick filled improvised hospitals—huts, dilapidated meetinghouses, and private dwellings. The swampy York River made Tripler hesitate before setting up new hospitals. Rather than let them hold up the advance, he sent the sick north. His decision helped create the false impression that a sick soldier was no longer in the army.

Olmsted urged the setting up of "flying hospitals" for the weary and homesick; in this way three-fourths of those formerly sent north might be returned to their regiments. He called on Hammond for tarpaulins and the means of setting up sheds—anything to spare the wounded the added suffering from exposure. Each army corps before Richmond needed at least one "depot" behind the line of fire. Olmsted noted: "Such an arrangement would have saved many hundred lives after the battle of Fair Oaks." [1]

Early in April the Sanitary Commission had found the crudest of base hospitals at Newport News and Fortress Monroe. In "long, log-houses, dark and without floors" the patients lay on straw covering the ground. The Sanitary inspector urged General Wool to send the sick back to Washington instead of cluttering the base hospital prior to a major action. General Wool "didn't see it," because the sick would be put into hospital tents. Private Cox wrote his father from Fortress Monroe: "For neglect, incapacity, bullying of patients, starvation, and a hundred other meannesses that my indignant pen refuses to write, this hospital goes ahead of anything this side of all creation." [2]

Tripler established a base hospital at White House. He had no suitable buildings. One hundred tents housed 1,600 patients. Easily swamped and managed with "improvident consideration," this hospital had five surgeons, five assistant surgeons, one steward, but no detail to care for the patients. Convalescents served as nurses. Tripler's requisitions were cut in half, but he appeared satisfied with medical arrangements. Olmsted pleaded for a completely equipped hospital, not forgetting such immediate needs as cooks, kettles, pans, cups, spoons, laborers, canvas, nails, tools, pumps, filters, and water carts. Lack of foresight meant courting disaster, he reminded authorities at White House. But in what war were the sick as well taken care of? they answered. England did no better; suffering was inevitable in war.

The Sanitary Commission had to heed cries other than those of McClellan's army. Surgeons from the armies of Banks and Frémont called for supplies. The Annapolis gen-

[1] Olmsted MSS. F. L. Olmsted to W. A. Hammond, June 17, 1862, *Wilson Small*, White House, Va.

[2] Bellows MSS. [n.s.] Cox to his father, April 22, 1862, Fortress Monroe, Va.

eral hospital applied for as many shirts, drawers, and stockings as possible. Demands also came from Washington churches, which were being converted into emergency hospitals. Between June 22 and June 30, Washington headquarters distributed about 14,000 shirts, about 8,000 each of towels, handkerchiefs, pillow cases, and socks, about 6,000 sheets and pillows, 3,000 quilts, and over 2,000 bed ticks. Demands for drawers so far exceeded supply that the commission could distribute only 4,200.

The public knew little about Sanitary work on the Peninsula. Newspaper correspondents, noted Olmsted, were all at the front but showed as little care for the disposition of the sick as did the generals. Publishers wanted to devote every bit of space to the fighting; the story of relief had little appeal. How were the people to learn about floating hospitals? The undertaking seemed too vast for private resources. At times the commission seemed to bear the major burdens of the bureau; it had spent $22,000 from the end of April to May 25, when only $16,000 remained in its treasury. But the bureau shared its good things. It treated Sanitary transports as its own, furnishing cots, beds, bedding medicine, food, comfort, stimulants, and other necessities.

-2-

The secretary of war had arranged with New York and Pennsylvania for summoning civilian doctors whenever the occasion demanded; but he had neither sent considerable amounts of medical stores nor prepared transports nor engaged nurses. Stanton approved a Sanitary project to equip and use large steamers as hospitals. The commission was prepared to carry a thousand patients or more.

Tripler did not organize a hospital transport system because he had few medical officers with experience and "the faculty of rapid systematization." The quartermaster assigned the *Commodore* to Tripler. Surgeon General H. H. Smith of Pennsylvania took charge of the steamer, preparing it to receive 900 wounded. The *Commodore* and the *William Whilden* became government receiving ships.

On April 25, 1862, the *Daniel Webster* was steaming to Fortress Monroe while Olmsted supervised its conversion from a troopship to a hospital transport. The company of nurses, surgeons, carpenters, and passengers divided into squads. They knocked out bulkheads in the wings of the engine room to gain a draft; they divided cabins and upper steerage into six wards. One surgeon, two interns, four nurses, convalescent soldiers, and Negro helpers staffed each ward. The *Webster* carried 250 patients. Olmsted divided them into squads of 50 with a wardmaster who drew the rations. The *Ocean Queen* was the best ship for hospital purposes. Quartermaster General Meigs replaced it with the large but unseaworthy *S. R. Spaulding*, a cavalry transport, which served as a reserve hospital for the gravest cases. A later addition was the large *Daniel Webster No. 2*. *Wilson Small*, *Elizabeth*, and *Wissahickon*, all boats of light draft, were equipped to run up creeks and bring casualties down to the floating hospitals. The *Elm City* accommodated 400 surgical cases. On its wide decks the wounded lay on cots and mattresses. This large river boat carried its human freight up the Potomac to Washington. The *Knickerbocker* was very old, low between decks, poorly ventilated, and of small capacity; but it managed to transfer 250 wounded from White House to Fortress Monroe every twenty-four hours. A delight to the eyes, the *St. Mark* was a clipper ship drawn from the East India trade. It and the *Euterpe* carried their own surgical corps. Owing to their large size they stayed at Yorktown, while lighter boats brought them the sick and wounded.

According to the agreement of June 20 with the bureau, the commission would receive only the permanently disabled;

government transports would take all the other casualties. The direction of its transports was under the commission. In theory its duties began on board; in practice it had to care for those brought to base hospitals. Certain cases were theoretically confined to specified vessels, but demands of the moment ignored these distinctions. Military discipline supposedly governed the transports, but the task of pacifying mutinous crews—"superstitious, beastly Portuguese"—fell to Olmsted. His was the job of wheedling the pantry servants, humoring the cooks, and coaxing the captains. Quartermaster General Meigs might recall a ship; and as soon as Sanitary workers had removed patients and hospital fittings, he was likely to return it. Hammond and Tripler determined the destination of transports; medical authorities decided about the reception and distribution of patients; Olmsted judged the capacity of each ship and its time for sailing. He had nine superiors. Each had a different understanding of his duties and problems. Noon found the policy of the morning reversed, and following his hunch became Olmsted's rule for night.

Dependence without rights and command without authority were more than Olmsted could tolerate. He pursued duty with a "fanaticism" which distressed the commissioners; but he carried the bureau's responsibilities, said Hammond, and met the obligations others shirked. F. N. Knapp tried to keep camp and field hospitals in supplies. Tubercular Dr. J. M. Grymes alternated between listlessness and the "hawk-eyed" spirit of emergency. Knapp and Grymes, said Olmsted, were responsible for whatever the commission accomplished on the peninsula. Dr. Robert Ware and three medical students worked night and day, shipping patients and moving them from one boat to another. Ware and his assistants registered the names and listed all personal belongings; they looked after the dispensaries, keeping them well supplied; they gave medical and surgical services, dressing wounds, and often sat up all night with critical cases. Their bed was any available mattress where they could sleep.

Commission and bureau tried to guard against the evils of uncontrolled volunteer service. The government agreed to pay doctors and nurses with whom it was under contract. The commission selected and recommended candidates for examination by a medical board. Once engaged, they came under Sanitary orders. Contract surgeons proved something of a nuisance. One complained of being unable to change his shirt for two days; another worked with excessive fussiness. A New York physician of "immense pretensions" was "lazy, careless and deceptive"; his colleague was "unwisely fond of bourbon." A group of Philadelphians suddenly demanded special transportation home "to open hospitals and deliver lectures and friends' wives." "Magnanimous surgical pretenders" expressed enthusiasm for cleanliness, numbering, records of disease, and pure water, balancing zeal with neglect of mundane details. Meeting the fact of work and routine turned them "sour and seedy." Among the nurses, a gentleman of Pickwickian rotundity and bewilderment did little but get drunk. Forty Sisters of Mercy struck for a chapel and keys to their staterooms at the order of their chaplain. They sat on their trunks "clean and peaceful with their forty umbrellas and their forty baskets," but unable to help with the incoming tide of battle casualties. Soldiers in the uniform of Zouaves proved efficient helpers. Although dull and obstinate, they showed good sense and gentleness.

Life on a transport called for a gentlewoman of "delicacy and refinement." She saved worry and time by making haste slowly; she stood for severe order in the thick of confusion. The women of the Sanitary transports served as housekeepers, cleaning, setting mattresses on bunks and beds, filling closets with linen, hospital clothing, socks, bandages, lint, and rags. Untrained as nurses, they went to strange places with medications; on stormy nights they groped their way by lantern, carrying spirits and ice water, restoring the exhausted and catching the last whispers of the dying.

Soldiers low in endurance dropped from the march, making their way to the banks of creeks and rivers, where passing boats picked them up. In a hut at Bigelow Landing the sick, crammed into a small room, had to sit upright for lack of space to lie down. Ambulances frequently dumped casualties on the shores of a marshy creek without a single attendant; they lay for hours, devoured by gnats and mosquitoes. Soldiers reached floating hospitals "baked," in either a "stupor" or an "anxious delirium." Their martial bearing had drooped to a "dull, weary, and sad" air, as they let themselves be fed, undressed, washed, and put to bed. In the transport world groans, yells, and shrieks became the rule. "Rustic Sidneys" were so common that they lost their identity in this "republic of suffering." Types left a strong impression. The Irish frequently expressed the "pathetically despondent and lachrymose" when not severely injured, while the French looked "unutterable things."

The women of the Sanitary transports thought each man should have the essentials of medical attention, a place in which to sleep, and a daily allowance of warm food; but events generally canceled their plans. Without warning, officers might overwhelm them with new patients. The twenty or thirty buckets of soup from the subsistence corps rarely came on time. Shortages in pots and pans complicated the preparation of special diets. Over on the government transports lack of preparation was chronic; and when they had enough supplies, no one apparently knew where the stores were kept or whether they had been unpacked. Very likely the surgeon in charge was a poor planner; perhaps he shrugged off offers of food and stimulants, but beat a tattoo for help when his patient was sinking fast. The women of the transports laughed when most they felt like weeping. Work was better than rest for those who longed for home. Olmsted marveled at their industry and self-possession. The neat white uniform had no place in this setting. Dresses were "yellow with lemon juice, sticky with sugar, greasy with beef tea, and pasted with milk and porridge."

Mrs. Henry Whitney Bellows made a Lady Bountiful excursion with nineteen other women. Soldiers at Yorktown welcomed ladies most politely, but showed contempt for charitable errands. They patronized Mrs. George Strong, who insisted on the freedom to exercise her abilities on the ship of her own choice. Sent to the *Wilson Small*, Mrs. Bellows and two intelligent and experienced friends proved invaluable helpers. That most of the patients came from New York made Mrs. Bellows feel more at home. Only her Irish servants failed to appreciate the "glorious privileges" of helping the sick and wounded; they did less work than anybody else in proportion to their strength. Enjoying the breezes at Fortress Monroe, Mrs. Bellows forgot her delicate health. For the first time in her life she did not know where to pass the night.

Many sightseers at White House talked twaddle, half hoping and half dreading to witness scenes of pain and slaughter. Gentlemen attended ladies dressed in silks. A congressman moved about holding a rose to his nose. The overprotective male indulged his sensibilities, striving to shield his lady's eyes from the slightest suggestion of suffering. Ladies from New England failed to understand that they had come to work, but looked forward to attending church in Boston "unless it would be more convenient to do so in Richmond." Most of them confused the Sanitary Commission with the Institute for the Blind. Olmsted noted: "Any man without a clearly defined function about the army is a horrid nuisance, and is treated as such unless he comes with a peremptory edict from the Secretary of War that he shan't be; when aside swearing becomes the substitute for kicks and cold shoulders." [3]

- 3 -

McClellan asked Lincoln for more troops. The president ordered McDowell to move toward Richmond, but this march ended back in Washington. By May 25, Stonewall Jackson had driven Union arms from the Shenandoah Valley. His appearance on the Potomac made Washington skittish. McClellan had to look elsewhere for reinforcements.

Hammond continued to suffer from Stanton's inaction on inspectors. He had no way of learning needs accurately, but was obliged to rely on inefficient medical directors. Bureau affairs seemed worse than in the Finley era. By May 25 the Senate had not received the names of candidates for inspector.

The battle of Fair Oaks was fought on May 31. The evacuation of over three thousand wounded began on the night of June 1 and was completed on June 7. Surgeons packed living and dead like freight into boxcars with nothing to ease the jolting and bumping; but this was only the beginning of the inferno. When the sufferers reached White House the stench of rotting flesh was rising on the summer air. All Sanitary transports, except the *Spaulding*, were on hand. The *Commodore*, *Whilden*, and *Vanderbilt* took the worst cases. Besides being dirty, these government ships lacked provisions and equipment; but the wounded took up all available space, even on the stairs and gangways. Negroes carried in the shattered and shrieking, banging the stretchers against pillars and posts and walking over men just to dump the wounded anywhere. The commission rushed in supplies. Olmsted pitched a hospital tent on the riverbank by the railroad track. Here

[3] Olmsted MSS. F. L. Olmsted to C. L. Brace, ca July 3, 1862, *Wilson Small*, Hampton Roads, Va.

in a camp kitchen helpers warmed kettles of soup and tea. Trains arrived all night. Human cargoes had to walk or be carried on stretchers along a road lit up by candles and small fires; they had received no food in from one to four days. The slightly wounded received hot coffee. Brandy, wine, or iced lemonade went to those on stretchers. It took but a minute "to pour something down their throats and put oranges in their hands." In this way the commission worked to save the men from thirst and exhaustion. Much time must pass before helpers on government transports could feed them, because "the medical mind of the army" failed to provide not only nourishment but also a pail or a cup. Patients destined for shore hospitals found a night's shelter in the Sanitary tents; they frequently stayed there for three days at a time.

Congressmen visiting the floating hospitals at White House witnessed these scenes. They saw little reason in tumbling "bleeding, fainting men" out of boxcars and into ill-prepared transports. Back in Washington they asked why inspectors had not been appointed. Senator Grimes noticed that nearly two months had elapsed since the passage of the medical bill. Lincoln was reported annoyed at the delay. Stanton nominated half the surgeon general's candidates; the rest were his own choices. The Senate confirmed Hammond's preferences. It rejected Le Conte for inspector and approved Dr. Wood for assistant surgeon general. Hammond soon sent Wood to St. Louis; Major Joseph R. Smith took his place. Tripler was defeated for inspector general. Stanton seemed to be doing Senator Fessenden a favor by nominating his kinsman, Dr. Thomas F. Perley. Reports reached Sanitary headquarters that Perley—"the worst possible man for the place"—was known for his bad qualities, and had practiced medicine without distinction. By the waters of the peninsula, Olmsted lifted up his voice in wrath; the patriotic duty of every Christian gentleman called for "guillotining" the secretary of war. With Anglican restraint George Templeton Strong thought Stanton would do the United States "most service as Ambassador Extraordinary to the Court of Heaven."

- 4 -

At White House, one afternoon in June, Miss Harriet Whetten sat on the deck of the *Spaulding* writing letters. The heat was more than she could endure, but a Negro assured her that next month would be a "heap hotter." Puffing and panting tugs were moving from one boat to another, while the constant passage of large vessels churned the Pamunkey into a muddy stream. From the shore came the stench of dead horses and mules. Guerrilla bands caused fresh anxiety. One night they fired on the train bound for White House, wounding and killing some of the soldiers on board. In the darkness officers ordered all store and hospital ships to get up steam and move down the river a mile; but the danger quickly disappeared, and the boats returned to the landing.[4]

The strain began to tell on the Sanitary staff, sending them home close to the breaking point. Olmsted felt he could last out until the army entered Richmond, "subjugators or subjugated." Medical preparations continued a mockery, he said. The soldier could die by quick bleeding or slow starvation. But on June 22 the Medical Bureau sent more transports, twenty-five Sisters of Charity, twenty-five surgeons, and a company of male nurses. Olmsted instructed directors of the largest transports in ways to overcome the most pronounced difficulties.

The fighting at Oak Grove on June 25 started the Seven Days' Battles. On June 26 the wounded from Mechanicsville reached White House "without notice, without a report, a

[4] Maria Lydig Daly MSS. H. Whetten to M. L. Daly, June 15, 1862, White House, Va.

nurse, or a crust of bread." As early as June 21 orders had reached Tripler to evacuate field hospitals. On June 26, Olmsted received notice to leave White House. Mechanical disrepair made departure of the *Elm City* slow and halting. Signs of war turned strange the once-familiar landscape. Felled trees lay for a mile along the Pamunkey; boats pointed their guns toward the plain. Soldiers were dismantling two hundred hospital tents, while all articles of value went sailing down the river. By evening the Confederates had seized the railroad and cut the telegraph wire. Civilians and sutlers clamored for passage on the government transports, while locomotive and cars shot up in explosion. Invalid horses and mules driven toward Cumberland sent up a cloud of dust over the landscape. General Casey sat on the piazza of White House and signalmen on the roof waved messages, which were answered from gunboats. Escaping slaves crowded into forage boats. Negro mothers nursed their children, while through the din arose the singing of hymns. One slow-moving craft was "filled with women . . . in their gayest dresses and brightest turbans, like a whole load of tulips for a horticultural show."

Sanitary workers did not share in the battles that marked McClellan's move from White House to Harrison's Landing on the James River. Great difficulties attended the change of base. Daily requirements of the army called for six hundred tons of ammunition, food, forage, medical and other supplies. Command of the sea by the United States assured success for the Army of the Potomac. Troops were in good position for attacking Richmond and cutting off Confederate retreat, thought Olmsted. Soldiers "parched and haggard" set up headquarters on the James on July 1, 1862, having fought five battles in five successive days and repulsed hostile attacks at night. They had two days' rations of uncooked food; they slept on their arms in torrential rains, without tents, blankets, or fire. Men looked like veterans who had lost all taste for fighting, as they marched across the gently undulating country. Gaunt and gloomy officers boarded Sanitary transports, their hair stiff with dirt, their faces nearly black, and their waists "literally moulded in Virginia clay." Yet Olmsted could find no words to describe "the exultant confidence." The army's physical condition was worse than after Bull Run, but its morale was remarkably high.

Lincoln visited Harrison's Landing on July 8. The commission's workers knew nothing of the tactless letter McClellan had handed the president on his arrival, but saw only the surface of things. In a nearby boat president and general sat in "earnest conversation" for two hours. Miss Katherine Wormeley rejoiced that Lincoln had "sprung across that dreadful intervening Washington" and came to judge for himself. He stood on deck looking through a telescope, and soon scanned the floating hospitals. As he waved his handkerchief to spectators, a "great [observation] balloon was slowly descending" over headquarters.

The medical corps on the peninsula seemed caught between two worlds, one dead and the other too slow to be born. Authority was ill defined and divided. A medical director and his men could take their battle stations and set up field hospitals; he could command surgeons, hospital stewards, and nurses, but not provision base hospitals. The law, moreover, assumed that he had powers which it did not define. Many officers of the line failed to cooperate with the surgeons. Difficulties overwhelmed many surgeons, who knew nothing of actual conditions of warfare; they wasted time and effort looking for the men of their own regiments.

Medical directors like Tripler were of the old dispensation. He neglected preparations of suitable base hospitals; he seemed unaware of the urgent need for mobile organization; but to blame Tripler exclusively for medical chaos would be wrong. The commissioners were inclined to censure Stanton; his tardy appointment of medical inspectors had "crippled"

the surgeon general. Olmsted held Hammond partly responsible; the surgeon general, he said, needed no new staff to
inaugurate a preventive policy. Tripler had torn red tape to
tatters to get supplies; but the quartermaster corps treated
medical requirements as secondary. It blocked Tripler and
ruined him, said Olmsted.

Furious over the change in the Medical Bureau, Tripler
made no secret of hating the commission. Olmsted thought
him a poor administrator and lacking in moral courage. The
medical director changed plans and delegated authority
without notifying others. He leaned on Dr. Henry H. Smith,
surgeon general of Pennsylvania, giving him discretionary
power over all floating hospitals; but he neglected to tell the
Sanitary Commission and the quartermaster corps. Muddle
worsened; bitterness sharpened. Smith gave injudicious orders; he was nowhere to be found at critical moments.
Tripler followed a "hand to mouth" policy. He suggested one
"ready to fall into the sea"; struggling for balance, he jumped
on any plank, now here, now there.

Feeling was never cordial between Hammond and Tripler.
The surgeon general hesitated to recall him; Stanton might
hurry one of his own favorites into the empty place. With
the transports under Tripler's direction, time and events
played on Hammond's side. He told Tripler to order directly
from New York without sending to Washington for approval.
Their rows were constant; each blamed the other for failing
to make proper provision. Foreigners spoke of Tripler's lack
of foresight and charged him with "an overshadowing proportion of the wrongdoing and the non-doing." This member
of the old guard was apparently unequal to the occasion;
but undoubtedly he did his best to meet the needs of the
service.

Dr. Jonathan Letterman replaced Tripler as medical director on July 3, 1862. Letterman's "dry, taciturn, and impenetrable manner" promised nothing. What Tripler despaired of,

Letterman thought possible and worth trying. He would care for the well that they might be saved from sickness. Letterman smoked incessantly, noted Dr. Bellows, who was vexed by the medical director's determination to keep the commission in second place. Letterman's "forbidding" aspect prefaced a want of "personal humanity." Governed by "a strong professional ambition and zeal," he showed quickness of perception and promptness in action. Letterman reaped the whirlwind of others' sowing. Scurvy was appearing in troops long deprived of fresh vegetables. It undermined their fighting power, depressing those not sick enough to place on the sick list. Only rest and proper diet would cure them. Letterman wanted reinforcements for picket duty and camp police. He faced an ineffective medical service and an exhaustion of stores. So overworked were surgeons that he was reduced to estimates when he most needed careful surveys. The Harrison house plus a few wall tents made up his hospital. Government transports housed the wounded, but they carried away 14,159 soldiers, many of whom might have seen further service. Letterman successfully attacked the ambulance problem. Each army corps had its ambulances, whose officers were under control of the medical directors. Out of confusion Letterman fashioned order and a system. Never again would the commission have to serve as the bureau's crutch.

By August many citizens thought the Peninsular campaign a failure. A Unionist needed little insight to see that the affairs of the United States had grown worse. He had moments of wondering whether the nation could be restored. Had McClellan adhered to his original plan, said Olmsted, the United States would have been nearer victory; a "stupid Christian," the general was patient, industrious, and brave. His critics cut the ground from beneath him, making the citizenry pay for their folly. Stanton preferred fighting McClellan to crushing the rebellion, thought the commissioners. The campaign brought about a change of emphasis within the Sanitary Commission. The standing committee assumed greater importance. While Olmsted was directing operations in Virginia, the New York members took over responsibilities of leadership. They opened permanent headquarters at 823 Broadway.

- 5 -

The floating hospital service cost the commission about $20,000 a month. Increasing publicity sent contributions from $7,382.43 in June up to $24,381.46 in July. Expenditures went for supplies, special appliances, and upkeep of the flotilla. The branches experienced an unparalleled strain between June 22 and June 30. Even $100,000 could not have satisfied all demands, for the commission would still have to watch hundreds die from want. Commissioners concluded that they had run a futile errand. Officers paid little heed to their advice, turning a deaf ear on a group not officially responsible. The commission, thought Olmsted, had utterly failed to create a good army hospital system. That its floating hospitals were exceptional made no difference to those who wore shoulder straps. Medical directors chose army boats, because these were their own. Their decision showed neither disrespect nor hostility to the commission. The tumult of war made directors play safe. If the person offering help was not responsible to them, they would accept as little as possible. The commission ferried from 8,000 to 10,000 casualties, but daily its ships became of less service. Olmsted had to struggle to see that they were used. Whenever necessity forced officers to take a Sanitary transport, they gave it the treatment Dapple Grey received from the lady.

Even under Hammond's administration indifference characterized the government transports, which were still crowded, stinking, and ill supplied. On June 26, Hammond took over the commission's boats, and Letterman agreed to accept doctors of Sanitary recommendation. He took all male nurses, but left the question of women nurses up to the officers in charge of the boats; he readily agreed to accept all Sanitary hospital stores. The government had good reason for not stressing the transport service. Morale was suffering because of the system of easy furloughs and sick leaves. Malingerers took advantage of the floating hospitals either to shirk their duties or to leave the battle area.

The death rate in the Peninsular campaign was 165 per thousand. The commission took some of the credit for the comparatively small mortality. After the battle of Fair Oaks it had stepped between disgrace and the country, said Olmsted. "Persuasion, argument, management, and assumption" had brought Sanitary affairs a degree of success. Olmsted expressed the satisfaction of having played a worthy part. He disappeared down the side of the *Daniel Webster* "clad in the garb of a fashionable gentleman." Miss Wormeley said goodbye to the "unalloyed happiness" of life on a transport. On July 25 the act of donning a black teaspoon hat restored her to the "conventional and duly civilized" Victorian proprieties. Later she lingered long rereading *Hospital Transports.* One of her helpers asked:

"Colonel, what makes you study that book so?"

"My dear," she replied, "I am dreaming it." She could write to Olmsted, and he would fully understand when she said: "I really have lived not in remembrance so much as in the actual time itself." [5]

[5] Olmsted MSS. K. P. Wormeley to F. L. Olmsted, Aug. 3, 1863, Portsmouth Grove, R.I.

CHAPTER VIII

Battles within Battles

- 1 -

ON June 28, Lincoln had asked state governments for 300,000 additional troops: 501,663 were reported "present" with the army before Washington, but this number was plainly inflated; 49,990 recruits went to the Army of the Potomac. The Sanitary Commission proposed that recruits be distributed among veterans. Within three months experienced fighters could bring the new levy to good discipline by example. If 300,000 augmented the already formed regiments without creating new ones, the country would save "thousands of lives and millions of dollars." The Sanitary stand won general approval, thus obliging the government to accept some of its proposals. The commission also called for stricter standards of examination. Washington's intentions hardly inspired much confidence, thought the commissioners. Three hundred thousand fresh recruits did not cut the root of the difficulty, when reinforcements should have been sent to regiments depleted by battle and disease. Had training camps been set up over the country, pleas for more troops would have been unnecessary; had trained reserves been marching to the front, the devices of drawing lots and money payment to attract soldiers would have been pointless.

Public interest shifted to the Army of Virginia under General John Pope. His 77,799 men plunged into active campaigning before they could be organized properly for teamwork. To take care of ambulances in time of action Dr.

Thomas A. McParlin, medical director, proposed to have a subordinate in each corps, who would apparently direct the ambulances through corps directors and detail officers for general service on application from headquarters. The pressure of events kept him from inaugurating Letterman's improvements. Demands for ammunition, rations, and forage took precedence; medical supplies did not always arrive on time to be effective. McParlin had ambulances enough for a minor engagement but not for a major battle. With Alexandria as his central depot, the railroad became his line of communication and supplies. A few cars fitted up with shelves and stores served as a movable medical depot, until the Confederates later burned the supply train. McParlin planned to set up one large field hospital in the rear of the retreating army. The one at Bull Run stood too far from the wings to be effective, but houses, barns, and outhouses sheltered some of the wounded. The two hundred tents sent to Warrenton proved useful before McParlin sent the casualties back to hospitals in Alexandria. In Washington, Surgeon General Hammond prepared for the "heaviest battle of the war." His great difficulty was finding fit surgeons. The commission heard widespread calls for relief, while the stock of eastern storehouses was running low.

McClellan left Harrison's Landing on August 13. General Robert E. Lee had already snatched at the chance to defeat Pope on the Rapidan before the Army of the Potomac could reach Washington in battle readiness. He aimed to defeat Pope and McClellan separately. Pope's forces destroyed roads, bridges, and telegraphic communications as far south as possible, retreating slowly and giving stubborn resistance. Pope was sorely tried. Jackson, Ewell, and Hill operated in his rear, disrupting his communications. Reinforcements from the Army of the Potomac reached Manassas and Centreville; some of them saw action, but their transport and supplies arrived late. By August 16 the ambulances had been on constant call for many days. With forage scarce, the animals grew poor and weak; for use in the general service they would have to rest and regain their strength; but these August days shared no kindness with man or beast.

By August 29 the two armies battled around Gainesville, Groveton, Bull Run, and Manassas. From headquarters Pope surveyed "a most extended country" filled with soldiers and lines of campfires stretching for miles toward Thoroughfare Gap. McParlin telegraphed Hammond for more surgeons and supplies; but trains were not running, and little came from Alexandria by wagon. The wounded received medical attention at night; ambulances took them to a general depot near Centreville. The Confederates renewed their attack on August 30. Little more could be done for the wounded than feed them. Sanitary workers came on a field shrouded in dust and smoke. Wavering troops emerged from the murk to rally again, as the tides of battle swept back and forth. Dusk brought a slackening of attack. Pope retreated to Centreville, for the enemy had crushed his left wing. The blue and yellow dust settled "like a pall" on the field.

On August 30, Stanton issued a call through the Washington papers for doctors and male nurses. About a thousand civilians answered it. Many were drunk when the train pulled in at Fairfax after an all-night ride. The army had made no provision to carry them to the battlefield, so the majority went back to Washington. At the War Department doctors from other states learned that the army needed nothing; and so they returned home, while the wounded still lay strewn over the ground. The surgeon general sent out a fleet of wagons and hacks for ambulance service, but their progress swelled a tale of drunken drivers, broken-down hacks, and tired, hungry horses.

Held up by crowds and trains moving toward the front and rear, the two wagons of the Sanitary Commission reached Centreville after an all-night ride. Here Dr. Steiner saw Pope "careless and smoking," while General McDowell looked "gloomy and mysterious." Confederate capture of government stores at Manassas forced surgeons to beg from the commission. They came to an old hayrick for stimulants, bandages, lint, dressings, splints, chloroform, sponges, beef tea, chocolate, and condensed milk. The report of a Sanitary inspector read:

Not one of the twenty several kinds of supplies which our wagons took out but was eagerly sought, and did good service in some quarter or other. Every one of the seventy-five torniquets we sent was seized as a prize.[1]

Patients lay without blankets on wet ground or in the streets, where surgeons performed operations. Although already famished, the wounded faced a jolting ride back to Washington. Sanitary workers watched groups of tired and confused soldiers in the rain; they talked mostly of the "treachery and incompetence of some of their generals."

Inspector Coolidge of the Medical Bureau took over the job of removing casualties. Hired drivers, he learned, proved blatant thieves. Only physical force could make some give up provisions; others, who openly stole blankets, were "highly insolent" when Coolidge stripped them of their spoils. Very few helped place the wounded in the ambulances; still fewer would give them food and water. The patient's comfort was a secondary consideration, because the drivers had loaded the ambulances with "forage, camp kettles, personal baggage and subsistence." Pope's withdrawal from Centreville complicated Coolidge's problem. The remaining nurses, cooks, and hospital attendants pillaged the medical supplies. They were usually tipsy, and greeted the incoming Confederates with offers of swigs from whisky bottles. To the victor went the stores, but enemy officers shared medicines and food with Northern surgeons. Coolidge obtained at least

[1] Miscellaneous Documents [no title], Sept. 11, 1862, p. 5.

2,000 of the 4,000 blankets; for immediate use he received concentrated beef essence, mutton broth, coffee extract, sugar, milk, crackers, brandy, whisky, wine, and tea. These things did not stretch far. Not until ambulances arrived from Washington on September 5 was there anything like sufficient food.

The wreckage of war covered the battlefield. Under a flag of truce inspectors from the Sanitary Commission passed over ground strewn "with fragments of shell, with ruins of gun carriages . . . caissons, and wagons, and with the dead horses of the batteries lying where they were killed." Dr. John Foster Jenkins * counted forty-nine Union corpses in one spot. A. J. Bloor reported: "All our dead had been stripped of hats and shoes, fifty or sixty per cent of coats, twenty or thirty per cent of pantaloons, showing the comparative need of the rebels for these articles." [2] Confederate officers treated the inspectors well, and gave them about 1,500 blankets.

Union surgeons on the field snatched up the stores brought in by the commissary and the commission. When not operating they were preparing eggnog for patients. A barrel of tin cups from the commission proved invaluable, since most of the wounded had lost their canteens.

Inspector Coolidge seemed to treat reports of starvation as exaggerations, but Sanitary inspectors told of widespread suffering from hunger and thirst. Many of the doctors were starving. One seemed glad to eat a cracker picked up from the mud. Numbers of wounded had nothing to drink from Saturday to Wednesday; when at last water came, a thunderstorm brought it. Surgeons and Sanitary workers removed the last casualties on September 9, feeding patients milk punch and beef tea whenever the ambulance trains halted. Pale passengers rode by moonlight in a "long line of omnibuses, hacks, and ambulances."

[2] Box 834, Vol. II, pp. 641–42. A. J. Bloor to F. L. Olmsted, Sept. 8, 1862, Washington, D.C.

The commission spent over $6,000, while stores distributed came to "vastly greater amount." Defeat blew some good in Sanitary directions. Agents and medical officers worked in "perfect harmony." Dr. Hammond lacked proper organization to meet the disaster, said critics. But the surgeon general was one of the few "really alive to the crisis," answered the commissioners. His foresight had saved "regiments of lives." Within relatively few hours he had sent 5,000 convalescents from Washington to Northern hospitals. Hammond received an order for 2,000 beds in the Capitol, 1,000 on the supper floor of the Patent Office, and 30 to 40 churches and old barracks dwellings for hospitals. His asking for the White House was said to have roused Stanton's fury, although Lincoln himself had apparently offered it. The surgeon general sent for additional doctors, and collected a six months' backlog of supplies. He asked the commission to keep most of its stores in Washington, where the greatest demands would be felt. He saved many men from exposure and starvation by sending blankets and stores to Manassas.

Hammond's promptness and system, said the commissioners, repaid their exertions in reorganization and reform; he was their son in whom they were well pleased. Their blame fell on Stanton for haphazard preparations; he blocked Hammond's way for "free and greatly increased activity." The United States now ate "the bitter fruit of Stanton's suicidal course in stopping enlistments"; he had thrown "unarmed, uneducated soldiers" into "the clutches of rebel veterans." Confederates at Bull Run and Chantilly showed admirable discipline, appearance, and courage. They had risen from "immense defeat" to make good their boast of carrying war into the North. The season of humiliation had come again. Dr. L. H. Steiner noted: "We are losing our best officers . . . inspiriting the enemy and dispiriting our own men." [3] Europe was seriously considering recognition of the

[3] Lewis Henry Steiner, *Diary* (MSS.), Sept. 2, 1862.

Confederacy. The *Alabama* steamed out of England to start its raids on Northern shipping. Public criticism of the administration was mounting. Even the commissioners shared this mood. What was Lincoln's latest anecdote? Was he really a "first-rate second-rate man"?

- 2 -

Generals Bragg and Smith of the Confederacy now threatened Union control of Kentucky. Bewilderment swept Washington at the sight of the Army of Virginia within the city's fortifications. Lee at Chantilly had no intention of attacking, for he could neither invest Union fortifications nor properly supply his army. Presumably bent on destroying important railroad connections, Lee marched toward Pennsylvania. His move would draw the United States Army after him; their defeat might make falling back on Washington impossible.

The Army of the Potomac left Washington on September 5. McClellan moved to shut the fords of the Potomac and to cover Baltimore. A martial air covered a "slack and nerveless discipline," said Sanitary agents. Neglect of regulations threatened the health of every camp. The United States had been fighting for more than a year, protested one commissioner, but no sentinel had been shot for sleeping at his post. Far too few officers had been publicly disgraced for inefficiency. Sanitary workers fed the weary, feeble, and sick a more varied diet than coffee and hard bread. One of the commission's wagons stayed in the rear; to it the others periodically returned to replenish their supplies. From this simple beginning the commission began to develop its system of battlefield relief. Its wagons kept pace with the march and answered the loudest calls for help.

The Confederates marched without cadence, as their bands played "Dixie" and "Maryland, My Maryland." This motley crowd showed a will to win; they entered Frederick, Maryland, where General Howell Cobb failed in an attempt to start a riot. Dr. Lewis Henry Steiner watched him shake his fist and threaten the "damn'd long-faced Yankees." One citizen revealed the hiding place of Sanitary stores to Confederate officers, and only orders from General Stuart saved these supplies from complete destruction.

Letterman had no time to repair the bad luck that had undone much of his work at Harrison's Landing. Surgeons arrived exhausted at Washington. Stores lay either at Fortress Monroe or behind on the countryside of Virginia. Letterman lacked time to equip many of his officers, who apparently did not bother to provide for themselves. He knew nothing of the troops formerly under Pope's command. Medical reorganization had to be done "almost in the face of the enemy." Seventy doctors answered Letterman's appeal for one hundred additional surgeons. His efforts raised the number of ambulances to 315, an insufficient amount for the coming conflict.

Washington hospital accommodations expanded from 2,000 to 20,000 by the end of September. Barracks and tents began to replace old buildings at Meridian Hill and Armory and Judiciary Squares. Hospitals in Baltimore, Philadelphia, and New York held large numbers. The Medical Bureau began to heed Sanitary protests against using buildings of faulty construction for permanent hospitals.

Confederate destruction of the railroad bridge over the Monocacy River created a traffic jam. Government and Sanitary stores were held up somewhere in twenty miles of cars behind ammunition and subsistence; but because the commission had its own transportation, its five wagons reached the battlefield twenty-four hours ahead of anything else. According to Sanitary agents, the Medical Bureau had not one-tenth the necessary stores; these were either switched to sidings or did not leave Baltimore, and not until September 20 did they begin to trickle into the battle area. Shortages did not stop Letterman from organizing a hospital system. He distributed ambulances as fast as the moving army would permit. Between ravines and in buildings near the front Letterman set up seventy-one hospitals. He preferred barns to houses because of their greater space; simple structures allowed surgeons to attend large groups more easily. The wounded without shelter supposedly found compensation in good weather; but according to one doctor, many died for want of blankets and warm clothing.

September 17, 1862, has been called a day of "isolated attacks and wasted efforts." The Union Army of 75,000 tried to smash the 51,000 of the Confederacy. One observer marveled how men could "charge up hill after hill and over narrow bridges and through narrow defiles" against the musketry and heavy cannon of a powerful enemy. A surgeon later remember a field so carpeted with dead and wounded that the cavalry could scarcely move without doing further violence to the fallen. Troops took their positions in a confusion that prevented the removal of the wounded, who were consequently under fire for many hours. Cries went up that would have "softened the most hardened heart."

Letterman overcame immense difficulties in fashioning an ambulance corps. The original Army of the Potomac still followed his scheme adopted at Harrison's Landing, but troops under Pope had no well-organized system. Yet the medical officers at Antietam removed the wounded to Frederick, a tedious and painful journey to the suffering. The ambulances halted at Middletown, where food prepared at the right time was fed to the wounded. Drivers made an effort to see that their horses did not break down. Surgeons tried not to overcrowd the improvised hospitals at Frederick or keep their patients waiting before transferring them from ambulance to railroad trains. The Union wounded numbered about 9,000. Many who had been shot in the upper parts of the body walked some eighteen or twenty miles to Frederick because of the scarcity of conveyances. McClellan repeated the error of Shiloh, when he allowed certain states and well-meaning individuals to withdraw the wounded.

Letterman's account of the supply problem stood in bright relief to the Sanitary picture. Before the battle he ordered the preparation of supplies at Baltimore, which were to be sent on notice by telegraph. The medical director visited every hospital in the rear and "in no instance" did he find "any undue suffering" for lack of medical supplies; the army had enough on hand to care for the wounded of both armies. The food shortage, he conceded, was a graver concern, but only for a short time.

The Sanitary experience made a frantic background for the calm of an official report. Not even the genii of the telegraph could bring "one one-hundredth part" of what the surgeon needed, noted Commissioner C. R. Agnew. For several days the commission dispensed only essential relief. Olmsted spent $3,500 in Philadelphia and sent large orders to Hagerstown. He urged New York physicians to send by wagon and avoid the choked railroads. The commission sent 10 pounds of chloroform, 28,763 pieces of dry goods, shirts, towels, bed ticks, and pillows, thirty barrels of old linen and bandages, 3,188 pounds of farina, 2,620 pounds of condensed milk, 5,000 pounds of beef stock and cured meats, 3,000 bottles of wine and cordials, and many tons of fruits, crackers, tea, sugar, rubber, tin cups, cloth and hospital conveniences. Besides its agents and inspectors, the commission brought surgeons from New York, Philadelphia, and Boston. It found out where additional professional aid was needed, and sent surgeons to supply the need; it gave aid to more than 5,000 wounded.

Hospitals from Williamsport to the mouth of Antietam Creek housed nearly 10,000 of both armies. All around lay the dead. Surgeons partly made up with energy for lack of supplies. Hospitals on the right bank received little, while those on the left were furnished in part from various sources; but everywhere surgeons snatched up chloroform, opiates, instruments, tourniquets, bedpans, stimulants, and concentrated food. Patients were without proper facilities. The shortage of anesthetics meant the neglect of critical operations, frequently with fatal results. The terribly wounded had much to endure without opiates. Barns were heavy with the harvest of casualties. Lying on straw, patients "with lacerated and broken thighs had to be carried . . . into the open fields to answer a call of nature."

Sanitary agents tried to distinguished between avoidable evils and those inseparable from war. Traditional warfare, they said, did not contemplate such bedside care as nineteenth-century civilization demanded and the means of "alleviation furnished by science" could provide. For men to lie in fields for days unattended seemed needless, and every patient ought to be well fed; as it was, a little water the first twenty-four hours was followed by a diet of coffee and crackers. Surgeons did not organize nursing and food supply; they failed to convert barns into model hospitals. Because they were overtaxed they did not always reach their gravest cases in time. Wounds frequently became infected for lack of proper nursing. The sum of all these wants added up to a "depressed" state which was "eminently unfavorable to recovery."

After the battle the army moved to a new camp two miles distant; but for want of its own transportation the medical corps had to leave its stores behind—"a solitary pile in the midst of a deserted camp." If the Medical Bureau could not have its own supply wagons, the Sanitary Commission must provide the transportation. With proper personnel the commission could see that the wounded rested comfortably. One doctor noted: ". . . it is . . . possible to follow our army with sufficient tent accommodation to be used for hospital purposes, and stretcher beds with bed and pillow sacks to be filled with straw together with the necessary sheets, pillow slips and bed shirts to enable us to put into comfortable beds (under shelter though well ventilated) all the severest cases." The commission should plan to provide good hospital attendance, which meant "shelter, warmth, and stimulant; sufficient and prompt surgical assistance; nursing and the moral stimulus of care." [4] If the commission did not act on all these suggestions, they nevertheless gave direction to Sanitary thinking about field hospitals.

Perhaps the commission talked as though it had borne the burden of Antietam; but its inspectors and agents believed in Letterman's greatness, which had brought method and order out of confusion. Although only partially organized, it was his ambulance system that collected the wounded. Never before had surgical and medical provisions been so promptly forwarded in spite or delays, noted Commissioner Elisha Harris. While every hospital called for stores, Letterman summoned every means of relief at his command. Certainly the medical accommodations at Antietam were vastly superior to those at the second battle of Manassas. But why should Letterman's report differ so markedly from the many Sanitary accounts? He apparently saw the commission as a critic and must defend himself from its intrusion. There were probably differences in points of view. As an administrator, Letterman's concern was the general condition of the army; he did not necessarily share in the particular experience of surgeons and Sanitary inspectors.

Letterman's improvements continued through the fall of 1862. To guard against the waste of stores he set up supply tables with definite allowances for given periods and restricted the issuance to brigade surgeons. Dr. Steiner praised the measure for economy and efficiency, but Dr. Douglas

[4] Bellows MSS. E. R. Dunning to H. W. Bellows, Oct. 1862, [n.s.]

objected to the policy of scarcity. His coat pocket would hold the medicines of each hospital, said Douglas, while a barrel would contain the stores of a field hospital.

To develop a more responsible corps Letterman had surgeons learn their battle stations and precise duties. He directed the establishment of a field hospital for each division, and so gradually superseded the regimental hospital. Letterman did not give systematic organization to the service in the rear, evacuation hospitals, transport columns, and lines of communication. Since he left each of these aspects to its own devices, the result was generally unsatisfactory.

- 3 -

August and September, 1862, brought daily visits from the surgeon general to the commission's Washington office. Hammond and Olmsted worked closely together to solve the problems of ambulance corps and independent transportation, even though Quartermaster General Meigs objected to any move that would take business away from him. An ambulance corps free from quartermaster control would supposedly take good care of the animals and see that a certain number were held in reserve for the general use; it would also pay attention to its own vehicles and keep them from breaking down, and so ensure better service in camp and field. An ambulance corps improved morale; a trained personnel took pride in its work and was loyal to duty. These considerations would apparently have an effect on the troops, for the knowledge that he was being well cared for usually made the soldier show respect for his officers and government.

Olmsted wholly approved the surgeon general's memorandum to the secretary of war of a project for an ambulance corps made up of trained noncombatants. Hammond rehearsed old arguments: In no battle had the wounded really received proper care; soldiers carried them off the field as an excuse to leave the ranks; trained personnel subject to military authority would remove the need for taking men from the line to serve as nurses, cooks, and attendants, and in this way the army would stand to gain by 16,000 men. But the War Department turned thumbs down. The plan was too expensive; its large corps of noncombatants increased immobility and was detrimental, for "most panics and stampedes" in the army started with them.

Because of the " frightful state of disorder" after the second battle of Bull Run, Hammond again applied to the secretary of war. For want of an ambulance corps 600 wounded still lay on the battlefield, dying of starvation or exhaustion. Just adopt "*some* system," pleaded Hammond. Get the wounded from the field and avoid this kind of suffering in the future. But General Henry Halleck, commander in chief, thought present arrangements quite satisfactory.

The Sanitary Commission set out to change his attitude by discussion and persuasion. General Halleck appeared before nine commissioners on the evening of September 17. This short, stout man of dark complexion had a low, bald forehead. He appeared cordial and solicitous about meeting each commissioner. Halleck dressed carelessly and plainly. He was an incessant smoker and held a cigar in his fingers throughout the evening. His manner of speaking was hurried; his opinion of everyone poor. Halleck respected the Sanitary Commission but not those philanthropic nuisances that had created mischief after Shiloh. McClellan couldn't travel more than six miles a day because of some six hundred wagons. Better burn baggage trains and let the army march faster. Half-naked rebels fought better than Federals who wore shoes, shirts and drawers—"effeminating comforts" that made soldiers sluggish and self-indulgent. Commissioners would do well not to give 'em things. Why, a regiment refused to move until each man had his tin cup! But even that wasn't enough. The men had to wait for the governor, who wouldn't let 'em go until he'd given every man a handshake.

Halleck's jests were in poor taste, thought Strong and Bellows. The War Department, he said, had been debating to make "either Bishop Hughes or Bishop Bellows a Major General to offset [Bishop Leonidas] Polk!" "Weak, shallow, commonplace, vulgar" Halleck, concluded his Victorian hosts. He was not the man for his exalted post. Low in "natural humanity," he expressed his slim budget of ideas with immoderate emphasis; he had no comprehension of the spirit of the age, but showed signs of "bon vivantism," his manners moving from ". . . arrogance without dignity to . . . familiarity without ease, from reticence in public to the most unguarded garrulity in the audience chamber." [5]

Hammond despaired of getting an ambulance as long as Stanton stayed in office. To ask help from the president seemed useless. Reports reached the Sanitary Commission that Lincoln merely tolerated outside volunteer organizations, because "the pressure of public sentiment" left him no other choice. From Judge Skinner came accounts of interviews of a "most frightful and doleful import" between Lincoln and Stanton after Antietam. Olmsted wrote:

. . . the President has said that he was "under bonds" to let Halleck have his own way in anything in regard to the army; to make no appointments or removals, even, without his advice or consent; the President goes about wringing his hands and whining. He can depend on nobody. He don't know what to think of anything. He has even groaned out with a sickly smile, which showed that he was more than half in earnest but was too cowardly to acknowledge it. "It is now a fight for boundaries." Is this Halleck or Seward? [6]

[5] Bellows MSS. Interview with General Halleck as reported by H. W. Bellows, Sept. 18, 1862, Washington, D.C.
[6] Box 641. F. L. Olmsted to H. W. Bellows, Sept. 22, 1862, Washington, D.C.

Dr. Henry Ingersoll Bowditch of Boston took up the ambulance problem for Sanitary. In October, 1862, he came to Washington with a Mr. Pierce, who had apparently taken his plans from foreign treatises. According to Dr. Steiner, Pierce, a "nobody" and "humbug," wanted to "manoeuvre a most important medical subject" in hopes of riding into power "on the backs of some politicians." Stanton agreed to anything that Halleck might recommend; he was willing to authorize a draft on the Treasury, believing that Congress would support so humane a proceeding. Bowditch and Pierce bored Letterman, said Steiner, but he expressed interest in their plans, which fitted in with his own. Their ambulance corps called for "specially enlightened and instructed" men but not detailed soldiers. McClellan accepted their views. He agreed to sign any letter of general principles and asked that a detailed plan be forwarded to Halleck; but the commander in chief acted like a *giaour*. He seemed to have forgotten his earlier promises, but was adamant about demanding the proposition in writing—a proposition which had already been written three times. Pierce withdrew, this faithlessness filling him more with sorrow than with anger.

By the middle of November the commission saw the futility of urging the trained ambulance corps and independent transportation for the Medical Bureau. That men had to suffer was just too bad, said officials of Halleck's stripe, and humanitarian appeals could neither alter this condition nor change human nature. Military conservatism meant little, since medical directors like Letterman did pretty much as they pleased. Letterman's ambulance scheme continued to operate in the Army of the Potomac; its staff was neither trained nor civilian. General Grant introduced it in the Army of the Tennessee on March 30, 1863. Probably Sanitary influence was later helpful in creating an ambulance corps based on Letterman's plan for all armies in the field.

- 4 -

Surgeons of the Army of the Cumberland felt much abused, reported Dr. Newberry from Louisville. The armies of the Potomac and Mississippi had completer medical arrangements than theirs, but what army had seen as much hard and continued service? Any advances had come from their own "unaided efforts." Washington shed no guiding ray; General Buell clung to the dark of his prejudice, permitting each brigade but one wagonload of medical stores—an inadequate amount for a large-scale military operation.

The battle of Perryville on October 8, 1862, made Louisville safe for the Union, as Bragg withdrew from Kentucky. The medical director set up a division hospital, where the surgeons came with their wagons; but the army had no regular ambulance organization. Buell's indifference plus cold weather brought on keen suffering; the lack of ambulances, tents, hospital furniture, and food crippled surgical labors. Since medical officers had no power to transport sick and wounded by railroad, the commission fitted up hospital cars and operated them in this region for over a year. General Rosecrans replaced Buell on October 16. With a new command came a more humane attitude toward medical necessities.

November 9 saw McClellan out of a job. He had failed to press the campaign during the bright Indian summer. Popular approval greeted his departure, but soldiers gave him up with reluctance. McClellan's "power of detailed observation" had fascinated men; his personal attention to the sick and wounded and his refusal to fight a battle that might be avoided brought him popularity. McClellan's "wonderfully broad and well knit pair of shoulders" added to his physical charm, suggesting the bows of a ship that set off the "unguiding figurehead." But he wanted drive and confidence, said critics. Fit to do battle with unchanging fossils was this Napoleon, who had failed to learn that a new day was dawning. The general was one of those who "wanted God to wrap flannel around his thunderbolts, and then to slide them only in conservative curves." [7] Major General Ambrose Burnside took McClellan's place; it was said that this "clear translucent soul" wept when he received the command.

Burnside marched south toward the Rappahannock River, where Lee had taken a position in and around Fredericksburg. Union forces crossed the river on December 13, but the enemy drove them back. Letterman had made all necessary preparations before battle. The Medical Bureau's depot at Aquia Creek and subdepot at Falmouth kept the medical directors well supplied. Letterman's ambulance corps removed all the wounded beyond the enemy picket line within twelve hours, and carried more than 10,000 to tent hospitals north of the Rappahannock. Serious cases went to Washington by railroad; casualties lay on open cars bedded down with hay or boughs of pine and cedar. They suffered from the cold, although many of the exposed received Sanitary blankets. Steamers carried cargoes of wounded from Aquia Creek to Washington. The ambulance corps alone compared favorably with that of France, thought a Sanitary inspector. Walt Whitman, however, caught the note of human misery and found fault with hospital arrangements near Falmouth. Near "a heap of amputated feet, legs, arms, hands" lay corpses covered with brown woolen blankets. Within the hospital was confusion—nothing in readiness and men in old clothes, dirty, and bleeding. Patients sheltered in poor tent hospitals were lucky if they had leaves and pine twigs between them and the ground. Medical Inspector Thomas F. Perley protested against the high rate of sickness and criti-

[7] Bellows MSS., T. S. King to H. W. Bellows, Feb. 12, 1864, San Francisco, Calif.

cized Letterman for negligence. Behind his strictures loomed the feud between Stanton and Hammond, who was waiting for the right time to suspend Perley.

What struck the commission was not the human misery but the progress of the bureau. An inspector reported: "Great as the improvement of Antietam was over preceding battle-fields, I think that in every respect this has been an improve-men upon Antietam in the promptness and perfection of the care extended to the wounded." [8] For the first time the Medical Bureau stood as a peer among the divisions of the War Department. It was now "a compact organization, with personnel and material ready to take the field" and successfully tackle the problem of removing the wounded. The commission's work was wholly supplementary. At Aquia Creek it tried to make up for the lack of an evacuation hospital, and organized a relief station with kitchen and attendants. It contributed 1,800 blankets, 900 quilts, 5,642 woolen shirts, 4,439 woolen drawers, 4,270 pairs of socks, and over 2,500 towels. In one week Sanitary branches sent 16 barrels of dried fruit, 10 boxes of soda biscuit, 6 barrels of crackers, and nearly 1,000 pounds of concentrated milk to hospitals. The quartermaster set up stoves in tent hospitals, while the commission provided stovepipes. On the first night of its existence the station on Aquia Creek fed and cared for over 600 men. An occasional soldier spoke of the commission as indispensable. One wrote: "I would rather have Mr. Olmsted's fame than that of any General in this war since the beginning." [9]

In a northeastern storm General Burnside moved the Union left wing and marched upstream. Fourteen to twenty pairs of horses pulled the heaviest artillery out of mudholes, while rain-soaked soldiers looked "stupid and dejected." Weather defeated Burnside's second attempt to strike at the

[8] Box 835, Vol. I, p. 710. J. F. Jenkins to the Executive Committee, Dec. 17, 1862, Washington, D.C.
[9] J. S. Woolsey, *Hospital Days* (1868), p. 158.

Confederacy. His resignation came on January 25, 1863. General Joseph Hooker took over command of the Army of the Potomac. "Injudicious Hooker!" exclaimed George Strong in his diary. Bellows learned to give the new commander his due. Hooker worked with an excellent staff, and Union officers generally praised his administration. Never before had the Army of the Potomac been "in better discipline, [more] rigid accountability" than under Hooker. Only enthusiasm was wanting. Soldiers seemed to rely as much on themselves as on the general. Neither cheers nor sneers went up when he rode by. Apparently the "days of man-worship" had passed, thought Bellows.

On December 31, 1862, General Rosecrans was left in possession of the field at Murfreesboro, while Bragg withdrew the remnants of his 34,000, leaving a reported loss of 14,560. Out of 41,000 federal dead numbered 1,533; wounded totaled 7,345. Rosecrans' medical facilities did not equal those in the Army of the Potomac. Surgeons had to do without the "leading and simple articles of medicine." Officers and Sanitary agents tried to stretch meagre hospital accommodations and limited supplies that they might soften suffering in cold weather. Because the Confederates had broken the Louisville and Nashville Railroad, commission supplies failed to arrive in adequate quantity. Shipments came by the Cumberland River to Nashville, from where they were carried thirty miles to the battlefield. The Sanitary Commission later called on farmers from the northwest for vegetables, when the Army of Tennessee showed symptoms of scurvy. Within a month it had gathered 15,000 bushels without cost, and furnished eight barrels a day to each field hospital.

General Rosecrans cooperated with his medical corps. Signs of improvement came after the battle of Murfreesboro, when a newly appointed board of medical examiners removed several incompetent surgeons. To offset the competition of Western groups Olmsted urged Newberry to ask General

Rosecrans for a recommendation of Sanitary "zeal and promptness and generosity." According to Strong, the *Post* of February 16 carried a letter from the general certifying the commission's merits. Rosecrans had his excellences, said Olmsted. A "deep plotter and arranger," the general rode a wave of ambition, overconfidence, and vanity; but he was noteworthy for fighting with anger and religious enthusiasm.

The Emancipation Proclamation of January 1, 1863, confirmed the antislavery aspects of the war. Commissioners set limits to their sympathy for the freedman; as long as he served in the armed forces, they would help him. The plight of the emancipated Negro called on the sympathies of philanthropy; but his claim for government care seemed uncertain, and only by chance was he free to press demands on the commission. The Conscription Act of March 3, 1863, drafted all men fit for military duty, except those who paid $300 for commutation. Sanitary agents were not subject to the draft. Trained help was essential if the commission was to be effective. If it lost two or three hundred agents, the soldier would be the sufferer.

CHAPTER IX

The Ledger of Battle

- 1 -

THOMAS STARR KING of San Francisco threw California behind the Sanitary Commission. After the second battle of Bull Run he denounced the "supine temper," goading the city to wake up to the cries of the wounded, his oratory turning men "nearly frantic with enthusiasm and loyalty." Starr King promised to send monthly payments for the duration of the war. He followed one draft for $100,000 by another a few days later; the Western Sanitary Commission received $50,000 from the first draft of October 13, 1862.

The United States Sanitary Commission did not give St. Louis anything with good grace. King's words proved important in making the allotment: ". . . let . . . [Eliot] have a fair bite when it gets there—and all other branches too, if there are still other subsidiary organizations whose cash treasury is distinct from yours." It was neither right nor best, said Olmsted, to give a cent to St. Louis or any organization other than those under his direction. Westward flowed a stream of letters from Bellows and Eliot, each pleading his right to the greater share of money. Bellows argued for the necessity of symmetry; Eliot drew on pathos. For King to have ignored St. Louis entirely would have brought on a fruitless row with the Missourians in San Francisco; but he chose to give the greater support to the United States Sanitary Commission. He read only parts of the competing letters to the finance committee;

San Franciscans knew only the good things Starr King told them. Eliot applauded their help, and they were pleased; Bellows ennobled them in rhetoric, and they felt "like a big Newfoundland petted by Duke." [1]

The Sanitary Commission proposed calling a convention of branches at Indianapolis to discuss Western needs. The executive committee in New York nominated Judge George Hoadly * of Cincinnati to the board. He presently showed a lack of sympathy with the West, demanding exclusive control of supplies for his city; the new wealth must pay for Cincinnati's increased operations. Olmsted defied Hoadly, for all branches were but parts of one mighty whole. Cincinnati alone would prove unequal to the demands of a nation-wide problem. The central treasury allotted fair shares to all, giving special work special pay. On the battle line the commission took precedence of section, state, or city; this was the position that California supported.

The Cincinnati "wilding" had grown through its own efforts, answered Hoadly. Now an ungrateful parent demanded money and supplies in return for neglect. The plan for making the United States Sanitary Commission distributor of stores came as an afterthought begotten of greed. The commission had armed St. Louis with $50,000 and set it in position to assume real leadership. To treat the West ungenerously might explode and scatter the branches, warned Hoadly. Olmsted would reduce them to little more than receiving stations. This was the sin of consolidation; it erred against the national principle as much as secession did. To persist in such a course would justify the waywardness of St. Louis.

The commission was self-constituted, a voluntary society recognized by the government, said Hoadly. It existed to fill

[1] Bellows MSS. T. S. King to H. W. Bellows, Sept. 18, Nov. 24, Dec. 10, 1862, San Francisco, Calif.

a need and would die when government took over its functions. It was not a representative body; its members spoke for the East and the centers in the Great Lakes area; no one sat for the Southwest. Its spurious nationalism was presuming on the branches. To become a national commission St. Louis needed help from powerful auxiliaries like Cincinnati; their withdrawal would puncture the United States Sanitary Commission. Eastern avarice threatened to cut out Cincinnati and St. Louis from their share, continued Hoadly, while a Western council would limit the extent of Cincinnati's activities. The supremacy of one central body set competition in place of cooperation, and meant wasting the accumulated experience of a particular group; it would insult those who had built up a reserve fund through their own exertions. President Lincoln was the Sanitary focal point, answered Olmsted. What the commission took from one it returned to all. Cincinnati would take from all to glorify itself; to this end it would have its own agents distribute from the common stockpile. It denounced a Western council, although it had backed the scheme before the California gift had arrived.

The commission always worked through local machinery, noted Olmsted. This point had escaped Hoadly's memory. No one had ever doubted the national character of the Sanitary Commission. At the time of the California donation Judge Hoadly seemed no champion of localism; that came later. Emergencies demanded the opening of more depots and greater financial support from the people. Let Cincinnati join St. Louis, if it opposed efficiency; let it join those who mistook the shadow for the substance; but to accuse the commission of greed was to brand it with trickery. Neither Cincinnati nor St. Louis had rights over any other branches with independent treasuries. Cincinnati's treasury was not independent like that of St. Louis. To soothe wounded feel-

ings the commission made the following allottment of
$50,000:

Cincinnati	$15,000
Chicago	10,000
Louisville	10,000
Cleveland	10,000
Columbus	5,000

Cincinnati refused its share, although it kept the draft; but
by March 11, 1863, it quietly yielded. Why it backed down
was not clear. Jealousy of St. Louis might have been a factor.
Perhaps Cincinnati had learned that the time had passed for
building a machine.

California gold saved the Sanitary Commission from exclusive reliance on the poor, the ignorant, and the prejudiced.
September receipts were $20,916.80, but expenses came to
$26,646.01. Receipts rose to $213,964.23 at the end of October, when disbursements added up to $43,876.93. Of this
income $206,837.65 came from settlements west of the Rocky
Mountains. Thereafter the Sanitary treasury held enough to
ward off drastic cuts in operations. Contributions from December, 1862, to July, 1863, ran as follows:

December, 1862	$168,154.14
January, 1863	49,981.66
February	21,091.50
March	65,676.63
April	2,630.38
May	15,491.60
June	29,172.31
July	28,628.54

At the end of the war money from the Pacific coast had
totaled $1,473,407.07.

Western support placed the Sanitary Commission ahead
of all other relief agencies. The power of money dramatized

the commission before the public; it awakened confidence in
Sanitary ministrations, rousing other sections to give on a
large scale through fairs. These large sums helped perfect
the inspection system. Louisville became the center of operations in the Mississippi Valley. West Virginia, Kansas, and the
Northwest were brought more actively into Sanitary operations. Memphis and Nashville built new soldiers' homes,
while Cairo and Louisville enlarged their centers. Hospital
visitors went out to feed the morally and spiritually hungry.
The commission spent $7,000 on hospital cars, and chartered
a supply steamer late in 1862. The branches purchased stores
which they forwarded for distribution; but the costs for men,
horses, transportation, and distribution fell on the central
treasury. The more money the branches had the more supplies for the whole organization, although costs rose proportionately for supply and distribution. Sanitary accounts balanced at $301,997.66 on January 23, 1863. In that month the
commission distributed daily goods worth more than $2,000.
Early in February, 1863, Strong wrote: "Our work at Washington and at Louisville, our two chief nervous centres, is on
a big scale, employs some two hundred agents of every sort
and costs not much less than $40,000 a month." [2]

California's golden apple struck a note of discord within
the commission itself. Olmsted's demands of extraordinary
powers for the executive officer alarmed the "shrewd and
worldly wise, self-opinionated" commissioners. In ordinary
times he would have made "a crushing rupture inevitable."
Enlarging offices and increasing services in Washington, New
York, and Louisville disturbed members of the executive
committee. Money matters, said Olmsted, should be the least
of their cares. Their reputations backed the Sanitary name;
the deeds of trusted workers were its testament. Hold to

[2] G. T. Strong, *The Diary of George Templeton Strong*, edited by Allan
Nevins and Milton Halsey Thomas (New York, 1952), Vol. III, p. 264.

rigid accountability, and you increase expenditures. Those who loved the commission saved its expenses, because they shunned the appearance of waste.

Olmsted must submit all proposals for raising salaries of employees, said the Sanitary Commission in October, 1862. If the general secretary spent over $1,000, he must have approval from the executive committee. This order harmed efficiency, protested Olmsted. The executive committee must revoke it. Theirs was not the power to annul a resolution passed in "solemn council," they answered. The general secretary executed the wills of the commission and the executive committee; he confined his duties to the hired agents. The power of the purse belonged to commissioners and committeemen; they bore the responsibility. Critical groups were watching for flaws. Let cautious procedure be the Sanitary shield. What if Wall Street whispered that the commission treasurer paid out money without asking questions! In instances where the ruling proved inconvenient, Olmsted had only to telegraphed New York; the executive committee would try to help him.

Was red tape to bind him to the fifth wheel? asked Olmsted. Sanitary effectiveness depended on his flexibility. Could the commission afford conformity to Wall Street canons? Try it, and see the commission, shorn of "those little members," grow lazy, fat, timid, and "long of horn and short of stride." The executive committee modified their resolution, allowing the general secretary to spend over $1,000 but only in case of emergency. Olmsted bowed to what he believed a wrong and a slur, cast on his "practical sagacity." Needs had heretofore determined the kind of agent to be employed; costs now took precedence of quality of service.

Olmsted was mentally sick, all nerves and "morally morbid," thought the commissioners. At his office he turned night into day, and worked feverishly over things which were

never done; but what could one expect of a man who break-
fasted on "strong coffee and pickles!!!"

- 2 -

Organized in November 14, 1861, at Bible House in New
York, the Christian Commission represented Protestant ministers, the Y.M.C.A., and the American Tract Society. This
gathering elected George H. Stuart permanent chairman.
Public indifference at first worked against the Christian Commission. Inadequate organization kept it from assuming
nation-wide proportions; but December, 1862, showed it a
threat to the Sanitary Commission. Without privileges from
government, it carried the good message to the soldiers. St.
Louis had never been like this competitor!

Christian expenditures came to $6,291,107.68 from 1862
to 1864. To the front went its 95,000 boxes of stores and publications; this did not include 1,466,748 Bibles and other religious reading matter. The Christian Commission provided
8,309,052 pieces of knapsack literature. Its 4,859 agents were
called "delegates." They preached 53,304 sermons, held
77,744 prayer meetings, and wrote 92,321 letters for the sick
and wounded. Delegates took no pay, ran the boast. In reality they earned $50 a month. A minister on leave from his
pulpit received his monthly salary from home. This stipend,
added to the amount paid a substitute preacher by a congregation, plus the delegate's expenses paid by the Christian
Commission, reached a total that amounted to more than the
cost of a Sanitary relief agent for a similar period.

An "evangelical mountebank," George Stuart revealed the
"shallowness, fussiness, and humbug" of religious enthusiasm.
But connotations of "Christian" carried a powerful talisman,
seducing the believer to behavior unchristian. Whatever was
Christian was best; before this word the zealots forgot all

ideas of fitness, usefulness, and efficiency. "We have made the word commission a human word," wrote the troubled Bellows. "Add Christian to it, and the two will be invincible." [3]

In December, 1862, the two groups agreed to cooperate, but representatives did not meet until February and April, 1863. Men who were moved by the spirit proved erratic in business. These enthusiasts broke their pledged word. Decrying the ungodly Sanitarians, Christians were blind to the wide religious representation of the Sanitary Commission; Bellows they damned for not believing in Jesus as the Christ. Orthodox audiences in western Pennsylvania refused to hear one with Unitarian affiliations. The Christian Commission would not buy and distribute prayer books and objects of devotion for Catholic soldiers. At Annapolis the Sanitary Commission assumed this duty on application from the Fathers of St. Mary's Church in 1864. A gift of $500 from Pope Pius IX in the same year came to the Sanitary Commission through John Bishop of Buffalo. If treatment of Leo Eloesser of the San Francisco *Abend Post* was typical, the Christian Commission set aside Jews as "incompetent to act" for religious reasons.

Christian auxiliaries were apparently spontaneous in origin and organization. Their methods varied in detail, but all were one in aim. Christians did not scruple about the means to conquer aid societies, charged Sanitarians. They claimed important differences from the Sanitary Commission; their agents worked for nothing, and their stores reached the patient without the mediation of a medical officer. Besides, the Sanitary Commission destroyed the individuality of boxes by scattering their contents, and its central offices kept no account of expenditures. Loyal Sanitary aid societies accused their rival of bullying, when it could not win by falsehood.

[3] Box 835, Vol. I, pp. 430–32. H. W. Bellows to W. E. Dodge, Feb. 12, 1863, New York.

For "cant, illiberality and blasphemy" the First Annual Report of the Christian Commission was more than some Sanitarians could bear.

Could balance and thoughtfulness possibly counteract this contagion of sentimentality? the commissioners wondered. Some despaired of converting the "unthinking mass to right views"; others insisted on making the effort because the commission drew on the humble for supplies. Forceful and intelligent women kept many aid societies in the Sanitary orbit. Miss Louisa Lee Schuyler * of New York City, Miss Lydia Wallace of Syracuse, Mrs. Emily Barnes of Albany, daughter of Thurlow Weed, and others fought the commission's battles in New York. In the Women's Pennsylvania Branch, Mrs. Bloomfield Moor and Mrs. M. B. Grier brought the commission into closer touch with remote towns.

Christians did not bear all the blame; Sanitarians had to fight their own inertia. Sneering Sanitary agents stirred intracommission hostility. Masculine rigidity failed to meet the challenge quickly. Gentlemen in Philadelphia asked their wives to stay home rather than give aid to the Sanitary Commission. Like Dickens' Mr. Gradgrind, commissioners wanted facts, but frequently failed to scan their larger significance; they made too little of "occasional sensational information." Many Sanitary contributors hungered for the personal touch and the warmth of conversation. Commissioners themselves did not reach out to rural communities; they did not cultivate men of influence in distant hamlets; they failed to forge bonds of intimacy between city and countryside. But the Christian Commission had a missionary and resident agent in nearly every orthodox clergyman.

- 3 -

The Sanitary Commission kept on good terms with the Lincoln administration. Olmsted wanted the commission to wind up affairs, because Washington refused its confidence. Samuel Gridley Howe charged his fellow commissioners with doing too much. If they had not shielded officialdom from censure, citizens would long ago have blamed authorities for shortages in hospital stores. People should not be urged to do the government's work, said Howe; palliation of non-doing only made affairs worse for the future. Officialdom was a great swindler; trust it and the most solemn promises lay shattered.

The secretary of war never mentioned the commission "without a curse." In August, 1862, he refused government printers permission to reprint certain Sanitary documents, which were needed for the care of recruits. In October a commission inspector asked for transportation to the army at New Bern, North Carolina. Generals Hammond, Banks, and Halleck approved his request, but the secretary of war withheld permission. In December, Stanton placed the Western Sanitary Commission on the same national footing enjoyed by the United States Sanitary Commission. He did this to spite them, thought the commissioners; they now feared that other organizations across the continent would make similar application.

With few exceptions, members of cabinet and Congress expressed confidence in the surgeon general. "Big, burly, and genial," Hammond seemed everything a surgeon general ought to be. Doctor and officer, he knew his own worth. To old friends his manner could be cold and without grace; but his energy and accomplishments filled others with admiration. For 1862, Finley had tried to stay within a budget of almost two and a half million dollars; in striking contrast Hammond asked for over ten millions and spent over eleven millions. He allowed medical directors like Letterman great freedom of action. His efforts regarding the ambulance corps eventually met success. The increase of personnel and transport ran into thousands. Hammond sought increased rank

and pay for officers other than medical inspectors. He saw
to it that the pavilion-type hospital was set up wherever
general hospitals were needed. By November, 1864, the
United States had 190 hospitals, containing 120,521 beds.

But Hammond had watchful enemies. Senator Wilson refused to sponsor legislation distasteful to the secretary of
war, who thwarted plans for ambulance and hospital corps
and for an army medical school. Hammond's plans might
have been carried out better had old surgeons been friendly.
Sanitary inspectors objected to Hammond's careful regard
for seniority; he would have done better to get willing surgeons instead of taking the old medical officers.

The Sanitary Commission cooperated as closely as possible
with the surgeon general, fulfilling its original function of inquiry and advice. By fall of 1862 it was sending about fifteen
inspectors to the armies; instead of reporting to the secretary
general, they sent their findings to the commission which
confidentially informed Hammond of what was wrong and
lacking. The commission also sent out a set of experts to examine military hospitals and report their conditions. At the
special request of the surgeon general the commission carefully studied the wants and prospects of disabled soldiers.
It invited a distinguished Bostonian to visit the best institutions in Europe and submit a report. The commission also
examined for the Medical Bureau men who had applied for
nursing jobs in hospitals.

The secretary of war told Hammond to give up the commission. This could indicate that Stanton feared to make war,
thought the commissioners, but the surgeon general might
have wanted to heed his advice. The Sanitary Commission
bragged a lot about the indispensability of its supplies. Shouting Sanitary tidings seemed necessary, if public support
counted for anything. The surgeon general was lucky to have
strong and close allies among the commissioners, who stood
between him and "lamentable failure." But the commission

was not the army's beginning and end, protested a Sanitary inspector; self-praise puffed it up, making the surgeons seem short in contrast. For its harvest the commission was reaping the hatred of men who should have been its friends.

The surgeon general understandably wanted to think his corps up to the job. Hammond openly said he saw no reason for Sanitary continuance, since the Medical Bureau performed all necessary services. If the commission chose to limit its duties to the collection of statistics, he would aid it. He appeared to think the Sanitary hospital directors an intrusion on his affairs. The surgeon general was candid and friendly, but the commission's very presence seemed a source of embarrassment; jealous and envious surgeons were waiting to distort the slightest sign of friendship into charges of favoritism. Hammond tried to improve his relations with the secretary of war; but since he still relied on the commission, he only gained Stanton's contempt. Stanton seemed to loathe the Sanitary interloper much as the Anglican Church despised Methodism, remarked Bellows; his behavior, "inexplicable but characteristic," suggested a motiveless malignity.

- 4 -

Americans, tired of the waiting game in September, 1862, were reaping the rewards of contempt for politics, thought some of the commissioners. Their government resembled a ship whose pilot was a "poor whining broken-down idiot." Republican leaders, thought Olmsted, were the "damnest fools and rascals out of asylums and prisons." "Contemptible Chase!" . . . "a mere ward politician with a clean face." Lincoln answered for a cat, when the country needed a tiger; he had the obstinacy of the weak. The country must grow much worse before it showed any sign for the better.

Autumn, 1862, brought Democratic victories in New York, Pennsylvania, Ohio, Indiana, Illinois, and Wisconsin. New

England, Michigan, Iowa, California, Minnesota, Oregon, and the Border slave states saved the Republican majority in Congress. Some blamed Lincoln's Proclamation of Emancipation for the upset, because they believed a war to free the slave was ignoble; others blamed the military defeats and McClellan's failure to follow up his victory at Antietam. At any rate, the lukewarm took heart and Copperheads raised their heads. Before the elections Olmsted had felt free to excoriate the Republican administration; but now rose the frightful thought that Northern defeatism might clear way to Southern victory. He blamed the electorate for its faithlessness, noting: ". . . I haven't seen a man with a pleasant face today that it hasn't cost me a strong effort to overcome the attraction of my walking stick for his skull or my fist for his nose, or my boot for his coccyx. (And this is Sanitary education.)" [4]

To protect the loyal states from internal enemies the government imprisoned those who helped the enemy by speech or written word. Peace Democrats played on the dangers of tyranny and loss of liberty, weakening the Republican control of Congress and distracting attention from the war effort; they longed to summon from the vasty deep a never-never land, where reconciliation had been achieved through a convention of states. Men of this stripe threatened to rend the national fabric, the commissioners feared. The time called for an examination of attitude. Middle-class respectability was setting its "teeth in the old revolutionary way," wrote Olmsted; it would stamp out treason, even though the war took "seven years" and the citizens put up a "gallows in every town."

Secretary Seward urged his countrymen to take up the cross of patriotism. In January, 1863, Willard's Hotel became the scene of a dinner party, at which Seward dominated the

[4] Box 914, Vol. I, letter 268. F. L. Olmsted to J. S. Newberry, Nov. 5, 1862, New York.

conversation. Never before had the guests known him "so free, so brilliant, and so easy." His loud voice mixed "earnestness and naturalness," as he seemed to bare his official life for inspection. Seward spoke as though his reputation had suffered. The statesman of crisis must adapt himself to every conceivable situation; but citizens demanded consistency of him, even though they rarely showed an understanding of the meaning of patriotism. Let him who loved his country put down rebellion by upholding President Lincoln, "the lawful head of the nation and the incarnation of the Government." Set the country above the Constitution, said Seward; a nation on fire made any debate on the sanctity of law out of order. Merge private rights with the common danger and defend the state.

Seward held up Lincoln as a leader of admirable judgment, comprehension, and "infallible right mindedness." More willful and ambitious men had greater intellectual drive, which in the president was a "little weakened by gentle, mild and candid qualities and affections." His only recreation came with hearing and telling stories; often he interrupted the work of a cabinet meeting just to joke awhile. To Lincoln a jest was good on any occasion; laughter was all, if a man wanted to save his personal life. Yet the president suffered from depressions, and bad news robbed him of sleep. Open to conviction, he learned quickly; once a problem had been clearly explained, he became its master. Lincoln feared injustices and hurting the feelings of others. A servant of the people, he believed he held office to hear complaints. Since the president was always accessible, he paid too much attention to the trivial, said Seward; but waste of time was an "inevitable evil" in a democracy. Lincoln could dispatch matters of state in five minutes, for generally he accepted the opinions of the department heads.

George Bancroft, the historian, sat "cowed and silenced," except for an occasional interruption. Bellows noted:

. . . Mr. Seward maintained that the government had put forth a financial and military energy, never witnessed in the history of society—and had conquered more territory than all Europe (to which Mr. Bancroft said, 'Oh!' but Mr. Seward reasserted it). That no problem since the fall of man and the restoration of a ruined world equaled that proposed to us; that no republic had ever yet saved itself—and we were called upon to save a Republic with thirty-six sub-republics jealous of it and each other in its bosom! (Mr. Bancroft said thirty-five.) Mr. Seward over and over compared Mr. Lincoln's task to our Saviour's and Mr. Lincoln to the Lord. Indeed many of his comparisons were very scriptural and ecclesiastical without being at all pious or becoming—specially as he proposed to send various interests to hell, and exclaimed every now and then, 'Damn the Constitution, damn the banks, damn everything that sets itself upon a level with the nation.'[5]

Bellows embodied Seward's ideas in his sermon *Unconditional Loyalty*. Olmsted called it a "grand work." Thirty thousand copies were distributed to the army. The commissioners now listened to administration critics with difficulty. The loose and harmful elequence of Wendell Phillips ignored the fact that Washington partook of "law and usage, not an ideal kingdom." In New York castles of comfort sheltered "rich and lazy do-nothings" who hinted dislike and hesitated in name-calling while leading assaults on public confidence.

But if the Sanitary Commission was going to preserve decorum in politics, what in the world would it do about Stanton? Energetic, able, and hard working, he settled twenty problems for every one the secretary of state solved. Stanton respected no man, said Seward. The president down to the porter knew him as "irritable, capricious, uncomfortable"; but Stanton was the best man for the job, and the country could not spare him. Bellows and Olmsted doubtless swallowed this with a vinegar face. They still set down Stanton

[5] Bellows MSS. Dinner party of S. B. Ruggles (early 1863); H. W. Bellows to Mrs. H. W. Bellows, April 23, 1863, New York.

as a bully and a "blunderer upon good things"; but if Lincoln liked him, the commission would not demand the secretary's removal. Strong wrote: ". . . be to his virtues (whatever they are) very kind and be to his failings very blind indeed and stick up for the national government; that is, the present Administration, Stanton and all, through thick and thin." [6]

"Unconditional Loyalty" rang the alarm for men of learning, virtue, and property rights. Commissioners in their role as citizen set out to infuse the respectable with heightened patriotism; they would exalt politics, making it an honor to those who would abandon it in disgust. Set the central government above the tripod and venerate it, they cried. Concentrate all thoughts, feelings, and "views on national subjects" in a club. Drawn from the worlds of wealth and power, members could ponder the "grandest and widest schemes"; simple and fervent minds "could qualify" for membership, while "large active" intellects should develop a distinctively American point of view.

The New York Union League Club first saw the light of day in February, 1863, although Philadelphia was the first to organize a similar group. Bostonians called theirs the Union Club. New Yorkers urged other cities and towns to form Union Leagues. According to Seward, these clubs did much to save the United States from insurrection in the West, restoring confidence and doubling resolution.

Olmsted wanted the commission to distribute Loyal League publications, for whatever advanced the country's cause was a Sanitary aid. The Union League paid printing costs of Stillé's *How a Free People Conduct a Long War*, a pamphlet which won Abraham Lincoln's admiration. Sanitary agents distributed copies among the soldiers. Let history be your guide, it reminded citizens; sacrifice was the price of

[6] G. T. Strong, *op. cit.*, p. 314.

victory. The South had won battles, but North would win the war. Stillé supplied "a forensic shield and buckler" against croaking and malice. Out of 1,200 auxiliaries the Woman's Central Association of Relief heard few discordant notes; one called the administration "miserably feeble" and Lincoln an oath violator. The cousin of the governor of New York mourned the prostitution of the "Heaven born" Sanitary Commission for self-seeking partisan ends.

Bostonians planned to spread sound political principles, advertising their publications in almost a thousand newspapers and advancing plans to publish the *Army and Navy Journal* by mid-April. In New York, Olmsted and Edward Lawrence Godkin considered editing a review of high order. Subscriptions would finance it. Dana of the *Tribune* doubted its success, but Surgeon General Hammond thought it a potential power in the land. In August, 1863, Olmsted withdrew; the project seemed uncertain, he said, and the editor would scarcely make a living wage. Not until May, 1865, did James Miller McKim support the weekly, making the *Nation* a certainty.

CHAPTER X

Wheels of Battle

- 1 -

VILE, stinking, and miserable was all Aquia Creek, said Dr. Steiner—a town of wharves and mushrooming tents. Here the army kept ten days' provisions in advance. Six mules drew large and small trains of covered wagons; their going and coming was constant, they transported stores to various parts of the army. About 60,000 horses ate 800 tons of forage daily; the men required 700 tons of food. Government provisions came from Alexandria on some twenty-five vessels, besides many others engaged in delivering forage. Goods bound for Falmouth, the distributing depot, went from Aquia Creek by rail.

The commission set up headquarters on a hillside—living quarters, kitchen, dining room, storehouses, and stable; workers and guests found themselves as much at home as "pigs in a sty." Dr. I. N. Kerlin knew no end of interruptions—perhaps a half-drowned man, then one with a stomachache, and now three ladies in the kitchen clamoring to go to bed. There were deserving cases to feed and there were parasites—"bespectacled sutlers and chubby newsmen"—to keep from the trough. A dozen doctors added to the din, arguing the "eternal nigger question." In days of battle "straggling wounded soldiers and a heavy percentage of clericals, doctorates, and hospital stewards" filled the lodge. Such was the pressure, said Kerlin, that the commission's demand for a "weakly" report seemed very unjust.

Soldiers pitched their tents up and down the Rappahannock for about twenty miles. They had begun to camp next
the river; by mid-April they had moved two miles back,
burning up forests, fences, houses, and mahogany furniture
for cooking and warmth. Pickets could talk across the three
hundred yards of water, mutually agreeing not to fire on
each other. From Falmouth a spectator could see the battered gables of Fredericksburg. Now one could hear the
playing of a Confederate band; then the striking of a clock
followed by the voices of soldiers singing songs and hymns.
A good glass brought into view the monument to Mary Ball
Washington just above the town. Behind the first ridge of
hills camped the main body of Confederate forces; these
stayed out of sight as much as possible, although some of
their tents were visible.

For the "folly" of secession Virginia had "crippled" itself,
noted Dr. Steiner; the desolation was impossible to exag-
gerate. Southern desertion to Union lines was common. Run-
aways told of discomfort and disaffection. A pound of flour
with a little salt and two or three ounces of bacon made up
the ration. A good pair of boots cost $60. Because Lee's disci-
pline was very strict, deserters could tell something about
their own regiments but little about the entire army. "Des-
peration" made soldiers of the South "brave and fearful
foes."

Health and morale in the Union Army were excellent.
According to Letterman, the sickness rate averaged 8 or 9 per
cent for each regiment. The cleanliness of General Hooker's
camp and the martial bearing of his guards became a model
to the troops. Inspections included examination of ears and
feet; in some instances the soldiers had been ordered to strip.
Hooker praised the commission. He would "put his shoulder
to the wheel" to remove any obstacles, but Sanitary charity
could well "stand on its own bottom" and not expect a written

testimonial from him. General Haupt thought the organization obstructive, and wished Sanitary hospital cars at the bottom of the Potomac, until Dr. Elisha Harris changed his point of view.

For the coming campaign each man would be his own beast of burden, and bear eight days' rations, sixty rounds of ammunition, musket, woolen blanket, rubber blanket, overcoat, extra shirt, drawers, socks, and shelter tent—sixty pounds. Perhaps the commission misread Letterman's conformity to military orders on provisioning as personal animus. He refused its agents the right to advance with their own ambulances and military stores; he could not give them "any advantage over his own department." Sanitary stores would go with his on the line of march. This insistence betrayed "a foolish jealousy," thought commissioners; it seemed to imply that the commission existed only to remind the Medical Bureau of its deficiencies. Could Letterman be lacking in generosity? Certain of his subordinates more willingly admitted their Sanitary dependence for hospital clothing than he. The agents packed their stores on mules; this meant fewer supplies than wagons could carry. The quartermaster corps agreed to furnish the commission with eight days' forage.

Dr. Bellows visited General Hooker in the spring of 1863 along with Brigadier General Muir and Medical Inspector Taylor of the British Army.

At Aquia Creek, Hooker lived in a tent to which another tent, his dining room, was attached. About eight guests sat down to lunch that Sunday in April. Bellows noted:

Two beautiful nosegays just sent down by Mrs. Lincoln, one to Him, the other to Major General Butterfield (his chief of staff), were in the middle of the table. We had an oyster soup, Potomac shad, roast mutton, roast chickens, pudding, pies, champagne, cigars! I was too sick to eat anything and indeed with great diffi-

culty kept from vomiting at table! a feat I accomplished successfully the moment I got home.[1]

Hooker was about forty-eight and tall; his full head of
"clustering hair" had just begun to turn gray. Signs of in-
temperance marred a Beau Brummel in uniform; dreamy
eyes, loose lips, a "staggering and leering expression," all
bespoke the good-natured drinking man.

This bachelor had been educated at West Point. After the
Mexican War he left the army and went to California. There
Hooker won prominence in politics, until his "habits" brought
him low. Bellows wrote: ". . . Captain Sawtelle . . . a
quartermaster there, says he employed him on very mod-
erate wages to take care of a body of mules as a means of
support!"[2]

Bellows observed: " . . . [Hooker] has some slight literary
tastes; talked of Charles Lamb—perhaps out of deference to
me." His patriotism and antislavery sentiments sounded sin-
cere. The general gave no sign of religious convictions. He
had contempt for army chaplains, a band of idlers for whom
religion did "more harm than good." One of Hooker's
colonels made his chaplain "caterer of his mess"; and when
he failed in good provision, the colonel made him preach
the next Sunday. Hooker was a man of little faith. Bellows
warned Hooker that the country would not overlook the
mistake, if he did not find a chaplain and hold regular religious exercises. Only the best ministers in the Union should
be thought of as fitting candidates, if the commanding general was to have his own chaplain. With an eye on himself,
Bellows thought it would be "the greatest of services" to act
as Hooker's spiritual advisor and "obtain influence and exercise sway over the staff."

[1] Bellows MSS. H. W. Bellows to Mrs. H. W. Bellows and Anna Bellows,
April 19, 1863, Washington, D.C.
[2] Bellows MSS. H. W. Bellows to Mrs. H. W. Bellows, April 19, 23, 1863,
Washington, D.C.

Hooker had a direct manner, a sense of humor, and intelligence. He never slept until he had "fulfilled" every duty. McClellan was an "incompetent" and Burnside "a child," said Hooker; but his own was going to be "the biggest kind of a fight." Whipper or whipped, Hooker didn't get "scared." Victory would crown him, once the army was well over the river; and what's more, he ought to be able to march straight through to New Orleans! Hooker lacked the grand scale of inspiration and command, thought Bellows; this man counted on the luck of his throw. The United States had to take a chance and trust Hooker, even if he risked the whole Army of the Potomac. Hooker "was better than he seemed and had best not be seen but heard of," said Seward to Bellows; "for . . . he did not inspire by his personal presence the sort of confidence we desire to feel." [2]

The Army of the Potomac crossed the Rappahannock twenty-seven miles above Fredericksburg. Hooker's offensive folded when Lee counterattacked. The Sanitary Commission could give little help. To avoid blocking troop movements, Letterman stationed medical wagons in the rear; stores near the firing lines were scarce. The Confederate advance placed Union hospitals within gun range. Sanitary agents shared in the confusion. Surgeons ran in all directions; occasionally they fell to avoid the shells. The slightly wounded hobbled through the woods distractedly. At headquarters a wooden pillar fell, stunning General Hooker. To dispel the rumor of his death he appeared before his troops, but scarcely able to sit on his horse. The transportation of wounded back across the river started before the Union lines returned to "their old stenchy camps" on May 4. More difficult was the problem of aiding 1,200 casualties in enemy hands. Opposing generals worked out an agreement, and twenty-six surgeons reached the wounded with medical stores. The wounded totaled 9,518; of these 1,160 were restored to Union lines. Serious cases found places in tent hospitals, while Letterman sent 2,000 of those less grave to Washington.

The Confederates seized the commission supplies. Agents met no success in getting federal authorities to carry out their promises; surgeons called for extra aid, but Sanitary stores could not leave Falmouth. The Medical Bureau successfully cared for its own, although commission agents found much to supplement. Suffering might have been further relieved, they thought, had their 2,000 pounds of material been put to freer use. For a week after the battle Eastern money contributions were large, although spontaneous offerings were not enough to cover expenditures. Branches sent wines, liquors, crackers, beef preparations, jelly, sugar, condensed milk, canned vegetables, bed ticking, and blankets. One worker later remembered distributing 1,000 loaves of bread cut in slices and buttered, 1,000 gallons of coffee made on the spot, and 30 barrels of soft crackers. Like the "locusts of Egypt," delegates from the Christian Commission swarmed with pails of water, canteens of brandy, and such simple appliances "as Christianity or humanity dictates."

Hooker, said Dr. Steiner, was too pigheaded for his post. Officers and privates damned him for an incompetent braggart. Yes, Chancellorsville had its discouragement, but the gloom of 1862 had lifted. The South no longer seemed to wear a charmed life. The upward swing of economic prosperity joined with the dramatic campaign around Vicksburg to restore the confidence of citizens.

Events in the Southwest would decide the war, thought George Strong, not Richmond. In January, 1863, Grant became commander of the forces near Vicksburg. Dr. J. H. Douglas observed: "Grant is not a commander who looks out for his sick or who makes provisions for possible contingencies. He is ready to do so but requires a broad-viewed medical director at his side to suggest proper action." [3] In February, Sanitary inspectors called army hospitals "horrid" and "destitute" of proper facilities. Many regiments moved their camps daily to keep out of rising water. More sickness resulted from seepage water. General Sherman, it was said, ordered the arrest of every captain who allowed his men to drink it. By April army health did not come up to ordinary standards, observed Olmsted, but it was "amazingly" good considering the circumstances. Surgeons gave excellent care. Grant's commissary had no equal in the other Union armies. The men ate a variety of good food, said Olmsted. Nowhere had he seen troops so well "clothed, shod, and sheltered." Hospital accommodations were of the best. Soldiers seemed to be enjoying a holiday; they suffered trials enough to produce "an enjoyable nobility and overruling satisfaction on duty." In contrast the sailors of Admiral Porter's squadron showed the effects of a broken-down commissary. Scurvy was threatening the crews. The commission sent them 230 barrels of potatoes and onions, as well as some ale and pickled onions. From the end of January to June 1, 1863, it shipped 11,926 packages of food to the military forces before Vicksburg.

Sanitary affairs in the West were confused and complicated, complained Olmsted. Vague and uncertain duties and responsibilities killed efficiency. Grant gave the commission a chance to remedy its errors. His cooperation helped the Sanitary work against the opposition of its rivals. In March the commission was faced with supplying some 13,000 sick on transports on the Mississippi River. To apply to the government for a boat proved useless. Hammond said his hands were tied. How was he to give what the secretary of war and quartermaster general opposed giving? It took Grant to place a steamer under Sanitary control as storehouse and

[3] Box 840, Vol. III, p. 9. J. H. Douglas to F. L. Olmsted, March 3, 1863, Washington, D.C.

soldiers' home. The steamer *Dunleith* also brought relief to naval vessels on the White and Arkansas rivers.

No general was more loved than Grant. He depended on snapsure judgments of common sense and "simple, unselfish, humble purpose." May 1 signaled the start of his great campaign with the battle of Port Hudson. General Pemberton in Vicksburg opposed him with almost 40,000 men, while at Jackson, General Johnston commanded nearly 15,000 Confederates. Grant moved speedily with large detachments, defeating the enemy in detail. James Ford Rhodes summarized the military action as follows: "In nineteen days . . . [Grant] had crossed the great rivers into the enemy's territory, had marched one hundred and eighty miles through a very difficult country, skirmishing constantly, had fought and won five distinct battles, inflicting a greater loss upon the enemy than he himself sustained and capturing many cannon and field-pieces, had taken the capital of the State and destroyed its arsenals and military manufactories, had been for ten days without communication with any base or his government, and was now in the rear of Vicksburg." [4]

Here Grant stationed troops in ravines and on the slopes descending from the city. Soldiers lived "half burrowed in the ground" for protection against infantry fire. The air was stifling; water was not only scarce but impure. The number of sick slowly mounted. About 3,000 sick and wounded lay in field hospitals, whose conditions were "universally good." The high excitement was gradually declining, for the men were sure of their prey.

Early in June, Lee started for the Shenandoah Valley, with Hooker in pursuit. Over Letterman's protests Hooker cut down on hospital tents, mess chests, medical wagons, and other essential articles. Surgeons had great need of medical stores at Gettysburg, but the supply train parked twenty-five miles away at Westminster. The railroad between West-

[4] J. F. Rhodes, *History of the Civil War 1861–1865* (1917), p. 253–4.

minster and Baltimore was without sidings or telegraph and took five hours to travel; still the army managed to send through fifteen trains a day. The Sanitary Commission built up reserves in New York, Philadelphia, Baltimore, and Washington, placing Dr. Steiner in charge at Frederick, Maryland. The commission stationed agents at Harrisburg. The enemy captured Alfred Brengle, relief agent, and Dr. Alexander McDonald, inspector, and put them into prison in Richmond. Other Sanitary agents accompanied the army on its forced march, sending the empty wagons back to reload at Frederick, returning to Gettysburg either by way of Westminster or by the direct route.

Confederates marched unopposed in pleasant weather. By demanding tribute they enjoyed an abundance of food and helped themselves to horses and mules on neighboring farms. White men of wealth and black of poverty fled northward as alternating tides of Union and Confederate cavalry surged through the streets of Frederick. The thought of similar inundation turned Harrisburg panicky. To Olmsted, New Yorkers seemed without emotion, while Washington slumped in a blue mood.

Hooker resigned, and was succeeded by General George Meade on June 28. "Gaunt and stooping," the new commander satisfied the soldiers without arousing their enthusiasm. His face looked "oriental and yet Yankee"; his manner was stern and dignified, this veteran of "candid and receptive disposition." Meade had always been friendly to the commission. The battle of Gettysburg started on July 1. The armies lay about a mile apart. Fortune smiled on the Confederacy in the early stages. But Lee failed to take advantage of the morning hours on July 2; his attack started in the afternoon, when the Union VI Corps had reached Gettysburg after a forced march. The failure of Pickett's grand charge on the Union center on July 3 heralded Confederate retreat on July 4.

The United States Army started in pursuit of Lee on July 6. Gettysburg, "the best fought field of the war," left the Union Army with "hardly a breath in it," said Olmsted. He remembered a certain half hour when the Union was but "a hair's breadth from terrible defeat." Lee's caution and steadiness were possibly the results of training, thought Olmsted. The Confederate general's photograph suggested a "temperament" which hid its "fondness for desperate play." According to reports, Lee had scattered his forces; skirmishes were being fought on the "circumference of a moving circle thirty miles in diameter." Presumably every village in this isolated area was housing the wounded of both armies.

Letterman at once felt the effects of insufficient equipment in this country stripped of food and forage. Medical wagons had only a modest supply of anesthetics, dressings, drugs, and instruments. Only the XII Corps had avoided sending supply trains to the rear; here doctors gave care equal to that of Fredericksburg. Throughout the battle 650 medical officers worked continuously. Some thousand ambulances removed 12,000 to Union hospitals by July 4. General Meade let half the reserve medical trains approach the field on the evening of July 3. To have to care for abandoned Confederates in addition to the Union wounded strained the capacities of the Medical Bureau. The commission sent congratulations to Hammond; furnishing attention to 20,995 did not come within the power of a Medical Bureau "administered by anything short of arch-angels in prescience and resources"; yet the bureau's preparations had been on a larger scale and were more effective than theretofore.

As late as July 8, Bellows wrote Olmsted:

No energy you can use in forwarding by every possible chance can equal the demand here. If I were to spend a week, I could not fitly describe the horrors and suffering of our wounded men. The dead are not yet buried; hundreds are yet undressed of their wounds; thousands have not food. The country is stripped bare of ordinary supplies: there is not food for the well, and they will not sacrifice much for the sick. Indeed there is nothing to be had for love or money.

Forage is very scarce; forward it for our use.

Beef is the only thing of which there is enough at the hospitals. The men want succulents; not so much spirits as usual.[5]

Sanitary stores reached the battlefield hours before supplies arrived from other quarters; the first arrived at Westminster by railroad on the morning of July 1. By the next morning agents had distributed them to the field hospitals. From Baltimore came tons of ice, mutton, poultry, fish, vegetables, bread, butter, eggs, clothing, hospital furniture, and many other articles. The commission spent $20,000 the first week after the battle, but the public sent in as much money. Expenditures presently mounted faster than receipts. By July 23 the commission had $75,000 in its treasury. Dr. Agnew called on Olmsted and Knapp "to take in sail."

The wounded were crowded into houses, churches, barns, and tents. They received such attention as a farmer would hesitate to give a cow. Those without shelter suffered acutely from the rains. The critically wounded stayed at Gettysburg; all others went to Hanover Station in greater numbers than trains could carry them away. Olmsted and Inspector Vollum of the army found the wounded without food, shelter, and attendants. Here the Sanitary Commission set up a lodge furnished with tents, beds, kitchens, and nurses; it fed 16,000, sheltered 1,200, and supplied many with clothes. An agent distributed coffee and soup before the patients left for the general hospitals, while a surgeon and corps of dressers examined the wounded and applied fresh dressings. Each hospital train carried a surgeon and attendants. The commission provided the cars with large cans of ice water, bags of crackers, and stimulants.

Sanitary workers made Camp Letterman "a thing of won-

[5] Box 762. H. W. Bellows to F. L. Olmsted, July 8, 1863, Gettysburg, Pa.

der," winning the praise of surgeons. An agent noted: "The most fastidious surgeon could not mangle . . . flesh or bones more splendidly for scientific purposes than this continuous battle has done. Every class and character of contusion and fracture and penetrating wound from shot and shell of the worst description is to be found under the three hundred tents which constitute Camp Letterman Hospital." [6] Conspicuous was Sanitary help to the 6,802 Confederate wounded, suffering from a shortage of food and medicine. Houses, barns, and dilapidated tents made up their hospitals. Camp police was deplorable, but Southern surgeons were intelligent and attentive. The Sanitary Commission made every provision for the comfort of the patients, feeding those placed directly in its care. The Southern doctors in return petitioned General Lee for the release of McDonald and Brengle in Richmond.

Gettysburg killed foreign efforts to recognize the Confederacy, but Meade failed to follow up his victory, letting Lee escape across the Potomac. Neither side assumed the offensive. Vicksburg fell on July 4. When Port Hudson on the Mississippi fell, the Confederacy lay cut in two. Better than these triumphs, thought Olmsted, was the drafting of 300,000. The city poor had a different idea; they expressed it in riots. New York mobs stormed and burned houses, but Sanitary work went on without hindrance. Violence had not ebbed when California silver reached the Broadway headquarters of the commission. To the commissioners this gift reaffirmed the united efforts of the nation.

- 2 -

Rosecrans remained inactive for nearly six months, while he fortified Murfreesboro and resupplied the Army of the

[6] Box 767. G. Winslow to L. H. Steiner, Sept. 25, 1863, Camp Letterman, Gettysburg, Pa.

Cumberland. His campaign against Bragg got under way in June. Skillfully outmaneuvering his foe, Rosecrans marched into Chattanooga, which with Vicksburg and Richmond formed three key points of the Confederacy. He did not stop to consoldiate his gains and plan for the future, but pursued an enemy who had no intention of retreating. Bragg won a Pyrrhic victory at Chickamauga on September 18. Only General Thomas' corps stood its ground, while the rest of the Army of the Cumberland fled to Chattanooga.

Deep in hostile territory, Union officers turned all available houses and buildings into hospitals. After the battle the Sanitary inspector entered a large church, where a congregation of wounded lay "without even a candle to shed a glimmering light over their destitution." War had defaced dwellings, grounds, and groves. Men ripped out fences and cut down fruit trees for firewood, while they set up huts and tents in empty lots. Fortified lines surrounded Chattanooga, strong fortifications crowning the more prominent points.

One route remained connecting the Army of the Cumberland with the North. It wound its way over the mountains and afforded no forage; the round trip from Stevenson to Chattanooga took nearly two weeks. But over the rutted road starving animals hauled ambulance trains to unload patients and reload with supplies. The commission stationed agents at various points, one surgeon observed, "making a species of entrepot for the aid of the passing ambulance trains, or such soldiers as might be returning to their commands; and in this way much assistance was rendered." Transportation difficulties limited Sanitary activities. The commission succeeded in sending through ten wagons full of stores, although the Confederates destroyed many others. It moved its mountain lodge from Jasper down to Kelly's Ferry and opened an agency at Bridgeport after Union arms had opened the Tennessee River.

Commanding the Departments of the Ohio, Cumberland,

and Tennessee, General Grant relieved Rosecrans in October. With reinforcements from the armies of the Potomac and Tennessee, Grant himself took command. The soldiers did not wait for orders, but drove the enemy from his entrenchments on Lookout Mountain on November 25, 1863.

At this time Dr. Newberry offered Surgeon John Moore "luxuries" not available elsewhere for the wounded. Moore thought it mortifying to have to depend on outside charity, when the government was in duty bound to provide these essentials. The commission made Chattanooga its most important agency in the Mississippi Valley for 1864. To combat an outbreak of scurvy it hired fifty workers to distribute potatoes, onions, sauerkraut, pickles, and dried fruit. The estimated value of these distributions from April to November, 1864, was $66,375.70. The commission paid the same attention to the forces under General Burnside at Knoxville.

CHAPTER XI

The Wheel of Fortune

- 1 -

AFFAIRS went from bad to worse for Olmsted. Members of the executive committee made "unbearable" men of business, he said; they submitted to no plan or discipline, but worked part of the time on their own business. Their grasp of Sanitary matters was not complete, because they lived far from actual operations; preoccupied with the possible misuse of money and power, they created resentments whenever they meddled in practical affairs. The committee countenanced a divided authority, and produced contradictory plans and announcements. In Olmsted's absence Dr. Agnew heard the complaints of agents, and dismissed two valuable men instead of referring the disagreement to the general secretary on his return.

The commission had never clearly defined the relations between the general secretary and the Western secretary. Newberry had acted as Olmsted's equal, not his subordinate. He invariably sent an excuse for not writing reports—ill-health, want of time, too much business, or the insignificance of his efforts. Without Western reports Olmsted could present no survey of operations. Ignorance of Western operations left an "enormous vacuum," said Bellows; it "vitiated" Sanitary statistics, supply estimates, and plans for monthly allotments. The commissioners viewed "such a defect . . . on so huge a scale . . . with a mysterious wonderment." On the other hand, Olmsted marred his own "glorious" qualities. His brain was "impracticable," thought Bellows. Human mediocrity and inertia tried Olmsted's patience. He had the pride and self-reliance of Lucifer, and his "passion for uniformity" was worse than Archbishop Laud's.

On January 24, 1863, the Sanitary Commission passed three resolutions. They paid respect to Newberry but disapproved "the separation of the Western Department from the superintendence of the General Secretary." In February they sent Olmsted on a tour of the West. This was a blunder, protested A. D. Bache. He spent much time soothing Olmsted's hurt feelings; but now the commission renewed what should have been forgotten. Olmsted would burn with criticism, because he could not compromise; he must be all or nothing.

Vaster than the Eastern seaboard, the West was fiercely local and full of rivalries. Westerners believed that states should work for their own soldiers. In the East the commission refused to make special distributions; but in the West energetic, reliable, and well-informed aid societies stood ready to defy any denial of their right to correct a reported distress. Westerners liked to do things in their own "rushing way." It was difficult for Easterners to understand "this tremendous tide of life and feeling," whose devotion to an immediate goal bade all else "clear the track." The commission in Chicago helped Westerners on their way; at the same time it protested against the swarms of civilians who visited camps bearing gifts. This policy of nonobstruction won friends and contributors. Collecting supplies was a difficult problem for Western branches. Indiana and Iowa had their own aggressive state agencies; Ohio and West Virginia cared little for Sanitary federalism; they all stood to profit if the Sanitary Commission struck at localism. By compromise Chicago had got the better of the Illinois agency. Wisconsin and Iowa in time became valuable tributaries.

Westerners found much in the commission to criticize. Inspectors should receive no salaries, they said. The commission never held a board meeting in the West. Eastern commissioners rarely went near the Mississippi Valley, but showed too great a fondness for the Army of the Potomac. Dr. Newberry was popular because he followed the line of least resistance, letting such local enthusiasm hang itself. Generals, legislatures, newspapers, and even critics spoke well of the commission. Cincinnati no longer thought of separating; St. Louis had given up trying to compete. Now Olmsted refused to treat the Westerners as a different breed of American. He praised the soundness of their patriotism but called them ignorant. They lacked faith in individuals and men, but showed "excessive confidence in movements and masses," and so became dupes of politicians who exploited their provinciality. But with patience and "long views" the West would agree to "federalize" once it understood Sanitary aims, said Olmsted. What Western branches called a broad policy he denounced as slovenly. The commission should not abet citizens in their pleasure jaunts to the army, but must teach them to mind their own business and follow a stricter division of labor. More women than men were pretending to do sanitary work; this "meddling under false colors" was more than Olmsted could bear. In Chicago he made few friends. Some admired his mind; others prized his integrity; but everyone agreed that Olmsted was arbitrary, inaccessible, and cold. Among Western surgeons he had given offense; his alarming reports to the surgeon general supposedly exaggerated the number dying from hospital gangrene.

Back in Washington, Olmsted worked out a plan of reorganization according to the specification and division of labor. He made the supply department indivisible and under one law. Each branch would enjoy local rule and authority; a secretary of supply would coordinate the work of each branch. When the plan came before the commission in June, Newberry threatened to resign. Beyond the Appalachians rumblings of rebellion became audible, for the scheme smacked too much of centralization. Chicago would have nothing to do with a plan that made it part of the Western Sanitary Commission. On the other hand, certain inspectors threatened to resign if reorganization failed to go through.

The majority of commissioners saw the issue in terms not of conformity but of historical development. It had never entered their minds in the beginning that the war could assume such vast proportions. The Sanitary machine had mushroomed to meet needs. Commissioners originally hoped to be the exclusive ministers of supplementary relief; but Washington did not dare suppress other charitable agencies. Since the commission had been unable to meet all extramilitary wants, the Christian Commission had enlisted personal and religious sympathies in a manner foreign to the impersonal attitude of the Sanitary. Headstrong Western organizations had never been more than relief associations, but the commissioners hoped to present them with ideas impossible to learn elsewhere. The West followed the East, copying what was easiest in Sanitary methods, but "always very unsatisfactorily." Yet when the commissioners looked at all they had done, they took heart; at least their organization was uniting the sections in its charity.

Since Olmsted's plan invited friction, the commissioners did not accept it. Newberry had promised to submit reports; instead, he issued the *Sanitary Reporter*, a newspaper containing information that should have formed a part of a general survey. Olmsted was ready to forget all vexations except Newberry's disposition to make the West a wheel within the fifth wheel; but the commission did not support its general secretary. Dr. Newberry had clearly won, and affairs went on as before.

In August the Mariposa Company of California offered Olmsted the job of superintending its estate. His would be "absolute, unqualified control" of a county with quartz mines, mills, a railroad, and a population of 7,000 tenants. He accepted the offer. On resigning from the commission he added up the credits and debits for two years in Washington, and he seemed to come out at the short end. Never did he enjoy a footing of intimacy with the government. Chase and Stanton had put him "out of the way with falsehoods." Europe had shown him respect. Members of the British Parliament as well as French and German economists were familiar with his views; a foreign minister even took the trouble to hunt him up. But Americans? For every American who had read his books there were twelve foreigners. The government could offer him nothing. Washington loved mediocrities, especially in high office. That the commission rejected his guiding principles was especially galling to Olmsted. He saw himself a greater failure than Jefferson Davis, who still had a chance of winning. Olmsted closed the door of his Washington office in the belief that he had "led nothing to nothing."

The commissioners, countered Bellows, had every right to doubt Olmsted's qualifications. This man—fastidious, over-wrought, his brains "ever teeming and brooding"—could no longer inspire confidence. The government wanted practical men, regardless of limitations. In the American crucible of surprises and crises leaders must be robust, flexible, and of a ready wit. The time was out of joint for Olmsted, who was fitted for "a more patient and deeper kind of work." He became a difficult subordinate. His domineering temperament made cooperation with lesser men impossible. The commissioners had been patient, respectful, and enlightened. Bellows had had to take the buffeting of mutually hostile winds and keep an even keel. Statesmanship, he said, was accomplishing what was practicable, not what was best.

Olmsted's resignation, however, filled Bellows with foreboding. Would the commission be able to escape injury by this act? asked Bellows. Considering the rapid growth of the Christian Commission, perhaps the time had come for the Sanitary Commission to close its doors. In August, Bellows wrote Olmsted:

Dr. Hammond tells me of the inimicalness of the Secretary of War and of his impending struggle in which he thinks it not unlikely he may lose his place. Why might not his withdrawal or removal be the appropriate moment for ours? You see how seriously I regard your loss to the Commission.[1]

Yet it soon became clear to the executive committee that the absence of this "positive and earnest mind" made for greater harmony. By the time October had arrived, Bellows had changed his text to "Comfort ye my people"; for without Olmsted the fifth wheel no longer rode in rough places and the highway looked straight.

But when Olmsted left, the light blew out that once had lit up the Sanitary house. The commission no longer had a man who held its affairs in his grasp. Each person could see his own job, but never the sum of the parts. With Olmsted went a sense of security for workers like Steiner, Knapp, and Louisa Lee Schuyler. Olmsted's bitterness slowly ebbed. The commission made him a member on October 17, 1863; but it went the way of Dr. Newberry. He became associate secretary for the West; Knapp became associate secretary for the East, a post he did not fill well. Dr. Jenkins took over the post of secretary general. With limited powers he went to New York to work with the executive committee.

In the Sierra Nevadas, Olmsted looked back on his Sanitary past as a previous age, when he had done "a nice bit of civilized workmanship." To Knapp he gave advice which he himself might have followed: ". . . you are cast down by that which was inevitable . . . for human nature and the

---

[1] Olmsted MSS. H. W. Bellows to F. L. Olmsted, *ca.* Aug. 12, 1863, Walpole, N.H.

constitution of human society are as much facts as the tides and as inevitable in their flow and reflow." This would have been chastening, had fatalism sat easily on Olmsted; but his words brought a "gripe" to his side which was like "a blow on the head" to his "constantly regerminating hopes and ambitions." [2]

- 2 -

Friends of the Sanitary Commission called the Christian Commission "fierce and vindictive" in its abuse of Sanitarians. Because wounded men on the battlefield needed little consolation of spirit, the Christians worked to make all stores flow their way. They took credit for "nearly all desirable operations carried on at Gettysburg"; in the ways of relief they proclaimed originality while copying their rival in plan, system, and rule. The Woman's Central Association of Relief found the Christian Commission a source of malicious rumor. Sanitary agents and inspectors squandered money in lives of riot, said gossip; and soldiers had to pay for what was really free; and agents sold hospital stores in the open market and sold slave maps to deserters.

The Sanitary Commission could count on cities in New England and the Central states; but Evangelical inroads in rural areas caused a sharp drop in supplies. From Buffalo, New York, and Toronto, Canada, came complaints; commissioners never visited those who were expected to wage cheerless contests against religious enthusiasts. Not until November 21, 1864, did Sanitarians in Philadelphia send out agents to correct misrepresentations, while they themselves drew nearer such Protestant leaders as Phillips Brooks. Henry Ward Beecher spoke at a Philadelphia rally for the exclusive benefit of the

[2] Olmsted MSS. F. L. Olmsted to F. N. Knapp, Sept. 28, 1864, San Francisco, Calif.

Sanitary Commission. Bishop Potter mentioned the Sanitary work at a Christian mass meeting, at Stillé's insistence. The Sanitary Commission accepted the cooperation of the American Tract Society as "more nearly in harmony" with its principles. Bellows called on support from the Pacific coast; he saw that the *Saturday Evening Post* and the *North American Review* carried favorable articles. The Sanitary Commission published the *Bulletin* as its official mouthpiece in September, 1863. It first appeared with E. L. Godkin as editor. In its pages Sanitarians tried to answer insinuation and half-truths with facts and figures. In the state of New York circulation came to 2,600 by the end of the war.

The Christian Commission did not stand alone in its criticism. Isaac Harris, an energetic Sanitary worker, wrote: "There is so much corruption existing throughout the land and people are so very suspicious that they cannot understand how any body of men in whom so much confidence is reposed and so much entrusted can prove aught but rascals." The government, said average businessmen, created the Sanitary world, for "shiftless, extravagant, unpractical people." To have educated men at the head was proper; but for gentlemen and scholars to work as porters and errand boys was too much of a good thing! Give money to the Sanitary, and it went into the pockets of a lot of "sawbones." Yessir, those sawbones were "making a good thing out of charity." Why, go to any Washington hotel, and it was always stocked with Sanitary Commission goods. Public benevolence passed by everything, except the Sanitary Commission. Soldiers' families were of no account. Let 'em starve! Private charity was sacrifice to public show. The people had run the Sanitary Commission into ground, and all because the government didn't live up to its duties. Yet frequently the commission could count on its critics for contributions. Isaac Harris explained: ". . . [People] are so purse proud and jealous of each other that one cannot give five cents without another thinking he will lose caste by not doing likewise." [3]

November 5, 1863, brought the opening of the first Sanitary fair at Chicago. Mary Ashton Livermore said: "The Fair is my suggestion, and I am largely concerned with all its various departments." [4] For once the Christian Commission seemed to be forgotten, as people flocked to Chicago in a mood of unbridled enthusiasm. Gate receipts were double the amount expected; presents ranged from "pianos to potatoes, from threshing machines to oats and corn; from deeds of land to gifts of sheep and pigs and chickens, from bulls . . . to buttons, from watches to steam engines." A fever for holding fairs quickly swept the North. By the middle of December, Boston was in the "agony of a Fair." Brooklyn went "crazy," and raised the battle cry, "Let us beat Boston!" A friend of the commission described preparations in Brooklyn:

The churches and Sunday schools are begging for money. The theatres are giving benefits. The nigger minstrels are crowded nightly in the same noble cause. Parlor concerts where a lot of children squeak to the unfortunate audience at fifty cents a piece are the rage. Regiments are giving promenade concerts, and billiard tables and bowling alleys are open to the lame.[5]

Bellows started the drive in New York City to raise funds for the Metropolitan Fair. To help the cause his parishioners gave up the money they had collected to provide All Souls Church with a steeple. Money raising proved nettlesome. The standing committee of the Sanitary Commission objected to raffling. People took sides and rushed into print. Bellows

[3] L. H. Steiner MSS. Isaac Harris to L. H. Steiner, Feb. 11, 1864, Brooklyn, N.Y.
[4] Schuyler-Post MSS. M. A. Livermore to L. L. Schuyler, Sept. 24, 1863, Worcester, Mass.
[5] L. H. Steiner MSS. Isaac Harris to L. H. Steiner, Feb. 11, 1864, Brooklyn, N.Y.

issued "manifestoes" against raffling but not without "great inward suffering." Only when the managers of the fair supported his position did he sense the "moral triumph."

Preparing for the fair brought many vexations. Especially trying was the strife between the two managerial committees. Although the committee of ladies made the plans, the committee of gentlemen advisers tried to override them. The ladies "bubbled and fizzed," and only by calling on the Sanitary standing committee did they succeed in carrying out their wishes. The grand opening of the Metropolitan Fair took place on April 14, 1864, but the gentlemen's committee remained incorrigible. They reserved no place for the ladies' committee, leaving them to buffet the crowd; they failed to escort General John A. Dix, one of the principal speakers, through the crush and up to the platform. Mrs. August Belmont of the ladies' committee nearly wept. George Templeton Strong fumed in his diary. Lloyd Aspinwall and Griswold Gray of the gentlemen's committee were "louts" who had more money than social position, and Richard Grant White, their colleague, was an "invertebrate" and a "poor shoat." But most wealthy New Yorkers lived for the excitement; it was after the fair that they felt a fatigue "beyond expression."

To the commissioners Sanitary fairs were scarcely a blessing. Supplies would abruptly double in quantity, creating new problems in transportation and distribution for Washington and Louisville. Then just as suddenly supplies would fall off; for their collection depended on "quiet, persistent, methodical work," not on these "gigantic spasms" which exhausted the energies of regular contributors. Someone like Louisa Lee Schuyler could create a permanent force from volunteers of the day; but organizers with her abilities were hard to find for the rest of the country. From California, Olmsted warned: ". . . [It will not] be easy to keep the little rills running after the flood has subsided. Yet that is the essential point." [6]

The commissioners did what they could to harness the "momentum" of the fairs. Bellows explained: "As we do not expect to touch the money directly, we are just concluding that the way to utilize these resources, while allowing them the feeling of entire control, is to call on our branches very loudly and definitely for supplies; basing our call on our experiences of last winter and seeking to accumulate in advance such stores as we may and shall require at points as advanced as safety will permit us to use." [7] The Sanitary fairs raised a total of $2,738,868.84. Boston, Brooklyn, New York, and Philadelphia turned over part of their proceeds to the central treasury.

Receipts in 1863 were low. Expenditures came to $64,634.28, when accounts balanced at $41,725.28. Starr King again roused California, which pledged $30,000 a month for the duration of the war. Collection boxes at the San Francisco polls garnered $10,000, while Nevada sent an equal amount. By February 12, 1864, San Francisco paid over $200,000, but drought brought low returns from inland farmers.

On March 4, 1864, Starr King died. This was almost as bad as a battle lost for the commission. King's devotion to the poor and the Union had crowned him with unique prestige, said Olmsted. Even after death his name carried an enchantment, as Californians seemed to see the Sanitary Commission in his lengthened shadow. Dr. Bellows agreed to occupy Starr King's pulpit for six months, and also plant the Sanitary Commission in California. Californians enjoyed more civilization than he had expected. Their moral tone bespoke New England, and San Francisco, the hub of the

[6] Bellows MSS. F. L. Olmsted to H. W. Bellows, March 5, 1864, Bear Valley, Calif.

[7] Box 710, Vol. I, p. 106. H. W. Bellows to J. S. Newberry, Dec. 18, 1863, New York.

Far West, became the radiating point of Sanitary influence.

What made California remarkable was its absence of accumulated capital. The mines paid little. People gave the Sanitary Commission more than they could afford. The generosity of picknickers at Sacramento brought $17,000 in gold. The strength of a merchant's credit showed in the amount of his contribution. Californians did not always give without complaint. Money might grow scarce and patriotism look wan while waiting for victories. Could the North do nothing to help itself? grumbled these Westerners. Why should they carry the heavier burden of the war effort? Country districts were jealous of the city. Raising funds meant a week's furor surrounded by an interval of sleep in San Francisco, where the Sanitary Fund Committee worked hard to get monthly assessments. About five members used to sit down before a reluctant contributor; there they stayed until he paid the amount they demanded.

Their business procedures failed to satisfy Bellows. The committee was not the exclusive agent of collection for the Sanitary Commission; it was not treated as the central agency in affiliation with city and country groups; it kept accounts with negligence. Bellows turned the fund committee into a regular Sanitary branch, and changed it from a city to a state group. A "carefully packed" committee worked with Bellows without asking questions. He planned to put villages and counties under a ten-cent monthly contribution; each town would give according to its population.

The Bellows committee opened up headquarters and hired a resident secretary. They prepared special publications—"a series of short pithy tracts that a man can read in ten minutes at lunch (the great California institution)." The committee chose ten agents to campaign in the forty-four counties. California had given $175,000 to Bellows alone. What would it yield under stricter methods of collection? By May, 1865, aid societies tributary to the Sanitary Commission numbered 286. About 200 sent in a monthly contribution, while some 70 worked with vigor and earnestness, bringing in thousands of dollars.

In Oregon, Bellows played peacemaker between a group of angry citizens and the Sanitary agent, Amory Holbrook, whom Oregonians charged with "drunkenness and political defalcation." These Pharisees, he answered, accused him to excuse themselves for never having given the commission a dime. Holbrook welcomed Bellows to Portland, and placed $2,020 in the visitor's hands. What was a man to do? Dismiss this faithful worker and bearer of gifts, or keep him and anger the community? Bellows sidestepped the issue. He created an Oregon branch, whose members were the leading citizens. The branch reconciled differences and gained a popular following.

Bellows met his gravest threat in the Christian Commission. Starr King's emphasis on "unsectarian Christianity" had alarmed the Evangelical. Their clergy banded together to put down the Sanitary Commission as a "monument and perpetuation of Starr King's influence." Among the "cautious, sly, and wily" was Bishop Willam Kipp; of him it was said that he knew more about every lord in England than about the Lord God. Eventually Bellows and Kipp became friends. "Earnest allies" of the Sanitary Commission were the Catholics, Jews, Baptists, and "unchurched thousands." Christian hatred blazed in September, 1864, but it came to nothing.

In Europe, William * and Charles Bowles * set about organizing Sanitary branches. They met with Richard Hoe, John Bigelow, Edward Brooks, Robert M. Mason, William S. Thompson, G. T. Richards, and Henry Woods on November 30, 1863, in Paris. The chairman they elected was Dr. John McClintock, Methodist minister at the American chapel; they chose William Bowles secretary, a post he held for eleven months. These Americans raised 60,000 francs, and shipped a good grade of brandy for medical purposes. American ministries and consulates came to the commission's aid. By mid-March, 1864, a total of 270,000 francs had been raised in addition to presents for the New York fair. But the majority of countrymen cared little; business and sightseeing claimed their allegiance. Efforts to convert the press to Union views promised little without their strong backing. In marked contrast, the Confederates banded together, freely spending time and money on the French newspapers.

But central headquarters in New York were greatly heartened. From time to time individual Americans in India, China, the Sandwich Islands, and Chili had sent in money. Here was the first instance of their forming a group for Sanitary benefit. The European Branch, said the commissioners, must become a beacon of democracy; for what was the Sanitary Commission but "the people's solicitude for their army, submitting to method and plan and successfully working against all known rules"? The European Branch must give expatriates the chance to prove their patriotism and advance "the cause of free institutions and of humanity."

Europeans themselves were reaching certain conclusions about battlefield relief. In his *Souvenir de Solferino*, Jean Henri Dunant had done much to focus attention on the need for care of the wounded. Ever since antiquity, he maintained, the personnel and material of army medical services had been inadequate for their purposes; in the nineteenth century volunteers to aid the wounded would have to organize and receive the sanction of their governments. In Geneva, Dunant enlisted the support of the Society of Public Utility, which appointed a special committee to study the problem. In February, 1863, this committee—later known as the International Committee of the Red Cross—issued invitations for an October meeting in Geneva. Thirty-six delegates met at the appointed time; eighteen were officially accredited by fourteen European governments, while the others were non-

official. None came from Portugal, Greece, Turkey, and the
Papal States; absent were any representatives from any Asi-
atic, African, or American country.

The proceedings covered four days. The conference recommended that each government authorize the formation
of a sanitary commission and offer it protection; that each
government in time of war grant neutrality to the medical
service and its personnel, and to the inhabitants who cared
for the wounded in their houses; that the universal insignia
and flag of personnel, ambulances, and hospitals in all armies
should be "a white flag or band with a red cross." Since no
government had sponsored the conference, its effectiveness
depended on European governments adopting its recommendations and making them part of international law. The
declaration of neutrality for sanitary or medical personnel
was already in harmony with many European precedents
and in accord with American practice.

The commission received three copies of the conference
report from an English friend. What Bellows read amazed
him. Long ago the leading medical journals of England,
France, and Germany had fully described the commission's
activities; but not a word from Geneva about the American
Civil War and its organized volunteer groups! The United
States had solved problems that the conference called "dark
riddles." History, said Bellows, had never seen so many hospitals and sick and wounded as in America; it had never
known "more systematic and more successful attempts to
alleviate suffering." The suggestion that future conferences
confine their services to Europe drew his scorn. Had the
United States Sanitary Commission known of this gathering,
it would have sent delegates and made the conference
"ashamed" of excluding them. Had the commission been able
to present its documents, they would have modified and
advanced the discussion. America could teach Europe a practical lesson that would "astonish" if it did not "delight" her.

In January, 1864, the European Branch was sending documents to all European governments. France, Holland, and Spain expressed interest; but the European Branch had to overcome a mountain of indifference to things American. Henri Dunant was soon speaking favorably of the Sanitary Commission. He apparently had never intended to exclude the United States; but apparently the unflattering truth said that the United States held no interest to the conference, no matter what the leading journals published. At the end of April, Dunant had received all the Sanitary documents; he spoke English with difficulty but read it with ease; yet he knew as much about the commission as "a native of Van Diemen's Land."

No American doubted Dunant's wish to organize an international sanitary commission. The visitor generally saw Dunant's problem in terms of the American scene, where the newspaper brought the horrors of war into the parlor; the telegraph made battles seem close and immediate; and railroad and steamship rapidly carried relief to the field. Soldiers did not suffer less, but the world no longer seemed indifferent to the fate of the rank and file. European states, however, did little more than express their "grand sympathie" with conference aims. The most interested governments agreed on the insignia and the neutrality of men who wore the insignia; and that the army occupying a given territory should care for all hospitals. But these governments would not allow the camp and hospital inspections of a sanitary commission; their bureaus performed this service.

A European sanitary commission on the American model was not feasible for other reasons. The soldier's life counted for little, although he received better care than those who stayed at home. Poverty kept the people from supporting a commission; supplying daily wants took all their effort. Women were the mainstay of the United States Sanitary Commission, but in Europe women meant little. The generosity of the wealthy could not be relied on; to them a sanitary commission seemed utopian. They gave nothing to Dunant, who by May, had spent 25,000 francs on publications. He had his followers, but they did not work for him. The various governments were almost of one mind about an international sanitary commission. Prussia had a commission that was state directed. Great Britain told Dunant that its own arrangements were sufficient for any emergency and could not be improved on; other countries entertained the same conceit.

At Dunant's suggestion the commission translated some of its documents. French scientists approved them but not without reservations, because Sanitary publications swelled with self-praise. Failing to quote directly from army doctors, the documents repeated well-known authorities; their attitude was fractional, when it should have been catholic.

Success with the English depended on the Americans in England. British aloofness would yield, if Americans were generous. In the interests of the Sanitary Commission, Frederick Milne Edge * wrote a tribute to Florence Nightingale, who had other matters than the American organization to think about. A few elderly Englishmen spoke in public for freedom and the Union, but the old were generally cold, lazy, and without courage. Charles Bowles set out to form an English Branch and raise a benefit fund. Manchester and Liverpool needed little prompting to take up the Sanitary cause. In London a few Americans had already formed a committee to aid the Metropolitan Fair. Their gift of 1,000 tons of coal of best quality arrived with freightage and insurance paid by London and Paris, and was sold to New York gas companies.

A new association in Great Britain would have to seem a spontaneous expression. Charles Francis Adams, the American minister, gave Bowles's plan his blessing but refused any part in it. The English were suspicious. If they thought that

Adams had promoted the scheme, they would very likely brand it as Washington inspired and not give a cent. So in February, 1864, William M. Evarts launched the English Branch; Cyrus W. Field, R. W. Weston, and James Mc-Henry added their influences. The election of Joshua Bates as president, C. M. Lamson, vice-president, and E. C. Fisher, secretary, gave the branch an air of influence. Fisher became secretary through Bowles's connivance. Bates of Baring Brothers was a sick man, but he accepted the honor. This was perhaps unfortunate, because the branch needed aggressive leadership. Yet Bowles and friends of the commission could point to quick results, for by April 1 they had raised £2,000 by subscription.

The branch pleased Adams but not other Americans. They seemed to fear the bully, English conservatism, whose hauteur, coldness, and indifference they aped, peering at the future "through the obscuring thickness of a cotton bale" set in "iron-clad spectacles." To the Bowles brothers came rumors that American bankers thought the Union doomed and told the British government as much; their words professed love of country, while their deeds fed on business with secession. Wealthy Americans had helped launch the branch to keep up appearances of loyalty. Only Adams' intervention had kept them from breaking it up, until they organized a new committee where theirs was the dominant voice. Jealousy of the Paris Branch and hatred of Charles Bowles allegedly consumed them. Their committee accomplished little. Fisher resigned, but New York headquarters hired him as its London agent.

- 3 -

In April, 1863, an order from the War Department seriously curtailed the commission's privileges to transport stores. Bellows raged. The secretary, he said, must undo this mischief; otherwise the president of the Sanitary Commission would resign and openly wage war on the secretary. Bellows discussed the matter with his old college friend William Whiting, solicitor of the War Department, who brought the issue before Stanton. The secretary had neither intended to attack the commission nor had he foreseen that his order would do any injury; but he refused to revoke the order. Detestable commission! He would do nothing to advance its cause. According to Strong, the following conversation took place between Stanton and Whiting, one which set the mark of "caitiff" and "scoundrel" on the secretary:

"But why, Mr. Stanton, when . . . [the Sanitary Commission] is notoriously doing so much good service, and when the Medical Department and the whole army confide in it and depend on it as you and I know they do?"

"Well," said the Secretary, "the fact is the Commission wanted Hammond to be Surgeon-General and I did not. I did my best with the President and with the Military Committee of the Senate, but the Commission beat me and got Hammond appointed. I'm not used to being beaten, and don't like it, and therefore am hostile to the Commission." [8]

The secretary of war sneered at the Medical Bureau, calling it a branch of the commission. The surgeon general objected. He wrote Bellows: ". . . you and the Commission have done less to influence me (except by your example) than any other set of men in the country." But had he had "ten millions more of money," he would have spent it on the sick and wounded. "Where would I have been but for the voluntary contributions of the people?" he asked. [9]

Early in 1863, Hammond asked three times for permission to leave Washington. Twice Stanton denied permission; he ignored the third request. The surgeon general sent Dr.

[8] G. T. Strong, *op. cit.*, p. 314.
[9] Box 640. W. A. Hammond to H. W. Bellows, Aug. 9, 1863, Washington, D.C. Olmsted MSS. W. A. Hammond to F. L. Olmsted, March 18, 1863, Washington, D.C.

Wood to St. Louis, but felt that Wood's sins of omission would be laid at his own door. Western surgeons seemed unreasonable, said Hammond. They were demanding, but they cared nothing about keeping him waiting for reports. Had he not answered letters from medical directors and purveyors within forty-eight hours? None could say that he had not dispatched liberal quantities of stores and approved plans for hospitals with the least delay. In January, 1863, Hammond sent more than two hundred doctors west, where he set up a special medical board. Western medical debts could not always be paid promptly, because Stanton had cut off funds voted by Congress for the Medical Bureau. Hammond apparently paid for much from his own pocket. He lacked power to force purveyors to purchase and distribute supplies. Whenever possible Hanmmond hunted out bad practice, but buying at inflated prices and from men set on cheating the government was unavoidable. Many difficulties resulted from enforced reliance on the quartermaster corps.

In May, 1863, the surgeon general upset one of the medical shibboleths of his day. Inspecting Grant's army before Vicksburg, Medical Inspector Vollum had reported the prevalence of mercurial salivation from overdoses of tartar emetic and especially calomel. This meant that quantities of saliva flowed from the patient's mouth, generally resulting in loss of teeth and mercurial gangrene. Rather than restrict its use, Hammond thought it safer to strike calomel from the supply table. In Boston, Dr. Oliver Wendell Holmes hailed his decision as of immense benefit to the medical profession; but average surgeons who believed in strong doses disobeyed the order and turned against the surgeon general. Other forces also worked to undo the surgeon general. Old-guard surgeons were clamoring for his head. The Evangelical element called him the appointee of Unitarians, Catholics, and "infidels," and urged his removal. Certain state relief agencies hostile to the Sanitary Commission wanted him out of the way.

Eager to attack the administration, Peace Democrats would possibly have liked to castigate Hammond's record. Perhaps Dr. Agnew had a measure of success in restraining the editor of the *World*. His note of June 29, 1863 to Manton Marble read:

Do let us have a talk over matters before you rush into type on the Surgeon General. Can you meet me at 6 o'clock this afternoon at Delmonico's for a quiet chop? [10]

In July, 1863, the secretary appointed a committee to investigate the bureau. This was a declaration of war, said Hammond. Committeemen were A. H. Reeder of Pennsylvania, Thomas Hood, and Major George O. Barstow of Boston. Hood was a "vulgar ignoramus," said the surgeon general. Reeder and Hammond had hated each other ever since the civil war in Kansas. Reeder, it was said, set out on his errand of revenge with eagerness. "Extra official and ex parte," the committee had but one object in view—to search out extravagance and negligence without hearing Hammond's story. It would try to prove official ignorance of business procedure, neglect of the West, and Hammond's responsibility for the suffering at Gettysburg. The Medical Bureau was no further behind than any other division, said the surgeon general. As stated above, Stanton had denied him the money to pay off Western debts. Direct testimony could disprove the charge of failure to provide for the Gettysburg wounded; but this evidence would never be heard, Hammond feared. The committeemen worked like the weavers of the emperor's new clothes, sewing together charges without substance and patching with the tales of malcontents; to piece out with certain information they reportedly offered to bribe a clerk. Their findings stood naked of qualifications; they failed to point out that certain articles could be purchased only in

[10] Marble Collection, Vol. 4, No. 841, Library of Congress. C. R. Agnew to M. Marble, June 29, 1863, New York.

specified plans, and that great battles demanded huge expenditures. Writing to the president, Bellows protested any move to unseat the surgeon general, but his letter was not sent. His colleagues feared it might be referred to Stanton, who would take action against the commission.

According to the Sanitary Commission, the secretary of war saw to it that nothing should embarrass his investigators. On August 28, 1863, he relieved the surgeon general of office with a cordial handshake. Hammond prepared to visit Hilton Head, New Orleans, and the West. The secretary also "banished" Surgeon Joseph R. Smith, Hammond's principal aide, to keep the accused from getting favorable testimony. As he ordered work stopped on the army medical museum, the president was heard to say that "he didn't know it was anything but a monument to General Hammond." Mrs. Hammond went to Stanton and asked whether he really intended to depose her husband. The secretary replied with astonishment; he had no intention of setting anyone in Hammond's place. To remove the surgeon general would have called for summary procedure. Stanton gave her permission to quote him to this effect. Colonel Joseph K. Barnes,* inspector general, became acting surgeon general. Dr. Steiner remembered that this "high-toned gentleman" used to be friendly with the Sanitary Commission; but others were sure of his "faithlessness."

Until early December, 1863, the surgeon general seemed to hang in mid-air. At Nashville he apparently performed the duties of inspector general. Were he to ask Stanton why he was not assigned to duty in Washington, Hammond might play into the hands of his foe, who would doubtless order him to resign. The surgeon general thought he would have to be in Washington when Congress met in January, 1864, to clear his name of any charges. He must also be present to block any of Stanton's tricks; for, according to report, the secretary was planning to increase the rank of surgeon gen-

eral to major general, but nominate someone other than
Hammond. This would leave Hammond a brigadier "with a
species of roving commission." Perhaps Stanton would dis-
miss him on the finding of the Reeder Committee before
Congress convened. A few friends came to Hammond's aid.
It was all very well to remove the surgeon general, said Senator Foster of Connecticut, but let him know the charges.
"There are many village doctors," he reminded President
Lincoln, "whose knowledge of medicine comprehends the
important facts that ipecac will puke and calomel will purge,
who feel themselves fully competent to perform the duties
of this office without ever making a mistake or neglecting a
call." [11]

December, 1863, began with Stanton's sending Hammond
a reprimand. Back in September the surgeon general had
made certain purchases from Philadelphia. Stanton himself
approved the measure, and now the surgeon general reminded him of this. Did relief from active duty mean that
the president and the Senate had stripped him of his powers?
asked Hammond. Who had placed him under arrest or deprived him of his commission? In what instance had he violated his duty? Stanton's original order assigned him inspection duties, commanding him to stay at Nashville until further
orders; but the secretary had never directed the surgeon
general "to abstain from advising or making purchases or
contracts on behalf of the Medical Bureau or anything else."
These unusual restrictions of a bureau head implied charges
of either wrongdoing or ineptitude. Hammond had suffered
slander, exile, and deprivation of rightful authority and
power; he called for a board of inquiry or a court-martial.

This stroke of imprudence, wrote a friend, would force a
crisis. Hammond had other friends in both houses of Con-

[11] National Archives, War Records, Record Group 107, Secretary of War.
Letters rec., p. 222, L. F. S. Foster to A. Lincoln, Nov. 26, 1863, Norwich,
Conn.

gress, but could he count on them? The Union League Club circulated a petition in his behalf. No member wanted to oppose the administration, so the petition received too few signatures. The Sanitary Commission had waited too long to strike; if Stanton was bent on crushing Hammond, the commissioners could hardly stop him. On December 23, John A. Bingham, the judge advocate general, submitted the Reeder Committee report to President Lincoln. Here was testimony sufficient to warrant Hammond's summary dismissal, said Bingham, but he recommended a trial. On December 26 the president wrote: "Let the Surgeon General be put upon trial by a court, as suggested by the Judge Advocate General." [12]

Letters to Lincoln met delay. Mr. Nicolay, his secretary, doubted the wisdom of Sanitary rebuke because of its threatening tone. Commissioners seemed ready to move against the administration, if the president refused their request. They ought to appear as private citizens to plead Hammond's cause. Nicolay was too cautious for the commissioners. Bellows ordered Knapp to present and read the letter to the president. Lincoln listened without comment. What word would Knapp have to tell the commissioners? The president spoke with sternness and "apparent study of phrase"; there would be a trial—at least that was his impression.

The standing committee sent a circular to each member of Congress. Stanton's was the unuttered name behind the rehearsal of Hammond's woes and the perfidy of the Reeder Committee. Let the surgeon general's honesty be questioned, read the circular; but let it be done openly by formal procedure and not in Venetian secrecy by an "anonymous commission." Wolcott Gibbs secured the signatures of the outstanding men in science, education, and medicine in Massachusetts. George Bancroft refused to sign, and so saved

[12] National Archives, War Records, Record Group 153, Judge Advocate General, MM 1430, Medical Department Report.

himself chagrin; for the appearance of the circular caused
consternation among the signers. Through Representative
Samuel Hooper they made their recantations to Stanton. Benjamin Pierce and Louis Agassiz could hardly deny their signatures; but these, they said, had been obtained by "misrepresentations" and by the addition of letters they never used.
President Thomas Hill of Harvard owned his name led all
the rest; but since the circular was not the paper he signed,
Hill pronounced his signature a forgery. Dr. T. S. Bell of
Louisville admitted signing that Hammond might have a fair
hearing. Only Dr. J. Mason Warren of Boston stood by the
surgeon general. Dr. Van Buren, "an unexceptionable authority," had given him the facts. Hammond's success had won
the admiration of the medical profession; he deserved a fair
hearing.

According to George Strong, the Sanitary stand made the
secretary hesitate. Indirectly he told Hammond that he was
ready to call quits, if the surgeon general was willing to let
bygones be bygones. Hammond would be glad to do so, but
Stanton must first apologize; if the secretary refused, the surgeon general must vindicate his honor by court-martial.
Placed under arrest on January 17, the surgeon general's trial
began on January 19. Bellows helped him secure legal services of Joseph H. Bradley and J. Morrison Harris. Hammond
spoke to old friends of leaving the army, whatever the outcome of the trial. At Nashville he had fallen and injured his
spine, temporarily paralyzing his legs below the knees. The
army, thought the commissioners, might use his physical
disability as a reason for retiring him.

According to the charges, Hammond was guilty of "disorders and neglects to the prejudice of order and discipline,"
"conduct unbecoming an officer and a gentleman," and "conduct to the prejudice of good order and discipline." It mattered little what he had bought under the first and third
charges; blankets, medicines, and beef extracts, all had been

purchased with intent to defraud the government. Hammond had removed George Cooper, the medical purveyor of Philadelphia, in a manner "unbecoming an officer and a gentleman," read the specifications; and Hammond had falsely said that General Halleck had asked for Dr. Robert Murray's appointment as a particular favor.

Hammond hailed the news of his trial with joy. No unprejudiced court could convict him of wrongdoing, he believed. He was given two days to prepare against an indictment that had been six months in the making. Stanton sat astride fortune's wheel. Although absent from the trial, he was master of the court. Judge Advocate Bingham set out to get a conviction, bitterly abusing the defendant in the four months of trial. Hammond's accusers treated language like Humpty-Dumpty. They read the law of April, 1862, to take from him the right to make purchases. Surgeon generals before and after Hammond never accepted this interpretation. He bought in excessive amounts, charged adversaries, who overlooked the emergencies of 1862 and 1863 which caught surgeons empty-handed. Did Halleck want Cooper's post for Murray? Halleck denied that he explicitly stated Philadelphia, but asked for an opening in the East. Murray had no doubt that Halleck wanted him in Philadelphia long before the general made this request.

Dr. Cooper, the chief witness, had long sought opportunity to betray the surgeon general. Hammond once wrote him a personal letter explaining Halleck's wish. Cooper, a petty Iago, sent Hammond's letter to the secretary of war; he began to collect records of seemingly suspicious purchases from as far back as May, 1862. Certain letters disappeared from the surgeon general's files during his exile at Nashville, so Cooper could deny receiving certain orders. In March, 1864, noted George Strong, an unknown person gave Hammond most of the correspondence for $1,500. The sessions grew stormy, when the defense showed up Cooper's repeated contradictions. Outside the court Cooper spoke to Hammond with "the utmost contrition." His testimony, he owned, was the product of cajoling, goading, and threats.

To see the surgeon general given "such a blanket tossing" gave Dr. T. S. Bell much pleasure. Bradley and Harris doubted whether their client could pay costs. Hammond's annual wage of $3,500 scarcely covered expenses. He had to borrow $6,000 from friends. By March 30 the trial record filled about ten reams of paper, foolscap size; the defense took up about a hundred pages, while the prosecution elaborated its charges far beyond specifications.

The Sanitary Commission enjoyed the respect of official Washington, but Judge Advocate Bingham accused it of furnishing supplies to district hospitals at great expense. By an agreement of spring, 1863, the commission spent close to $1,000 a month. Their system had saved these hospital funds at least 25 per cent on the cost of extra supplies; but the agreement had snared the commission in money transactions. Medical Director Abbot gave testimony that weakened Bingham's charges, while Knapp's evidence seemed to complete their overthrow.

Relations between the commission and the government appeared as good in a state of latent enemity as in avowed friendship, thought the commissioners. Hammond had done nothing for them in particular; and they needed nothing from Washington that they could not get themselves. Bache alone feared the secretary of war would strike the commission a mortal blow. Senator E. D. Morgan of New York happened to speak with Stanton, who wanted it understood that he ran his department. The Medical Bureau had been too long in the Sanitary interest, said the secretary, and the commission had "in a great degree control'd" the bureau.[13]

On May 6, 1864, Strong and Agnew set out with Morgan

[13] E. D. Morgan MSS., Letter Book, 1864, pp. 179–80. E. D. Morgan to C. R. Agnew, April 1, 1864, Washington, D.C.

in an effort to heal the breach with Stanton. The secretary received them with obvious distaste. Agnew read from a prepared memorandum, outlining the Sanitary work and expenses. The secretary interrupted. Where were the payments to the press for scurrilous attack, on him and the administration? He was referring to an anonymous letter written by Strong for the Sanitary *Bulletin*, proposing that the surgeon general not be set aside without a court-martial. The question, countered Strong and Agnew, bore on the bureau's efficiency; the secretary himself had taken the proposed action, they reminded him. But the commission had placed a copy of the January circular on the desk of each congressman, said Stanton. By fraud it secured signatures from eminent scientists. According to Strong, the visitors did not think it fitting to tell the secretary of the affidavits in New York; these told how the scientists had read the paper with deliberation, and how they carefully thought of its import before signing their names.

The commission, charged Stanton, had made itself a trade organization by its hospital supply system; Hammond had violated the law by ordering surgeons to buy extra supplies. The secretary apparently knew nothing about the hospital funds and the regulations that applied to its disbursement. The commission, he insinuated, had gone out to make money. But, answered Strong and Agnew, their books and vouchers showed an adverse balance from $5,000 to $10,000. Then the commission had wasted all that money, pursued Stanton. The balance, they answered, stood for the amount given to the hospitals. The commission turned over the stores it bought; it charged the hospital fund their cost price, and so cut out the middleman's profits and costs of transportation. Stanton changed the subject . The Sanitary Commission must carry out the "great trust" in its own way; the responsibility must rest upon its shoulders.

What the secretary knew of Sanitary affairs was phenomenal. Only the support it received from public curbed his destructive hatred, thought Strong. At the end of the interview the bully had turned spaniel. The commission, said Stanton, had won his "admiration" and "affection"; but he found fault with certain of its members. The secretary had done—and would always do—all that he could for the Sanitary Commission. The only interruption came from Abraham Lincoln. He said nothing but drew Stanton into a side room. Perhaps the interview blew the commission a little good. On August 6, Strong wrote Bellows: "We certainly stand well with the people—and the Secretary of War spoke well of us lately! We must remember to have a Feast of the Conversion of St. Stanton in the Sanitary Calendar." [14]

The trial ended on the day that Stanton received his two callers. Final decision rested with him; Lincoln seemed to have given the secretary a free hand. Hammond thought he had won an acquittal. Court documents had been suppressed, said one of his friends, for they might have injured the president's hopes of re-election. Lincoln turned a deaf ear to the appeals of Bradley and Harris; he refused to review the final argument of Judge Bingham; he would not see Mrs. Hammond, who went to the White House to plead for her husband; he ignored Hammond's appeal for an interview. The court pronounced Hammond guilty of all charges, though not on all specifications. Only in the Cooper-Murray incident was Hammond judged guilty without qualification. His conviction, thought Strong, was "little more than the technical sin of purchasing supplies too freely, and not in the way technically sanctioned by some Act of Congress half a century ago." The government dismissed Hammond; it barred him from ever again holding a position in its service.

Republican newspapers bellowed at the mildness of the sentence. Could there have been a fairer trial? asked Dr. Bell of Louisville. Hammond got what he deserved for hav-

[14] Box 642. G. T. Strong to H. W. Bellows, Aug. 6, 1864, New York.

ing joined "the McClellan-Buell gangs." In the West, Bellows heard Hammond set down as a "wire puller" in other men's speculations; critics said his questionable conduct on the frontier had come to its logical conclusion in disgrace. Sanitary inspectors thought differently. Hammond would stay damned until people wanted to learn the truth of his cause. The trial caused British doctors to speak with feeling, for Hammond was a favorite among them.

To the leading commissioners the court-martial was "as vindictive in its origin and as inconsequent in its action as any the world ever saw." Judge Bingham exercised the power of a lie, they thought, when he impugned their motives. After the trial he charged that the commission had acted in complicity with Hammond; that hospital supplies bought in Philadelphia were short in measure and bad in quality. The proofs of Knapp and Dr. Abbott counted little to this judge, whose court had found Hammond guilty of the specification. Bingham used derogatory language in a pamphlet which met with Lincoln's approval. The commission apparently took a public stand after the election; but in vain, on February 1, 1865, it begged the Senate to heed Hammond's plea of restitution and reverse the sentence of court-martial.

The Sanitary Commission had reason to take pride in Hammond's achievements. He had improved the care of the sick; the mortality rate had sunk "lower than had been observed in the experience of any army since the world began." His pavilion hospital was of immediate practical benefit; it saw widespread use in the East, but in the West suitable buildings were generally lacking. Surgeons met emergencies more easily by sending requests to military bases rather than distant centers. Government laboratories in New York and Philadelphia prepared the principal medicines and freed the Medical Bureau from dependence on commercial houses. By this innovation Hammond cut down on expenses, and produced better medications than outside firms. The bureau leaned less heavily on the Sanitary Commission, for he distributed clothing to patients, enlarged the supply table, and secured better qualified surgeons. He changed formalized reports to cover a comprehensive range of subjects; these provided the basis for a medical and surgical history of the war. He directed subordinates to collect and forward specimens for a projected army museum. The law set the number of inspectors at eight, but Hammond found competent civilians willing to make supplementary inspections. When his superiors refused him an enlisted hospital corps, he organized civilian nurses and cooks on a military basis. Dr. Hammond recommended the creation of an army medical school in 1862. Here medical cadets would receive proper training for their commissions. He proposed setting up a permanent general hospital in the District of Columbia. Throughout his time in office he maintained that hospital construction and control of medical transportation were functions of the Medical Bureau, not the quartermaster corps. His achievements won the bureau an international reputation.

The Sanitary Commission never wavered in its belief in Hammond. To his office he brought "vigor, courage, and humanity"; he left it with a clear conscience. Praise of Hammond has not withered with time. According to one historian, the surgeon general built the machine and set it going "in fifteen crowded months"; he made or asked for "every improvement carried out during the war, or for thirty years after the war."

Congress ultimately restored his rank, provided he yield all claims to pay. Congressmen had gained a better perspective on the Civil War thirteen years after 1865. The surgeon general, they agreed, might well have exceeded his lawful authority following the titanic battles; he could have been "technically guilty of 'disorders' to the prejudice of military authority." But the basis of all the charges was disproved by the defense, or given up by the prosecution, or ruled out by the court. There was one exception, but this charge was "in itself trifling, if not frivolous." The sentence of perpetual banishment was needlessly unjust and severe. On March 18, 1878, President Hayes signed a bill "for the relief of William A. Hammond, late Surgeon General of the Army."

CHAPTER XII

The Nettles of War

- 1 -

ON February 20, 1864, the Union forces suffered defeat
at Olustee, Florida. The Sanitary Commission furnished
all supplies, because the medical director had made no provision against attack. Agents met and cared for the first
wounded and carried the last from the field. Soldiers of the
54th Massachusetts tied ropes to the broken-down train
bearing the wounded and dragged it twenty-three miles to
Jacksonville. In April, 1864, General Banks came to grief at
Red River. New Orleans alone raised $2,000 to support the
Sanitary relief program.

Lieutenant General U. S. Grant took command of the armies
of the United States before the spring campaign. His freedom
from envy and vanity captured the popular imagination, his
wisdom growing from singleness of purpose. To Strong, the
general behaved like "an earnest business man—prompt,
clearheaded, and decisive"—who held out every encouragement to the Sanitary Commission. General Grant suggested
a New England farmer, said Bellows. His manners were
"plain"; his speech was slow and stumbling; his face expressed stolidity. Grant clearly felt like saying anything he
wanted, but he was neither "addicted to expression" nor did
he find it easy. His force lay in his judgment of men, thought
Bellows. The general surrounded himself with able minds
and willingly took their advice. Bellows concluded:

Some men are great from the absence of weaknesses, vanities and
self-conceit; from their freedom from cant, pretension and self-

seeking. I think Grant is like an apple stuck with cloves—that is, he draws the spicy folks about him, and forms an innocent, pure and simple center for such a concentration of ability.[1]

The commission's most important innovation was its Auxiliary Relief Corps, organized by Frank B. Fay of Chelsea, Massachusetts. From the original fifty these "educated, refined, whole-souled men" numbered almost two hundred by July 14. In squads of six they set out prepared to give the wounded first aid on the battlefield, to act as nurses in hospitals, and to set up temporary hospitals. Owing to its size and adaptability, the corps answered an immediate, practical problem. The commission had heretofore dealt with men in masses, with general conditions in moving armies; now through auxiliary relief it was reaching the individual soldiers.

Grant launched his campaign at a time when American doctors were discussing the recommendations of the Geneva Conference of 1863. In vain Elisha Harris hoped that the contending armies would adopt the usages of neutrality. Colonel John M. Cuyler,* acting inspector general of the Medical Bureau, became the advocate of "a limited, rational, and practicable neutrality." He would have a neutral ground near every line of battle, where the surgeon could attend the wounded and decide where to remove the patient at his own discretion. As it was, men with compound fractures died "almost inevitably because of transportation."

- 2 -

According to Dr. McParlin, medical director of the Army of the Potomac, medical arrangements were more complete that spring than at any previous period of the war. The Act of March 11, 1864, gave protection to the medical organiza-

[1] Bellows MSS. H. W. Bellows to Joe and Eliza Dorr, Dec. 26, 1864, New York.

tion and set it on a firm basis. The quartermaster corps still controlled the ambulances and horses, but the law forbade using them for any purpose other than to carry the sick or, in case of emergency, medical supplies. The distribution of ambulances depended on regimental size, not on the number of regiments; so the ambulances available for the whole army was lower than before. Since the number of men in a regiment varied continually, the medical director could not know what transportation he had for the wounded. The army at Gettysburg used 1,000 ambulances, but at the Wilderness it had only 600.

On May 4 the army left Brandy Station in clear and pleasant weather. The men enjoyed good spirits, but this interlude ended with the battle of the Wilderness (May 5–7). Grant was heard to say: "Well, if this is to be a Kilkenny cat fight, we have the longest tails." [2] Opposing sides crawled toward each through the dense underbrush and evergreen. Unable to see their targets, they fired blindly. Here and there the woods caught fire. Trapped, many soldiers suffocated or burned. The slightest noise or sign of motion caused the enemy to shoot. Stretcher-bearers could hardly find the wounded. As a rule, casualties received first aid a few hundred feet behind the lines, where Dr. Elisha Harris praised the improvement in the primary dressing of wounds. Ambulances usually gathered in one park, while at the advance stations surgeons generally held two or three ready to carry the injured to the rear. Drivers took byways, leaving the main-traveled roads to ammunition and troop wagons.

The Medical Bureau made preparations to receive the wounded at Rappahannock Station. When Grant made Fredericksburg his base, the bureau also redirected its stores and surgeons; but they arrived late at Fredericksburg, on May 10. The weakness of medical arrangements showed in the failure to provide for systematic removal from field hospital to the

[2] L. H. Steiner, *Diary* (MSS.), May 9, 1864.

base. Wagons and ambulances came to 813, an inadequate number to care for 7,000 maimed. This procession set out on May 7; the injured fell into the following classes: those able to walk, those able to ride in wagons, and the severely wounded carried in ambulances. On May 9 they arrived in Fredericksburg, where nothing was in readiness. The battle of Spotsylvania had started on May 8, but the vehicles were late in getting back to the army; they arrived on May 10 stripped of medical stores, the toil of seven days and nights having exhausted men and horses. Not all Wilderness casualties had arrived in Fredericksburg when casualties from Spotsylvania began to pour in.

Fredericksburg looked deserted. Shot and shell in 1862 and 1863 had made a shambles of eighteenth-century mansions; but anything with a roof now became a hospital. The wounded suffered as much as at Gettysburg, except that they were not left lying on the ground. Because of the shortage of food, nurses had to feed soldiers hardtack and coffee. From Washington came two medical supply steamers on May 10—the first boats of any kind to reach the new base. Surgeons sent away the most serious cases and set up some five hundred hospital tents outside the town. Some 26,000 wounded passed through Fredericksburg; by May 27 all had been shipped northward. The army used no evacuation hospitals, as at Antietam and Gettysburg, because battlefields were far away from railroads and guerrillas infested the land.

Commissioner Harris found much in Fredericksburg to criticize. Hospitals had been short of food and equipment, he said, because the medical purveyor and director had failed to keep Washington adequately informed. Wagons carrying the wounded had been thickly bedded down with evergreen boughs, while shelter tents and blankets gave some protection and comfort; but these precautions were not enough. Medical officers failed to issue instructions on the proper care of fracture cases during transportation. Patients often stayed twenty-four to forty-eight hours in wagons ill suited for ambulance service. Jolting rides frequently proved fatal. The long journey lowered vitality, leaving many men too weak to fight the effects of overcrowding and bad nursing. Harris criticized the Medical Bureau for making no special studies.

Dr. J. H. Douglas directed the commission's work at Fredericksburg. From a storehouse on Commercial Street it issued 200 tons of stores to hospitals. Divided into squads, 225 auxiliary relief agents were assigned to various division hospitals. Subject to the direction of surgeons, they helped care for patients and reported the wants of hospitals to Sanitary headquarters. Nurses like Miss Helen Gilson, Mrs. Arabella Barlow, and Mrs. Husbands ran special diet kitchens, serving soup, coffee, stimulants, soft bread, and other food for the thousands of passing wounded. Dr. L. H. Steiner, chief inspector, directed seven four-horse wagons transporting food, stimulants, bandages, and underclothing. Over forty four-horse wagons carried stores from Belle Plain to Fredericksburg, besides two steamboats and two barges. By May 24 the commission had spent over $100,000; it performed all these services in addition to doing for Sherman, the troops before Charleston, at New Orleans, and on the Red River. From May to June the commission spent $515,000 in Virginia alone.

At Belle Plain the army and the commission used one wharf. Many pressures attending loading and unloading created confusion. The Medical Bureau ran its stores ashore on a lighter, while gangs of Negroes placed them in a hospital tent or loaded them on wagons. Slowly down the right-hand side of the dock moved a single file of wagons filled with wounded. Standing by the gangway of a barge, Dr. Cuyler superintended their removal to the deck before transferring the barges to the left, where they took on ammunition and rations. Strings of men bearing litters crowded along a narrow margin to the gangway. This spectacle continued hour after hour, until it seemed as though the Army of the Potomac was leaving Belle Plain to overflow into Northern hospitals. Barges of horses landed beside the transports, and horses crossed the deck where helpless men lay. An observer wrote: "Mules, stretchers, army wagons, prisoners, dead men, and officials as good as dead are tumbled and jumbled on the wretched dock which falls in every little while and keeps the trains waiting for hours."[3] According to Dr. Agnew, Dr. Cuyler brought order out of chaos; at all times and in all kinds of weather he directed the rapid sheltering of the wounded. The quartermaster seemed to toil with almost superhuman effort.

All officers apparently took pleasure in aiding the commission. Under F. N. Knapp's direction the commission ran feeding stations at Fredericksburg, White Oak Church, and Belle Plain. Knapp wrote: "Not only did we feed these men as they . . . filed past our relief station at the base, or . . . waited on the shore until stretchers could be sent for them, or as placed in boats side by side—not only did we feed them thus, but bearing ample supplies we pursued our way from ambulance to wagon and wagon to ambulance out for . . . two or three miles, until we heard no groans beyond . . ."[4] Vehicles frequently plunged into quagmires, jostling their human cargoes. There was no pity in the clouds for the racked and screaming; thrown from side to side, they held to "extemporized straps suspended from the framework of wagons . . . sometimes dying in agony . . ." An average of six corpses to the mile lay beside the road, where drivers removed them—unknown soldiers with no marks of identification on the plain blue blouse. Fainting and starving, hobbling men dotted the way, acting like "ravenous wolves" to

[3] Quoted in J. S. Wolsey, *Hospital Days* (1868), p. 151.
[4] F. N. Knapp, History of the *Special Relief Service of the United States Sanitary Commission.* (MSS.)

get a little food. Many of these were stragglers and malingerers, complained Dr. McParlin. They took advantage of the Sanitary Commission for food and keeping, and then crept back home to show their scars and spread false rumors of suffering and destitution.

In Washington hospitals Walt Whitman caught the quality of individual suffering. Death lost its terrors for Whitman, but he had no armor against the exhaustion, sickness, and pain of others. Before Grant started his offensive, the hospitals seemed to be getting the "dregs" of hardship; now, with the fighting, human wretchedness moved from worse to worse. Whitman called the nursing poor and the attendants "unfeeling," fearful of touching the patients, and "cold and ceremonious." The misery of time faced the young man wasting away to a skeleton; far from his home he would probably die unknown and unwept.

Not only was the commission late in coming on the scene, but it also failed to organize effectively. Ten days passed before it seemed capable of meeting difficulties. This was Dr. Steiner's fault, said Dr. Agnew; he worked hard enough but without plan, ingenuity, or energy. Agnew himself had to unload supplies and send them ashore. But to blame Steiner exclusively would be grossly unfair. The commission was working against official hostility. When the campaign started, Sanitary stores stayed far in the rear, because the War Department refused to issue passes, and agents had to work without necessary privileges.

Many surgeons regarded the commission as Betsy Trotwood viewed donkeys: they would limit it to following the army and pressing forward its supplies after great battles. Medical Director McParlin made clear his friendship, but forebore to force Sanitary supplies on any corps that wanted to act independently. The commission met opposition at Bermuda Hundred, even though surgeons needed its stores. The Medical Bureau had abundant supplies, but because of transportation shortages surgeons could not always reach them. Transports at the base of operations often were without beds, basins, dippers, cooking utensils, food, clothing, and medicines. Yet the commission found supporters among the doctors. A member of the X Army Corps protested against excluding a group so incalculably useful; for want of it he and his colleagues must often send away the wounded "with torn and bloody garments on and sometimes half naked." Most surgeons kept the door open to Sanitary chloroform, morphine, stimulants, dressings, and sponges for the operating table, and food and clothing for field hospitals.

Sanitary workers were very much part of the campaign. They dodged bullets, but as civilians they could not fire back. They saw the ruin and desolation of Virginia, and shared the hardships of camp life without a murmur. Sometimes they slept in furrows or wherever else they might lie down. Perhaps the season had its compensations. The air was redolent in gardens lavish with roses, honeysuckle, columbine, and stars of Bethlehem. Vines clambered over verandas. Mockingbirds sang in magnificent shade trees. The long twilights were often calm and still.

The scene was a familiar one, when Grant made White House his base on May 28. The injured from North Anna River engagement came here. Either they stayed in ambulances or were placed in open fields; there they lay in the hot sunlight without surgical attention. Cornelia Hancock, a Quaker nurse, could not remember dressing so many wounds as at White House. The surgeons had no sooner cared for one group than another arrived; but, due to good organization, they set the wounded on transports and shipped them north. Grant lost some 7,000 at the battle of Cold Harbor on June 3. To find enough dry land for setting up a hospital was a major task for the Auxiliary Relief Corps there in the swamps of the Pamunkey. They sank wells, set up stoves and kitchens, landing tents, and supplies before ambulances brought in the wounded. Many surgeons at the front worked without anesthetics, until the commission's relief train arrived with chloroform. On June 15, Grant left White House for City Point, at the junction of the James and Appomattox rivers. Because General "Baldy" Smith failed to capture Petersburg, the Union Army settled down to a long siege. Exhaustion was lowering morale. Reinforcements scraped from the bottom of the barrel needed months of drill and discipline to make good soldiers. The period from summer, 1864, to spring, 1865, was relatively inactive.

- 3 -

The setting at City Point suggested the Bay of Naples, said one Sanitary worker. Smooth waters returned the image of the purple haze. Then calmness yielded to motion. Boats soon swarmed in the river, while troops kicked up clouds of dust. Wagon trains driven by Negroes rolled in all directions; everywhere officers on horseback, stragglers, camp followers, and disabled men moved in unison or against each other, weaving together and threading in and out. Barges lined the shore six deep. About a mile and a half away above the treetops rose the spires of Petersburg. Here and there in the distance little puffs of smoke broke out, followed by the rattle of musketry and the boom of cannon.

On the morning of June 18 the Sanitary Commission reached City Point. Workers spent the day setting up a feeding station, getting three large barges in position, and building a firm gangway. Moored permanently side by side, the barges were full of good things, said visitors. A pile of two or three hundred pairs of crutches decorated the upper deck. "Our boats at City Point are the state of endless activity," wrote Bellows, "every night brings from fifty to a hundred soldiers, refugees, officers, etc., going to or from camp without resources for food and shelter but such as we

afford them. We keep open table and ready lodgings for
soldiers white and black, officers and privates, provided
always they have no where else to go." [5] To Dr. Agnew and
G. T. Strong the commission's headquarters, anchored on "a
festering expanse of filthiness," made a horrid violation of
sanitary writ. They fastened on this disgrace as the reason
for the loss of twenty workers, forgetting the exertions of
the spring campaign which had sent the agents home.

By 1865 the commission was hiring about two hundred
workers and teamsters. A steamer tug moved up and down
the river carrying supplies. Various relief stations were scattered along the 30-mile battle front. Each army corps had
a Sanitary relief station and two four-horse wagons to accom-
pany any military move; in each a staff of agents looked
after the regimental hospitals and the soldiers' wants. Nurses
submitted their requisitions to the Sanitary stations, which
barge headquarters kept supplied. At the base hospital in
City Point worked forty members of the Auxiliary Relief
Corps. Dr. Alexander McDonald and W. F. Swalm directed
Sanitary business.

The backing of California and the Sanitary fairs showed
results in May, June, and July. By the end of June over
$515,000 had largely purchased 103 tons of canned tomatoes,
1,200 barrels of pickled cucumbers, 18,000 gallons of onions
and tomatoes, and 17,000 gallons of sauerkraut. Douglas
called for 1,500 barrels of potatoes. Each soldier could carry
one in his pocket without trouble. Ale helped restore him
who returned exhausted from the front, where a man risked
his life if he raised his head a few inches aboveground. The
commission restricted the use of spirits to special hospital
cases. Demands for woolen shirts, drawers, socks, and tobacco seemed without end. Officers from Grant down praised
Sanitary work. The issuance of antiscorbutics alone had
helped check scurvy. The commission, thought Strong, had

[5] Bellows MSS. H. W. Bellows to R. Bellows, Jan. 2, 1865, New York.

probably done much to influence the outcome of the campaign.

The frame pavilions and white tents of the army hospital stretched across a wide plateau. For a while it held 6,000 patients, although its bed capacity was 4,500. The four depot field hospitals were a mile from the City Point landing. A branch railroad ran directly from the main military line, through the center of the hospital grounds and out to the hospitals near the front. By using properly equipped cars the medical corps saved the sick and wounded the discomfort of travel by ambulance. Each hospital had a dispensary, a commissary storehouse, general and special diet kitchens, and a convalescents' dining room.

Of the many nurses calling for Sanitary stores, Miss Helen Gilson was a favorite with agents and inspectors. Her "indomitable spirit and immense good humor" made her an excellent attendant for the wounded, who loved hearing her sing army songs and hymns. Although she had been with the commission on the peninsula in 1862, her great work now was raising the hospital at City Point from a disgrace to an object of pride. The commission thought highly of Cornelia Hancock, who had traveled in Sanitary wagons from Fredericksburg to City Point. The plain Mrs. Husbands, granddaughter of financier Robert Morris, known for her perseverance and cultivated manners, was an excellent manager. Mrs. W. H. Holstein combined nursing with lectures and special appeals for the commission. Mrs. Arabella Barlow, wife of General Barlow, died of fever and exhaustion. The commission considered her a martyr.

Busy women nurses scarcely raised their heads to watch a medical officer pass. Perhaps one like Dr. Weir Mitchell commanded attention as he dashed by on horseback, "his long hair floating back . . . his yellow-lined cape thrown over his shoulder . . ." Men thought the woman doctor singular. Dr. H. K. Painter of New Jersey used personal influence to do her most effective work. She was small and of the "old time Quaker stamp" and wore "a little white cap, and the proverbial short gown and petticoat." Dr. Mary Walker, on the contrary, wore loose trousers down to her boot tops and then a skirt to her knees. Long skirts were unsanitary, she argued, because they swept the ground. She looked well in a close-fitting jacket and cape, a high collar and soft hat; but the battlefield was a man's world, and her masculine affectation went against the grain. Almost as strange was the sensitive male who worked with "a tear in his eye and a rose in his button-hole."

The Christian Commission was especially valuable after a battle, when the delegates fed the starving wounded. The Christians preferred to cook their own food and distribute it themselves. Surgeons generally wanted food prepared in hospital kitchens, and with regularity; they protested against the delegates' "desultory and fitful manner." Mrs. Holstein objected to the "windy" ways of the Christian Commission, which took Sanitary stores to glorify itself. Sanitary agents received orders not to honor Evangelical requests, unless they had approval from the Washington office.

The Sanitary Commission did not set itself above criticism. At least one employee complained of colleagues who made exhibitions of contempt and bitterness for the Christian Commission; they gave officers good care but seemed negligent about the enlisted man. Certain nurses were fed up with the Sanitary regard for the surgeon's demands; they liked the Christian Commission because it did not wait for requisitions. If a surgeon was "blind and deaf" to the Sanitary, a nurse could only call on the Christian Commission. General Patrick, provost marshal of the Army of the Potomac, objected to the Sanitary Commission for its "excessive releases" to surgeons; the general feeling was that it was too large and expensive.

Dr. Steiner found poor morale at City Point. Mutual

jealousy made common action impossible among agents.
"What a pity that the officers of the Sanitary Commission
do not more conscientiously carry out the duties of their
positions!" exclaimed the chief inspector. "I have so often
seen this want of attention to duty that it has become an
old tale." [6] In contrast to the God-fearing men of the Auxiliary Relief Corps were those of the Field Relief Corps, too
often the sweepings from cities. Here one got drunk on Sanitary liquor; there another sold the tobacco he should have
given the soldiers. Even friends of the Sanitary Commission
complained that its agents ate the stores that should have
gone to hospitals. Many soldiers consequently lost all respect for the commission; whenever they asked for anything
the agents made them feel like "beggars." Some who wanted
to write letters were known to refuse paper bearing the Sanitary stamp; others were reportedly ashamed to be seen using
a handkerchief from the commission. Sanitary Agent Isaac
Harris also complained about the motley crew of helpers.
But slanderers of the Sanitary Commission were numerous
among soldiers who never needed field relief, said Harris.
He wrote: "The Corcoran Legion; bummers; never saw any
fighting; never on the front; within the defenses of Washington; blowers not deserving anything from the Sanitary Commission." Sergeant Fitzgerald, the most "abominable liar" in
the Corcoran Legion, had "made out a terrible tale of corruption and swindling existing in the Sanitary Commission
and some of the 'Green ones' took his statement for Gospel
truths, because he was a soldier and of course ought to
know." [7]

But praise of the commission came from strange quarters.
Persons from remote areas often showed an understanding
of the fifth wheel, conceding that the supplies sent to hospi-

[6] L. H. Steiner, *Diary* (MSS.), June 29, 1864.
[7] L. H. Steiner MSS. Isaac Harris to L. H. Steiner, Feb. 11, 1864, Brooklyn.

tals were of the best quality. Agents of the Wisconsin relief society had become warm friends, praising Sanitary order and exactitude. The way the commission discriminated among applicants for help and kept a sharp lookout for waste and misappropriation won their admiration. To Cornelia Hancock the commission was "a God appointed institution" even though He communicated "very little with some of the agents."

But war and the labor of relief went on. Officers turned waspish; lines furrowed the faces of the young. Soldiers looked back on the Wilderness with "shuddering and pain," but with no wish to give up. Endurance was all. There were only two powerful armies trading blows. Sometimes men fought in the dust, and then again in the mud; in sunlight or in storms; at night as well as by day. Summer brought intolerable heat, but in spite of thinning regiments the armies fought on. War knew no Sunday. Now and then in the continuous bustle civilian as well as soldier felt "very, very tired." Wherever there were sick and wounded, the Sanitary work went on. The sight of suffering, Steiner admitted, made one callous. In all this blood and fatigue the toil of relief became mechanical, and its agents seemed like automatons.

Soldiers adopted a nearly uniform system of huts. They used shelter tents and bombproofs at the front. Bombproofs were long trenches, roofed over and covered on the side facing the enemy; soldiers left them exposed on the other side. In rainy weather, complained Dr. Elisha Harris, bombproofs became noisome "gopher holes" and one "continuous latrine."

Though ravaged by battle, Virginia was beautiful in autumn. At City Point nurses made a holiday of Thanksgiving and Christmas for the sick and wounded. At Beaufort, South Carolina, sheets borrowed from the Sanitary Commission served as tablecloths and furnished a homelike mood.

- 4 -

Now that Surgeon General Joseph K. Barnes ran the Medical Bureau, Stanton showed an interest in military health. The secretary invested the bureau with exclusive control of general hospitals and hospital camps. By granting the brevet commission he gave the corps ample recognition. His helpfulness brought about those monuments of American military medicine of Hammond's planning—the Army Medical Museum, the library of the surgeon general's office, and the *Medical and Surgical History of the War of the Rebellion.*

In 1864 the Sanitary Commission still thought itself an advisory body. It called for larger corps of surgeons and nurses, more hospital transports, and an ample transportation train; it still proposed giving the bureau exclusive control of army medical transportation. But there was no love lost between Barnes and the commissioners. Dr. Van Buren privately made out a set of charges against the surgeon general, but these were little better than gossip.

The new administration turned ardent Hammond men sour. Commissioner Elisha Harris, a leading figure in public health, mistakenly believed that the unhealthful atmosphere of the Potomac basin was killing the hospitalized. Surgeons like Cuyler, Hamlin, McDougal, and Rush Spencer agreed with him, and the fact that the Medical Bureau did nothing about setting up hospitals in a different climate looked like negligence. Harris' other criticisms seemed more to the point. The Medical Bureau began its studies of compound fractures of thigh and knee when half the fracture cases were in their graves. Tetanus allegedly remained unstudied, while hospitals and surgeons received no instruction about its history and control. Preventive sanitary studies seemed a thing of the past; apparently forgotten were the observation of causes, the collation and publication of statistics, and the study of measures for aiding and advising surgeons. Medical inspectors like Colonel Cuyler had made careful reports and specific recommendations, charged Harris; but the Medical Bureau neglected these findings and the inquiries of others. Barnes approved orders planned as part of the medical history of the war; yet to all appearances he lacked the vigor and imagination for opening new inquiries. He burdened medical officers with administrative details. Word came to Harris that the inspectors seemed little better than spies. The bureau made valuable information inaccessible to its own surgeons; surely it would bar the commission from using these findings, when the time came to write the Sanitary history.

Many surgeons hoped the commission would send inspectors to the hospital transports and ambulance trains, for the best source of information came from skilled and independent observers; the commission would have to be armed with fresh facts when the public asked for an accounting of the excessive mortality in hospitals. The War Department was responsible, said Harris; to be mild and charitable on this occasion was to sanction evil.

Surgeons also told Dr. Harris that the commission could not act because the bureau had it "blockaded." The secretary of war turned down the Sanitary application to inspect hospitals, and the bureau did not wait for possible attack. In November, "Satterlee or some other representative of fossil fogyism" furnished editorials in the *World* with material against the commission. Let the people rid themselves of a needless expense and pay for supplementary relief with taxes, the critic exhorted; let medical officers distribute the benefits of charity. A "feeble" band of citizens could never replace the power of government. The Commission—ha, a meddler! To this hive of avarice swarmed drones and workers "in all the splendors of shoddy or petroleum aristocracy." The commissioners protested against these slanders and asked the *World* to name names. Agnew had a conference with editor Manton Marble, and they patched up their differences.

But abuse from this Copperhead rankled. What he had printed for truth made the commissioners look like "members of the Common Council of New York." They dismissed Marble as "one of the dirtiest of our dirty dogs," but their fighting mood was gone. Hammond's court-martial gave sufficient ground for winding up Sanitary affairs, thought Dr. Van Buren. His colleagues talked about calling the attention of Congress to defects in the bureau, but that move seemed useless. They sat by while Barnes sent able doctors like Cuyler and Hamlin away from Washington. For supporting the Lincoln administration in the election the commissioners gained nothing, except the sense of doing their patriotic duty.

But 1864 spread their fame for distributing supplies, for finding out and ministering to cases of specific need. The fairs trumpeted the Sanitary across the land; as distributor of fresh vegetables, the commission received thanks from soldiers who had never felt its charity before. Families and officers in search of the mission knew its hospital directory. The statistical department grew larger; the Central Claim Agency reached into all parts of the country. While ignorant of other aspects of Sanitary work, soldiers and widows knew that the commission would collect for them their just dues.

Yet there were knocks in the fifth wheel, for it showed the effects of weak and absentee leadership. Wrangling divided the staff. "Oh! this worrying, wearisome life, full of toil and no satisfaction, a very treadmill which will wear the substance and pith out of a man's existence," Steiner confided to his diary.[8] Former friends now called the chief inspector meddlesome, bad tempered, and without ability. Knapp, his superior, took exclusive credit for ideas not his own, complained Steiner. In July, 1864, the executive committee ac-

[8] L. H. Steiner, *Diary* (MSS.), Sept. 10, 1863.

cepted his resignation "through the coloring of prejudice, costly judgment, and some resentment." The New York office was lax. The branches in London and Paris began to wonder whether they were really wanted. Why did their letters remain unanswered? Why did they receive no receipts for their remittances? Listless and indifferent servants let Sanitary interests slide. In Washington they were almost frivolous, leaving their duties in summer heat to enjoy cooler parts of the country. E. B. Elliott,* the actuary, lost his place by overstaying his vacation in England. Pride without self-control cost Alfred J. Bloor his job as assistant secretary. Jenkins and Knapp quarreled; Newberry, full of complaints, was spoken of as "disaffected." Bellows, who liked to think that the Sanitary Commission bore his impress and saw himself as the "lubrication and balance wheel of the concern," was powerless to stop the spread of ill-feeling. His ebullience ran low as he gained in fatigue. "I had a nice journey in, always accepting a crowd of soldiers in our car, sick and ill smelling but venerable in my eyes for their sufferings and services," wrote Bellows to his wife from Boston. "It was music in my ears to hear them speak of the Sanitary Commission as their familiar friend, although I kept dark and let no one know my connexion with it."[9]

War weariness was part of the American climate in 1864. Between the command and its execution fell a shadow. The executive committee had trouble making its force felt, but difficulties were greater than the clash of personnel. The Sanitary Commission badly needed persistent application to the thinking and carrying out of plans. Olmsted's policy of the disinterested pursuit of knowledge was a thing of the past; no one pushed his own "fancies in the place of some other men's facts." The commission became more an agent of supply and less an advocate of scientific progress. In England,

[9] Bellows MSS. H. W. Bellows to Mrs. H. W. Bellows, Feb. 20, 1865, Boston, Mass.

Edwin Chadwick, the leading sanitarian, criticized Sanitary documents because they gave no statistics to prove the actual death rates. Surgeons knew the relief agents, but the commission's medical men rarely visited regiments and army hospitals. Only Dr. Harris had made a special study of tetanus in 1864. The commission dropped publication of medical monographs, collecting those that had been printed and putting them out in an expensive volume with limited circulation. Tired, the commissioners—and especially those on the executive committee—stressed the proper order of detail and read a narrow literalism into their duties; their financial responsibility came to mean an overanxious accounting for every last penny. They took no new step without studying all legal aspects. They supervised what they should have delegated to subordinates, and turned the general secretary into an errand boy and chief clerk. Dr. Jenkins carried the burden of details and a weekly report. No wonder he fidgeted like "a hen on a hot griddle."

The sight of the Christian Commission growing in power and importance troubled the commissioners. People apparently felt that the Sanitary Commission had been too demanding. Nearly everywhere the Evangelicals were cutting in and boldly winning the contest. In November, 1864, the Sanitary had a reserve of $1,500,000; this would last, provided the war did not go on another year. The Christians planned to raise $1,000,000 for 1865; they were going to increase the number of paid canvassers and agents in the field. In December, 1864, they were paying delegates better wages than Sanitary workers received. In Chicago they demanded a share in the second Sanitary fair, although the Christian Commission evidently gave no financial backing.

But Lincoln's fifth wheel was not to end first with a shiver and then a spill. Even after the war it kept rolling without any management, thought critical Dr. Steiner, and all because the faith of the people was making it turn.

CHAPTER XIII

From Fifth Wheel to Red Cross

- 1 -

THE season arrived for the rip tides of politics. On June 7 the Republican convention at Baltimore renominated Lincoln, with Andrew Johnson of Tennessee his running mate. On August 29, Democrats at Chicago put up McClellan. Farragut's capture of Mobile on August 5 started the wave that eventually lifted the Republican party to victory. But the mood of summer, 1864, spoke peace at any price. Commissioners like George Strong shunned it, while Dr. Newberry thought gigantic preparations merely fed the maw of failure. The drafts took in more money than soldiers. Sherman dragged "a lengthening chain" for want of men to envelop and crush Confederate Johnston.

Earlier in 1864, Sherman had barred the commission from using transportation to the front. Railroad space should go to guns and ammunition, he reasoned, not Sanitary stores. In April, Sherman agreed to give the commission storage in Nashville; he allowed it one car of supplies a day, besides whatever the hospital train could carry; he would also furnish transportation to the front, provided the commission shipped the amounts specified by the medical director. To receive information from any other source was unmilitary and irregular, said Sherman. If the medical director failed to give him the correct information, the general could call him to account.

In preparing for Sherman's move against Atlanta, the commission sent 3,000 barrels of vegetables and large supplies of

condensed milk, beef stimulants, underclothing, and bandages to Chattanooga. From May to July, 1864, it moved forward about 100 tons a week of additional stores. The army
set up over 300 rude hospitals on the line of march. Agents
visited each one, distributing no less than twenty-four
wagonloads of supplies. Up to July 14 they had furnished
more than 17,000 meals at feeding stations in the rear. From
Chicago came reports that the commission stood in high
favor with men and officers.

Sherman crossed the Chattahoochee River on July 17. Jefferson Davis removed General Johnston, whose Fabian policy had denied the Union quick victory. Now under General
T. B. Hood the Confederates took the offensive only to meet
repulse. Sherman's forces besieging Atlanta sent up a cry for
Sanitary stores. The commission cut down on Eastern expenditures to supply the West. Protests rose from City Point; this
policy was robbing Peter to pay Paul. When requisitions
were cut to the minimum, incoming supplies lasted one week,
and gave soldiers cause for writing home that the Sanitary
Commission was played out.

Atlanta fell early in September. Perhaps the commissioners
remembered Olmsted's protest against those who visited
Western armies ostensibly as Sanitary workers, when Sherman abruptly excluded all civilians. Did the commission use
its privileges for the public or the army? asked General
Sherman. He had hungry soldiers to feed, and could ill afford
the herds of sightseers in their picnicking spirit. He temporarily cut off Sanitary transportation rights; he allowed no
other agents than those who came in good faith. Possibly
Sherman's dislike of the commission dated from this time;
but the commission was not the only object of his criticism.
Emphatic in profanity, he supposedly told a member of chaplains that he wanted no man in his army who did not carry
a musket.

In Atlanta the commission was "the general theme of

praise in every surgeon's mouth." It had pushed forward supplies so that hospitals were rarely caught shorthanded.
Agents furnished vegetables to 142 regiments and 25 batteries. Most of the men "had not tasted an onion or a mouth-
ful of cabbage for more than one hundred days." Sanitary
stores went to the care of 2,750 hospitalized when Sherman
decided to resume the campaign in October.

July and August had seen General Jubal Early sweep
Union forces out of the Shenandoah Valley. He carried
threat of capture to Washington and actual destruction to
Chambersburg, Pennsylvania. Lincoln and Grant sent General Philip Sheridan to defeat Early, ravage the granary of
the Shenandoah, but leave Virginians their eyes to weep
with.

Until Sheridan's appearance, the valley showed signs of
the ebb and flow of war—old camping grounds, fields without
fences, ruined houses, large cornfields haunted by the stalks
of ungathered harvests, here and there dead horses and
shallow graves. Occasionally one passed cultivated fields and
comfortable houses, where women sat at the doors and children flocked to the gates to watch the troops go by.

Sheridan's medical arrangements started from nothing.
At Harpers Ferry surgeons received medicines for immediate
needs; they took nothing too cumbersome for transportation.
The hospital at Sandy Hook expanded from 300 to 1,300
beds. Slight cases went to Frederick, and the more severe
ones to Baltimore. At Winchester nearly all shops were closed
and empty; their floors became beds for the wounded. Many
men were barefooted and shirtless. The arrival of three
wagonloads of Sanitary stores started a rush of surgeons,
stewards, and soldiers crying for help. Invoices consisted of
sheets, socks, shoes, drawers, and hospital stores. Both Medical Bureau and Sanitary Commission were poor planners at
Winchester, said Elisha Harris; neither bothered to consult
the proper authorities. But by the middle of October the

commission was spending $10,000 on Sheridan's wounded. A month later the bureau had improved its working order. Medical officers reported Winchester hospitals well stocked with clothing and furniture. Sheridan readily expressed appreciation to the commission for supplementing what the army could not supply.

- 2 -

Europe got a taste of the Civil War when the Union *Kearsarge* sank the Confederate *Alabama* off the French coast on June 19, 1864. So ended the career of the ironclad that burned, captured, or sent to the bottom sixty ships of the United States. In London, E. C. Fisher with the help of F. M. Edge continued the commission's quiet work. During the summer of 1864 they rented rooms in Trafalgar Square opposite the headquarters of the Southern association. Theirs was a halfway house, where Englishmen might forsake rebellion for the Union cause. The number of those willing to speak for the United States was growing; but none would sacrifice his comfort to canvassing, arguing with opponents, and writing. The backbones of members of Parliament needed constant stiffening, said Edge; statesmen lived in doubt, uneasiness, fear, and despair. Union propagandists could not reach certain levels of English society. Charles Dickens wrote a brief description of the commission in *All the Year Round*; but literary men tended to form impenetrable cliques. A writer would not act on his own; he must wait for the approval of the others in his "sanhedrin." The newspapers dwelt on the trivial and the special interests of critics. The Dundee linen industry made extensive purchases from the United States; but its moneyed men so hated the North that they would give nothing. The upper middle-class Englishman had apparently been suckled on the belief that nothing good could come out of America. How, then, could the commission convince them that the Americans were capable of putting into practice the noblest purposes, and advancing them "in the purest and most humanitarian principles"?

Yet signs of spring stirred in the freeze of winter. A few publishers were looking for fresh subjects. John Stuart Mill publicly expressed admiration of the Sanitary Commission. Leaders of the government such as Lord Palmerston, Earl Russell, and Gladstone sent notes of congratulation. Prominent among Continental visitors at London headquarters were Karl Blind of Germany and Signor Saffi of Italy. Chadwick and Rawlinson, the great English sanitarians, called for information on the hospital car as Elisha Harris had planned it. The Union and Emancipation Society praised the commission in an address sent to Lincoln. At least six newspapers began to describe Sanitary work. The commission could show that its journals, pamphlets, correspondence, and public addresses had helped to reduce British talk of "this barbarous war."

In October, 1864, Fisher enlarged headquarters to include a reading room. Only the Americans hung back from visiting. Some attacked Fisher's character; others wished to make him personally responsible for the small expense of his office and assailed people who gave help.

The standing committee made Charles Bowles "Foreign Agent in Europe," instructing him to communicate with Washington about the coming congress at Geneva. According to Secretary Seward, the United States stood ready to conclude unilateral treaties with one or all the powers, but could not bind itself by an agreement while fighting a "relentless and barbarous foe." The delegates had begun to gather when Bowles arrived in Geneva.

It seemed as though the United States would send no representative; but Seward directed George G. Fogg, American minister at Berne, to act informally. Because his instructions arrived late, Fogg did not appear until the congress had organized. For three days Bowles tried to fill the gap. Henri Dunant and the International Committee received him with "extreme cordiality." They had undertaken a great work and "absolutely" needed the support of a representative from the United States Sanitary Commission.

The first informal meeting took place on the Sunday evening before Fogg's arrival. Delegates vaguely knew what was expected of them. Were sanitary commissions practicable? someone asked. Should governments sanction and protect them? Delegations who were fully empowered to treat fell into dispute with those who had come more as observers. It seemed as though they might not bother to hold a first formal session when Bowles presented himself as "the real and palpable representative of an institution which they had all heard of . . . but which . . . they were still half disposed to consider . . . the unreal creation of an . . . incomprehensible people." Evidently the argument came to an end.

Bowles set out to win friends for the cause of sanitary commissions. His rooms facing Lake Geneva became an informal meeting place. He could tell them much about the American experience with insignia. How to distinguish its inspectors and agents from members of the armed forces had been an early problem of the Sanitary Commission. Secretary of War Cameron ruled against uniforms, probably regarding them as liveries. In April, 1863, Sanitary workers received cap badges; the wreath was described as beautiful, but the lettering and cloth were very poor. Members of the Field Relief Corps wore the raised shield of the United States and the title of the commission stamped on a gilt button. In 1864, the Auxiliary Relief Corps carried a white Greek cross surrounded by an oval band of silver on cap or coat. The badge, said Sanitary authorities, was neat, attractive, and not too conspicuous. Bowles was able to point out that Americans in

Virginia were wearing their white cross while delegates were deliberating at Geneva; he was also able to show that each relief station at the front could be spotted by a flag displaying the United States shield and the initials U.S.S.C. Bellows, on a tour of the Virginia lines, had written: "It is very gratifying to come upon the Red Sanitary Commission flag floating over those [relief] stations at the very front." [1]

Bowles doubtless told the delegates that the United States Army had been developing distinguishing marks ever since February, 1863. By 1864 badges identified officers and men as well as flags, wagons, and ambulances of the several corps. Soldiers cut a patch of cloth into a shamrock, star, square, triangle, heart, and circle. The VI Corps adopted a Greek cross, while red badges set off the first division; white, the second; and blue, the third. The V Corps took up a Maltese cross in the same colors. To make the strange familiar Bowles assailed the eyes and ears of delegates with medical and statistical reports, colored lithographs of the Philadelphia Fair, photographs of depots and buildings, and pictures of the field relief corps; he hoped to achieve a "full understanding of the subject which was so necessary to harmonious action in the session."

Fogg asked Bowles to serve as his colleague. Since Washington must be kept free from any shadow of commitment, they agreed not to share in the debates but to work through delegates sympathetic to the American point of view. This decision had annoying consequences in discussions over volunteer aid societies; it also kept Fogg and Bowles from clearing up the muddy thinking about democracies. Bowles noted many inconsistencies. The French seemed to speak for the military powers at the same time they backed the present congress and the idea of volunteer aid societies. Delegates recognized the neutrality of persons who cared for the wounded in their own houses; but they withheld this recog-

[1] Bellows MSS. H. W. Bellows to R. Bellows, Jan. 2, 1865, New York.

nition from sanitary commissions and volunteer nurses, who were prepared to go beyond primitive household charity. Certain proposals threatened to nullify the convention. The Spanish government proposed giving commanding generals the right to make their own exceptions; the French would deprive the sick of neutral rights. But a liberal spirit leavened the meeting; delegates followed their instructions but stretched their meanings to ensure harmony.

Presiding officer at the congress was General Dufour, general in chief of the Swiss Republic. The treaty provided for the neutrality of hospitals and ambulances as long as they contained "wounded or invalid soldiers." Belligerents would treat a medical worker or chaplain as a neutral while exercising his duties; they would allow him to retire with his own army, if the wounded in enemy territory no longer needed him. The medical worker could take with him only personal property. Belligerents would treat as neutral the person who was giving aid to the wounded. They would regard as hospitals those houses that received battle casualties and protect them; they would treat all wounded alike. A commander in chief was free to transfer the enemy wounded to their outposts, whenever circumstances permitted and with his opponent's consent. He could parole the wounded and also return those no longer capable of military service.

"Absolute neutrality" covered the evacuation of hospitals with the personnel in charge. Ambulances and hospitals must fly a uniform flag as well as that of their nationals; personnel could also wear a distinguishing badge. The powers left the execution of details to the generals of the opposing forces. By this last provision delegates hoped to show military authorities "that the Congress fully appreciated the conflicting nature of these innovations and allowed them latitude." Four nations active in creating the treaty were unable to sign, due to insufficient or improper instructions. On August 22, 1864, the representatives of Baden, Belgium, Denmark, Spain,

France, Hesse-Darmstadt, Italy, Holland, Portugal, Prussia, and Württemberg fixed their signatures to the "Treaty for the Amelioration of Wounded Soldiers of Armies in the Field."

Entertainment included fetes, regattas, illuminations, and excursions on Lake Leman. On August 17 the delegates singled out Bowles for attention. At the Hotel de l'Ecu the president of Switzerland presented the Red Cross flag to the representative of "the good of all humanity." From the window Bowles could see the spot where Tell shot Gessler; from the hall outside the Geneva Musical Society burst into a chorus from Rossini's *William Tell*. The honor and all the old associations of freedom's victory over tyranny were too much for Bowles; he wept.

So far as results were concerned, the steps taken by the United States government in 1865 differed little from the measures adopted by the Geneva Congress of 1864. Both the Geneva Conference of 1863 and the United States Sanitary Commission aimed to devise a plan "for aiding the medical services of the armies in campaign." Succor of the wounded was the concern of the Geneva Congress, which said nothing about the general health and comfort of the troops. Washington did not specifically refer to the succor of troops, but covered it with the phrase "preserving and restoring the health and comfort of the forces." The Geneva Congress conferred neutrality on army sanitary services and their personnel; but ever since the spring of 1862 the Union and Confederate forces had released all doctors and chaplains held as prisoners of war.

To Henri Dunant went the honor of having brought about the Congresses of 1863 and 1864. But without the American experiences Dunant's efforts might have been fruitless. The Sanitary Commission had solved problems of cooperation between civilian volunteers and the official medical service; it was proof that the people could be organized for relief as effectively as armies for war. The Congress of 1864 abandoned the proposition that it was lawful for committees of volunteers to aid battle casualties in active campaigns; but one would like to think of the Sanitary Commission as midwife to the Red Cross. Charles Bowles wrote Bellows: "We took *the lead* and kept it, and the undistinguished astonishment of the many different national representatives of this Congress at the results and *proportions* of your Humanitarian work, and the respect with which they afterward treated your representative showed not only that their eyes were opened but how much they had needed opening." [2]

The Sanitary Commission in Great Britain kept on winning friends and golden opinions. Its publications attracted new readers, while polite notes of recognition came from Benjamin Disraeli, the directors of the British Museum, and the bishops of London, Norwich, Lincoln, Worcester, Ely, Winchester, and Chester. In autumn, 1864, Fisher read a paper before the Social Science Congress at York. Although his speech followed a four-hour debate, the members called it an important contribution to social science. More gratifying was Fisher's address before the Royal United Service Institute in February, 1865, when the Sanitary Commission became of considerable interest to British naval and military men. Sir Harry Verney promised Fisher he would tell Florence Nightingale, his sister-in-law, of her influence on the Sanitary Commission.

Charles Francis Adams headed the spring subscription list with £100. His countrymen refused to attend the celebration of Washington's birthday, if the Sanitary Commission had anything to do with it. Fisher withdrew his support; so did the British friends who had been invited. The Americans enjoyed their private dinner, with General McClellan as presiding officer. Adams and Samuel F. B. Morse were there, but they seemed unaware of any unpleasantness.

[2] Box 638. C. P. S. Bowles to H. W. Bellows, Nov. 14, 1864, Paris, France.

The various chancelleries now spoke in compliments, but Europeans did not like being asked for contributions. The centuries had trained them to think in terms of mendicant friars and oppressive taxgatherers. Sanitary prestige was worth more than the few coins to be squeezed out of Europe. The American thought in terms of the dollar and gave with a magnificence; the European closely figured his sous and pfennigs; but the marvel was that the commission got anything from him, who seemed unused to this kind of spontaneous offering.

Europe was concerned with that aspect of the Civil War which would help shape military reform; it had given a fresh drive to the humanitarian impulse. One could see the reflection of the Sanitary Commission in a newly organized French Commission (1865). The British Sanitary Commission had carried the full weight and authority of government; its American counterpart remained extralegal, "without any infringement upon established prerogatives and discipline." The representative of the commission noted: "Our unflinching purpose as a people may have excited surprise, our increasing sacrifices astonishment, but it has remained for the Sanitary Commission alone by its charities and by its accomplished results to secure almost the only admiration which has been accorded to us in Europe since the beginning of the war." [3]

- 3 -

Lincoln's victory at the polls meant a vigorous prosecution of the war and the end of slavery. Sherman at Atlanta prepared to sever communications with the North. He loaded his wagons with ammunition, provisions, and forage, and sent all ineffectives to the rear. The commission withdrew its stations from Atlanta, Kingston, and Dalton. Chattanooga,

[3] Box 804. E. A. Crane to J. F. Jenkins, March 24, 1865, Paris, France.

again an advance post, became important for its hospital gardens. In the first week of December the commission distributed 2,045 bushels of potatoes and 7,663 gallons of pickles and kraut to 63,869 men. General Thomas restored it to the position of favorite, and boldly expressed his admiration in public. The commission took this for a victory, for Thomas was thought to have acted against the known feelings of Barnes and Stanton. On November 21, Hood rose up from Alabama to strike the Union at Nashville. Thomas bided his time and crushed the Confederates on December 15.

On November 12, Sherman's 62,000 had set out for the coast. Two Sanitary agents traveled with the army. Never did his sick average 20 per cent, as in the Peninsular campaign. Several divisions did not lose a man by sickness during the 350-mile march; death from disease took twelve out of every thousand. Measles spread after Sherman left Atlanta. Smallpox broke out, but vaccination checked its spread. Union forces had 14 hospitals, while 600 vehicles made up the ambulance train. One ambulance followed each regiment.

A medical officer directed the sick and wounded to report or be reported to the chief surgeon for transportation and treatment. A card admitted the bearer to a place in the ambulance. Here the footsore regained strength; even the seriously ill were known to recover while rolling through Georgia. Soldiers who died were mainly raw recruits. Every night the patients were put in hospital tents and fed; each morning before breakfast the doctors made their rounds. Each hospital had its organized foragers, who invariably returned with sweet potatoes, turnips, fresh meats, sorghum, and molasses. Milk, honey, corn meal, and sometimes flour found their way to the diet chart.

Military health improved all the way to Savannah. All traces of scurvy disappeared. Little rain marred the weather;

shortage of tents and medical stores caused no great hardships. Proud of their resilience, Sherman's men started the second campaign without having to rest several months after the first. Only the Union prisoners of war freed from Andersonville, Americus, Macon, and Millen showed the effects of suffering from starvation and poor health conditions. Novelty and excitement buoyed up the soldiers, who understood the importance of their errand and placed unquestioned faith in Sherman's leadership. Southern newspapers grew hysterical at his progress. By December 19 he had invested Savannah and gained communication with the Union fleet. On Christmas Day the mayor, Dr. Richard Arnold, yielded the city to Sherman.

Defeat at Nashville and Savannah meant that the Confederacy must soon lie down and die. The Union had one too many armies for the foe. To indicate the instability back on the Virginia front, General Grant lived in a rude board cabin of two or three rooms, wrote Bellows. Gone was the "luxury, parade," and "self-indulgent furniture" of Hooker and McClellan. The army was living "in a sort of demi-semi state, half summer, half winter arrangements—partly tent, partly hut," for Grant wanted Lee to know that a winter campaign was quite possible. The general "talked with a fine generosity about Sherman and Thomas." News of the fall of Savannah and Union victory at Nashville had just reached him. Success seemed certain to Grant, who spoke as though "the bottom of the Confederacy had fallen out." Now he chiefly feared that "Jeff Davis would sneak out and run away." Kindness and courtesy were native to the general. Since Grant's relations with the Sanitary Commission were excellent, Bellows "troubled him very little." Bellows noted that Grant depended on Southern newspapers for information, writing: "Reading to us like an unaccustomed reader out of the Richmond paper of the day (just brought in), he stumbled at the hard words and pronounced 'pabulum' pablum, as if he never met that phrase before." [4]

In January, 1865, the fall of Fort Fisher made Wilmington, North Carolina, useless as a Southern base for blockade running. In February, Sherman left Savannah with 65,000 troops. Again the army marched without a base, with no communications, and in a northerly direction, over swamps, marshes, and broad rivers. For two or three weeks the rain fell continuously; the enemy kept up sniping, but doggedly the army pushed on. Sherman avoided strongly fortified positions and heavy fighting. His soldiers laid waste the countryside, destroying the tracks of already useless railroads. Except for centers like Savannah, the places occupied by the Union Army fell back into Confederate hands after Sherman marched on. On February 18, Charleston fell to the pillaging invaders. At Fayetteville, North Carolina, Sherman established communications with Grant and Stanton by way of Wilmington; he joined the Union forces at Goldsboro, North Carolina, on March 21.

Ragged and destitute, Sherman's soldiers had covered 425 miles in fifty days. The Sanitary inspector in South Carolina thought that his foragers needed medical attention more than the hospitalized. Their skin was bronzed and "drawn tight over their pinched features." Like the damned, they knew no rest. Hundreds without blankets and overcoats suffered as the cold weather sharpened. If forage failed, the officer left his horse and marched on foot with valise in hand. Sanitary agents heard soldiers abuse Sherman as a hard master, but all agreed that he was "Nemesis in uniform" come to give the South the coup de grâce. So stay away! warned Sherman's lieutenants. That was the greatest kindness the Sanitary Commission could do this army. Only at coastal points should the commission try to reach it. The commissioners took this advice to heart. They ordered two steamers plying

[4] Bellows MSS. H. W. Bellows to R. Bellows, Jan. 2, 1865, New York.

between New York and North Carolina to attend Sherman's army whenever it made contact with the coast.

On March 11, Dr. Agnew set sail for Morehead, North Carolina, with 4,000 barrels of stores. These were but part of "great preparations against pending campaigns." Bellows said: "We shall lay out our whole strength in this coming campaign, which may be our last great opportunity of field service to the army." [5]

In March the combined forces of Terry, Schofield, and Sherman were threatening Raleigh, and steadily approaching the "last duct" that brought food to Richmond. They had entered southern Virginia about the end of March, while Thomas seemed to be moving toward Lynchburg. April 1 signaled Grant's grand attack all along the line, and two days later his forces entered Richmond. The Confederacy went up in a "cloud of impalpable dust," when Lee surrendered at Appomattox Court House on April 10. F. N. Knapp was at City Point when some horsemen dashed through the camp shouting news of Lee's surrender to Grant. A "storm of excitement" broke loose. Men half dressed or on crutches gathered round their corps flags, "sent up shout upon shout," and started bonfires with tar barrels. Knapp wrote:

. . . all the men who could move fell into one great procession carrying flags of all sorts: some were shirts, white and red tied onto long poles, some were sheets and bedspreads. . . . So they went from camp to camp all falling in, and passed on cheering every surgeon and steward and cook and darkey they could find. The bonfires continued—fences and shanties were torn down and piled on to make a blaze—the men were also firing guns and pistols—every form of noise that mortals could make those fellows made. They all seemed 'tearing mad.' Just then bright flashes were seen on the fortifications a mile or so beyond us; when all the heavy cannon there commenced thundering forth rejoicing,

[5] Bellows MSS. H. W. Bellows to Russell Bellows, March 12, 1865, New York.

we could see the flash and discharge of every gun—and as it came through the darkness followed by the roar, the effect was not to quiet the excitement of the men in camp. So the cheers and march continued till the guns ceased and every . . . man was hoarse with cheering and shouting victory.[6]

Miss Helen Gilson took Knapp to the "contraband quarters," where about a hundred Negroes were living. The shouting had awakened a few; but most of them were "sound asleep." The Negroes looked on Miss Gilson as a "guardian saint," said Knapp, and they obeyed her order to assemble in the tent street at once. Here they learned the news and praised God for their victory and freedom.

"Now," said Miss Gilson, "haven't you a song of rejoicing to sing?"

So one of the oldest darkies said, "Yes, yes, Miss Helen, we got one Hallelujah Song just right for dis-year 'casi'n—' when de Kingdom's coming!" So he led off in . . . a . . . song of praise and glory, and all the others joined in . . . the chorus, shaking hands . . . with each other . . . and kneeling down and praising God. . . .

Then Miss Gilson said, "Now who wants to lead in prayers?"

. . . One of the blackest of all Negroes said, ". . . I'se got a prayer dat's choking me now—bredren and sisters, let's pray to God Almighty!"

So every live soul there, except some half dozen white soldiers . . . and the camp general . . . kneeled down to the ground. . . .[7]

Word came from Sanitary headquarters in New Orleans that the news of surrender had struck the city like an electric shock. New York turned into a carnival. Bells rang; orators made speeches; groups passed resolutions. Nighttime brought illuminations. Steamship lines offered excursions to Charleston and Richmond. Money began to fill Sanitary and Christian coffers. The Civil War was now a ghost world for historians to haunt.

[6] F. N. Knapp MSS. F. N. Knapp to his parents, April 10, 1865, City Point, Va.   [7] *Ibid.*

Two agents and two four-horse wagons of the Sanitary Commission rolled into Richmond on April 3, when Union forces first marched in. Smoke and flames still rose from fires set by rebel hands. The rubble of fallen houses filled many streets. Paupers were everywhere. Even in humiliation Richmond still had the attractions of handsome trees and streets, large houses, and expansive gardens. A Sanitary agent praised the Jackson Hospital for its order and method of conduct; ration for sick and wounded was double that in Northern hospitals; but whenever possible, the commission furnished other Richmond hospitals which were in direst need.

Worn, dirty, tired in their suits of ragged gray, the defeated were figures of despair. Former officers of rebellion now packed Libby Prison and Castle Thunder. Those not behind bars flocked to the Spottswood Hotel. Silent and downcast, they walked without sidearms, a bitter sight to Union officers, who were ready to treat them as mortal enemies. True Union sentiment, said Sanitary agents, could be found among the lowly, for they had suffered from the "stern and grinding" rebel rule; but families of secession persuasion nursed their pride like the fallen Lucifer.

Among the ships crowding the Richmond wharves moved the Sanitary barges. The commission set up headquarters on the southeast corner of Ninth and Broad streets, and cooperated with the joint committee of subsistence. This was a group of Richmond citizens and Union officers who were supplying the families of the poor. "The wide benevolence and kindness" of the North surprised the conquered. Applicants to the Sanitary Commission came from a better class than the multitudes who gathered around the company offices. Women in black put Northern charity into their baskets, while pale children told tales of misery. The executive committee put an end to this "providing tea and sugar for sick rebels" as not legitimately part of Sanitary work. Charity fostered delusions among Southerners of "their own supreme dignity and the duty of Yankees to care for them." Sanitary stores belonged to the Union soldier, not to the defeated.

- 4 -

On April 14 the national religion found its paschal lamb, when John Wilkes Booth murdered Abraham Lincoln. Men opened their eyes to find their man of sorrows gone; the lonely hero rejected by one-third of a nation and tolerated by the rest had gone. Olmsted, in 1865, saw Lincoln as the one man who had consistently understood the people; he knew what they wanted, "what they could be expected to sustain, and what to renounce." He was the first great statesman to speak to the world in the language of the people. Bellows gave what solace he could to the family of Edwin Booth, the actor. Threatening letters demanded blood for blood, but Bellows reminded his countrymen that Booth, a loyal man, deserved their sympathy.

Leading members of the Sanitary Commission were among the eight hundred who attended Lincoln's funeral in the East Room of the White House. According to Strong, the "commonplace" service could not dispel the profound grief. One praised the dead; but glances exchanged across the catafalque showed that old passions still lived. Men divided into Pharisees and publicans. George Strong could not bear the representatives of the Christian Commission. They were at once "unctuous" and "vinegary," "an ugly looking set mostly of the Maw-worm and Chadband type."

What Lincoln thought of the Sanitary Commission seemed to have sunk with him into the grave. His minister, Dr. Gurley of the Presbyterian Church, said that Lincoln approved of charitable organizations and invited the people's generosity toward the soldier.[8] But a new president had stepped into the White House. Andrew Johnson always liked the

[8] Box 640. E. Harris to H. W. Bellows, April 23, 1865, Washington, D.C.

Sanitary Commission, and the commissioners thought he bore with firmness the greatness thrust upon him.

Americans said goodbye to war in a grand review. On May 23 and 24 travel-worn veterans and tattered banners paraded past the high officers of the republic. But a web of responsibilities still held the Sanitary Commission. The troops that remained needed relief. These numbered about 300,000 by June 20. Some 115,000 were Negroes, ignorant of self-care. Their officers could draw nothing, because all accounts were closed preparatory to making up the muster rolls. Since Quartermaster and Commissary bureaus were cutting down their issuances, cries for help sounded loudest in Sanitary ears. George J. Sicard noted: "Never in the history of this war, except only in the case of some of the largest battles, has such a sudden and immense demand been made upon our resources as now." [9]

The Medical Bureau apparently cared little for the wants of retiring troops. According to Elijah Harris, sanitary agents found traces of scurvy "in every regiment," and increased the supplies of fresh fruit and vegetables. The small supply at the Washington depot fed about 6 per cent, or 13,000 men. Surgeons made the minimum of requisitions and showed small consideration for the sick. Doctors seemed indifferent to everything that a sanitarian held dear. Soldiers lived in tents with dirt floors and slept on cots without straw-filled sacks. The sick feigned good spirits just to be mustered out with their regiments. Frequently they found themselves stranded in strange cities, because their illnesses had grown more complicated. Local charity often set up temporary hospitals, but large numbers of sick soldiers burdened Northern communities with problems of supply.

Five hundred cases of scurvy broke out among soldiers stationed in Texas during July, 1865. The army pushed for-

[9] Box 838, Vol. I, pp. 457–58. G. J. Sicard to Mrs. J. L. Colby, May 31, 1865, Washington, D.C.

ward vegetables, but difficulties hedged its system of distribution. The sick had to draw the vegetables according to regulations, a time-consuming process. The commissariat could
relieve itself only by a board of inquiry, which would "con-
demn the stuff so that it could be cast into the Rio Grande."
Military authorities thought the Sanitary Commission could
do this job better than the army. At once the commission sent
large quantities of fresh vegetables to Santiago, Brownsville,
and Indianola.

Proposals for future action filled the Sanitary letter box.
A madwoman suggested to Treasurer Strong that with the
commission's money they might live comfortably together
and for the greater glory of God. "Nobody" proposed paying
the national debt as the fitting and "crowning compliment
of the grand work of the Sanitary Commission." Enthusiasts
within the organization saw no end of fruitful courses. Men
like Dr. Joseph Parrish and F. N. Knapp would set up employment offices across the land, whose books would give a
sociological insight into America of postwar years. Let the
Sanitary angel look southward, where its experience could
re-create a moral setting in social chaos. But the commissioners had grown tired; they drew the blinds on views that
opened perilous prospects. The war had drained them of
strength. Bellows later wrote: "I think I crammed ten years
into the four, and shall never recover the vigour I then
squandered." [10] He asked Jenkins to resign just to speed the
closing up. On April 21, 1865, the soft-spoken J. S. Blatchford
of Boston became general secretary. This most efficient un-
dertaker laid out the winding sheets neatly and compactly.

The commission could not give up the ghost with good
conscience until it had tried to help the discharged soldier
back on his feet. The branches collected facts about persons,
back pay, bounty, and jobs, but the soldier must help him-

[10] Orville Dewey MSS. H. W. Bellows, Jan. 22, 1869, New York.

self. The incapacitated without friends and home deserved public support; one could expect many to exploit their scars for pennies. The commission denounced beggary of all kinds as corrupting. If the public could not understand this, the branches and aid societies must protect the community from its "own impulsive sympathies." To this end the second Chicago Fair, in May, 1865, raised $200,000; the central treasury, however, received proportionately little. The commission lacked funds to set up homes for the maimed and crippled. People felt small interest in their late defenders. In 1865 the lodge in Philadelphia met a steady refusal of employers to hire the one-armed and the one-legged, even for jobs that suited them.

And what of the lately furloughed, discharged, and disabled? The commissioners had to call a halt somewhere. Army officers thought the order to close the New Orleans lodge unreasonable. There were about 65,000 troops in Texas and New Mexico, while some 45,000 were stationed at various points along the Gulf of Mexico. Convalescents faced being turned out of hospitals with no friendly hand to help them afterward; this was "unjust" and "cruel." The commission apparently modified its order, and placed the soldiers' home at the disposal of the government.

The Sanitary balance came to $251,917.16 by July 1. The major administrative divisions continued with greatly reduced staffs. Consistent with order and good economy, they ended all business as soon as possible. The commission asked the branches to turn over all money to the central body by August 1, but few complied with this request. The commission limited distribution to stores on hand. By October, 1865, it was operating with skeleton crews in Washington, New York, and Louisville; it directed pension and claims agencies to receive no new business. To help in the writing of the official history the central office called for the books and papers of the various branches. The secretary general prepared to sell all wagons, horses, furniture, and other property; he asked all claimants to settle accounts.

As late as 1866 came many calls for the remaining supplies. Friends of Italian unification put in their bid; but the commission had already given its substance to the Southern and New York poor. The branches slowly wound up their affairs. The ladies of the Women's Central Association of Relief never mentioned the "last day," but thought a lot about it. On August 12, 1865, Louisa Lee Schuyler "waited to see the last cover put on the last box, the little flags taken down, and lastly the window curtains removed." Then she walked home. A few days later saw the end of the California branch. The London office closed its doors in late September, and Chicago in November. December came, and with it the last days of Washington headquarters. As one of its final acts the Sanitary Commission thanked Quartermaster General Meigs for his services; but the government never returned any official thanks.

The idea of the Sanitary Commission took the form of the American Association for the Relief of Misery on the Battlefield. Like the Red Cross, its insignia was a red Greek cross on a white background. Bellows was elected president and Charles Loring Brace was chosen domestic secretary on January 26, 1866. On the board were Agnew, Stillé, Olmsted, Gibbs, Harris, Strong, Blatchford, Van Buren, Knapp; these names showed a continuity of past aims. Added to these were W. E. Dodge, Theodore Roosevelt, Frank H. Hamilton, J. H. Cuyler, and others. Charles Bowles received the appointment of American agent in Europe. The association aimed to make the United States subscribe to the treaty of Geneva, especially to the clauses regarding the neutrality of hospitals, ambulances, doctors, and attendants. Once in 1866 and again in 1867 the secretary of state asked the secretary of war to recommend action on the proposals of the association; on both occasions the papers were returned without recommendations.

Bellows appealed to Senator E. D. Morgan of New York. America and Turkey, he pointed out, remained the two Western nations who refused to adhere to the treaty. Would the senator introduce legislation directing government policy into line with all other civilized nations? Since Bellows was going to attend a meeting of the International Committee in 1867, he hoped to avoid the mortification of having to acknowledge his country as one of the benighted. Morgan presented a resolution on March 22, 1867, instructing the Senate Committee on Foreign Affairs to inquire into the expediency of the United States becoming a party to the treaty. The committee refused to act. The session of the Fortieth Congress was late; five or six Northern states in addition to those of the South were not represented.

When the Franco-Prussian War broke out, Bellows wanted to see the machinery of the Sanitary Commission reproduced for international conflicts and their aftermaths. The American public showed little willingness to bind up the wounded of a foreign war, when Germany and France were equal to the task. In September, 1870, President Grant declined to sign the Geneva treaty, repeating the banality that America should avoid foreign entanglements. By 1871 the association had ceased to exist.

Before the end of the Civil War the Sanitary Commission had planned to send an exhibit to the Paris Fair of 1867. To check any "prejudicial interference," Bowles asked Stanton and Barnes in May, 1865, to allow the Medical Bureau to participate; but Americans in Paris suffered much chagrin, for their government refused to answer letters. Dr. Thomas W. Evans in Paris now came forward. He filled the teeth of the crowned heads of Europe—as well as his own pockets— with gold, said Bellows. Charles Bowles called him the "Foreign Historian of the Commission" because of a book Evans had written. Handsome and charming, he lived in elegance; his parlor resembled a jeweler's shop with the gifts of royalty. France gave him space on the fairground and the labor to erect a building, and Evans paid the cost of construction.

The magnificence of the Paris Fair never ceased to please Bellows. The industry of nations hummed everywhere. So skillful was the arrangement that he could see all aspects and not be distracted by the crowds. The display of the International Committee could not compare with the American museum. Other countries had bigger displays, but the commission apparently presented the most interesting and valuable exhibit. The judges awarded the commission a gold medal and twenty-five grand prizes. Representatives from other nations expressed displeasure at being ignored. The United States Sanitary Commission, they said, should have been part of the exhibition of the International Committee; but as it was, the commission took the honors for itself alone.

Since he had to leave Paris before the diploma and medal of excellence were conferred, Bellows asked Evans to accept the prizes. They were to be kept in Paris until called for. Evans sent the medal of the Grand Prix to America in October, 1867. The Imperial Commission, he said, had neglected to grant the diploma. Suspicion arose that Evans had kept the honor for himself. Evidently the dentist of kings boasted that he had founded the commission on a trip to the United States in 1861. The files do not show that the Sanitary Commission ever received the diploma. In April, 1868, Secretary Seward asked to display the gold medal—"simple, heavy, elegant"—but made no mention of the diploma. George Tempeton Strong considered the design of the medal inartistic and clumsy.

The ghost of the Sanitary Commission stayed on. Petitioners invoked it whenever scraps of leftover business called for settlement. On the evening of May 8, 1878, Dr. Bellows had laid the spirit to rest; but now and then a supplicant troubled its sleep. In 1890, Dr. Vollum of the medical corps asked the surviving commissioners to support him as a candidate for the surgeon-generalcy. At the same time rascally lobbyists in Washington tried to give them pensions. Enraged, Wolcott Gibbs exclaimed to Olmsted: "Imagine being *paid* for what we did!" [11] Agnew, Bellows, Van Buren, and other departed brethren would spin in their graves at the thought.

Clara Barton (1821–1912) preferred to work alone as nurse in the Civil War, but she cooperated well with the commission. On July, 1865, she applied for money to help obtain information about missing soldiers; she hoped that her findings would bring families and relatives arrears of pay, bounties, and pensions. Miss Barton merely duplicated the work of governmental and charitable agencies. Closer examination showed that her real motive was to gather up the incidents connected with each soldier's death and give them to surviving friends. This was Miss Barton's "inspiring thought"; the practical benefit to the survivors of dead soldiers was largely incidental.

Through her intercession the United States signed the Geneva Convention. President Chester Arthur and Secretary of State James G. Blaine secured its confirmation by the Senate in March, 1882. Bellows confessed having "ignominiously failed to get any encouragement in this measure from two administrations." The victory had passed to Miss Barton. Bellows must rest content with a Pisgah view, and die in the satisfaction that America had nothing to fear from extending mercy to victims of war.

[11] Olmsted MSS. W. Gibbs to F. L. Olmsted, July 28, 1890, Newport, R.I.

CHAPTER XIV

Conclusion

For time is like a fashionable host,
That slightly shakes his parting guest by the hand,
And with his arms outstretch'd as he would fly,
Grasps in the comer: welcome ever smiles,
And farewell goes out sighing.

William Shakespeare,
Troilus and Cressida, III, 3, 165–169

COMPARED with the British Sanitary Commission, said Bellows, the United States Sanitary Commission was born "paralytic." In the beginning the commissioners consulted the past to learn the conditions of people herded together in unhygienic quarters; but only the findings of inspectors could reveal the actual state of Union troops; and only theory hand in hand with inquiry could say what ought to be maximum security and efficiency. In direct relations with army officers the Commission tried to carry out the commands of the Medical Bureau; in conjunction with state governments and benevolent societies it worked for uniformity in plans and cooperation in action; for such extra purposes as the law did not provide, it had to find money and supplies.

Time and emergencies brought new duties, as the commission began to distribute supplies and develop the functions of relief. Before the end of 1861 it was recording the burials of those who had died in hospitals and battles. Enrolled as associate members, doctors prepared medical monographs, which reported the latest findings in medicine and surgery. But the commission refused to take on the duties and functions of government. It advised change, offered help, or temporarily accepted responsibilities not its own; it set out to work through government channels and by means of existing agencies. To supplement deficiencies formed the theoretical basis of Sanitary operations.

The commission was not a representative body, but its members were national in point of view. In its first year the board met every six weeks in Washington. Serving as a legislature, it exercised a supervisory function and set policy. With general supervision as its duty, the board defined policy and measures; secretaries and heads of bureaus carried out its will. The board met twenty-three times in four years; each session lasted four or five days. The secretary general presented them a sketch of the work based on the reports of bureau heads. The pressure and complexity of business soon forced the board to appoint a standing committee. Bellows, Van Buren, Gibbs, Strong, Agnew, and Stillé became members of this group. New York was their headquarters; they met every day, except Sunday, for four years.

The commissioners represented a broad range of interests. Bache, Cullum, Shiras, and Wood were government representatives. Bache was the head of the Coast Survey; Cullum came from the army engineers; Shiras spoke for the commissary; Wood represented the Medical Bureau. Skinner, McCagg, Binney, Stillé, and Strong were men of law. Science found spokesmen in Newberry, Gibbs, Van Buren, Agnew, Wood, Bell, Harris, Howe, and Cullum, representing geology, geography, chemistry, engineering, ophthalmology, medicine, surgery, and public health. Bache, Newberry, and Gibbs were members of the National Academy of Sciences and instrumental in its establishment. The religions of the commissioners ranged from Roman Catholicism on the right to Unitarianism on the left; Bellows, Heywood, and Clark were active churchmen. Stillé was the one student of literature, although Bellows and Strong took pride in their literary tastes. Bellows, Cullum, Bache, Stillé, Rogers, Newberry, Gibbs, Howe, and Bell either served as teachers or had taken active lead in education at some periods of their lives. No set lines kept the more vigorous minds to narrow specialization; training in one discipline did not stop them from participating in another.

The North was dominant on the commission. Bellows, Heywood, Skinner, Harris, and Newberry were born in New England but settled elsewhere; Olmsted, Gibbs, Howe, Wolcott, and Clark lived in New England most of their lives. The state of New York claimed Bellows, Strong, Agnew, Van Buren, Cullum, and Shiras; Gibbs and McCagg were born there. Philadelphia was the home of Stillé, Rogers, and Binney, although Bache and Van Buren left it for Washington and New York respectively. Bell and Heywood came from Louisville, Kentucky. Heywood chose it for his home. Bell was the only Southerner on the commission.

Executive responsibility fell on the general secretary, intermediary between the commissioner and officialdom. He supervised preparations for coming campaigns and the execution of orders; he proposed changes in plans, and coordinated the efforts of all departments; he determined the methods of relief and the best ways for transporting the wounded to hospitals; he chose inspectors, gave them instructions, and received their reports. The general secretary lived in Washington. On request he gave the government advice and submitted plans whenever necessary; he decided at what point supplementary aid should be given offering recommendations to the proper officials and asking that constructive changes be carried out. Olmsted, Jenkins, and Blatchford in succession held the post of secretary general; Newberry at Louisville carried out orders for the Western department.

In their early meetings the commissioners made no distinction between day and night. They turned their attention to a variety of subjects, and set up branch offices across the country. The commissioners served without pay. They made their own rules and regulations about the inspection of volunteers. The Sanitary life depended on the wish of the secretary of war, or it could will its own dissolution.

The commission went out to organize the enlightened element of the population. Articulate public opinion supposedly could strengthen and develop the various bureaus of the War Department. The commission stood between the government and its citizens. Through persuasion it would make officialdom more aware of what was owed the soldier and show the citizen the need for keeping military discipline, the importance of order and method, and the folly of good impulses when lacking control and direction. Stillé wrote: "If there had been no enlightened public opinion . . . and no Sanitary Commission to direct it aright, we should probably never have heard of the re-organization of the Medical Department, of improved hospital buildings and administration, of a system of thorough inspection, of humane methods of transporting the suffering, or of the numerous other methods of mitigating the horrors of war, of which we have set the example in history." [1]

The commission became "an expression of intense nationality—an instrument for conquering state lines and local prejudices." People mistakenly believed that Sanitary duties were wholly supplementary. This had been the original idea, when New Yorkers were arguing the lint and bandage question; but the founders placed sanitary or preventive service before relief. Prevention meant adding many thousands to the fighting forces, said Olmsted, who thought this aspect of Sanitary work would serve as guide in future wars.

The eyes and hands of the commission were its inspectors.

[1] C. J. Stillé, *History of the United States Sanitary Commission* (1866), p. 514.

The success of preventive service depended on these men, who were always doctors. They carefully observed all requirements of military etiquette, advocating strict discipline; they honored the surgeon for his heavy duties; they answered 180 questions about campsite, ventilation, drinking water, rations and cooking, discipline, character of officers, causes and rate of sickness, mortality among troops, and the nature of hospital accommodations. To make up for hospital shortages inspectors drew on the Sanitary stockpile. They distributed to army surgeons about 50,000 monographs on recent medical and surgical developments. An inspector enjoyed no official position or military rank. He constantly visited the hospitals in his area of duty; he took note of wants, defects, and dangers, and pointed them out to the surgeon in charge. By coaxing and urging changes for the better, the inspector frequently taught the medical officer the importance of his duties. Systematic inspection was successful from the first. Not a single inspector, said Olmsted, "was even so much as charged formally, individually, and specifically with a misuse of his privileges; with conveying information that should have been withheld; with offensive officiousness, or with undue zeal in any respect." Olmsted recalled that all injurious accusations concerned people wrongfully assumed to be in Sanitary service. The words of Generals Grant, Meade, and Rosecrans showed that the commission's inspectors were absolutely necessary to the army.[2]

Reformation of the Medical Bureau—a major act of prevention—put an end to "incompetency, inefficiency, and contracted ideas." The building of the first pavilion hospitals led the way in setting up a defense against the spread of disease. The government adopted the Sanitary models but improved them. In soldiers' homes the commission protected the public by caring for an average of two thousand a day

[2] F. L. Olmsted, *Books and Papers Relating to the Concerns of the United States Sanitary Commission in the War of the Rebellion* (1890), pp. x–xi.

over the four years of war. The commissioners planned their system of hospital steamers and railroad cars to keep state and local partialities from taking over a national concern.

During the Peninsular campaign agony by boxcar profoundly distressed Dr. Elisha Harris. To prevent further suffering he planned a hospital car, which carried patients over long routes without delay. Elastic tugs and other fixtures secured the litter beds, making a safe and easy couch; pillowed, it seemed free from jarring motions. The commission equipped the hospital car "with the outfit and attendance of a well managed hospital," and transferred it to the Medical Bureau, paying the wages of many attendants and furnishing much of the equipment and stores until the end of the war. The Harris car received a prize at the Paris Exhibition of 1867. The Prussian government adopted it but not without modifications. According to critics, the motion exhausted patients. Men with thoracic injuries suffered from the "excessive elasticity" of the berth supports.

Most people did not share in the preventive aspects of Sanitary work. They accepted the commission as distributor to the nation's soldiers, for experience taught that supplies sent to special regiments and persons were invariably lost. The commission successfully formed over seven thousand aid societies, uniting many women in a common front. They contributed supplies estimated at $15,000,000 for the four-year period. Their members seemed to work with little masculine interference. Instances of masculine cooperation were numerous; but masculine condescension annoyed serious-minded women.

Commission branches set up supply depots on a capital outlay of $50,000, plus $5,000 a month. New York, Boston, Philadelphia, Washington, Providence, Cincinnati, Cleveland, Wheeling, Louisville, Chicago, and Cairo were the main centers. In New York capable women like Miss Louisa Lee Schuyler and Miss Ellen Collins brought the Woman's

Central Association of Relief into prominence, collecting
stores from their state as well as eastern New Jersey. New
England's Women's Auxiliary with the help of Miss Abby
May made New England and even Nova Scotia, in Canada,
its tributary. Mrs. M. B. Grier and Mrs. H. Bloomfield Moore
united the efforts of some 350 aid societies in western New
Jersey, Pennsylvania, and Delaware to support the Pennsylvania branch. At Cleveland, Miss Mary Clark Brayton and
Mrs. Rouse built up northern Ohio, and drew on distant
counties in Michigan and New York. Mrs. Mary Ashton
Livermore and Mrs. Jane Hoge let the public know all that
they had done to develop the Northwestern branch at Chicago. In Michigan, Miss Valeria Campbell and, in Wisconsin,
Mrs. Henrietta Colt worked effectively but in a quieter vein.

Each branch served as a shipping agency. Here workers
sorted articles, stamped them with the Sanitary mark, and
then repacked them. If the army needed certain things it
called on either Washington or Louisville, the central distributing agencies. At these two points the commission tried
to build up reserves for great battles. Each branch submitted
inventories to the central office, where relief agents accounted
for supplies and their distribution.

Through its reserves the commission absorbed the shock
of urgent calls on the branches, easing local strains and
giving the storehouses time to build up backlogs. The way
was never free from obstacles; rising prices soon made contributions hard for poor villagers, while benevolent persons
and rival organizations later lowered the streams feeding the
Sanitary current. The system of supply proved so costly that
several thoughtful women viewed the opening of new depots
with misgivings; the money spent on rent, porters, printing,
and advertising was enough to make them "wish to do twice
the amount of work."

To the soldier went many kinds of comforts. The Sanitary
Commission forbade the sale of its stores. Generally it dis-

liked sending special boxes to certain troops, believing that its good things should be distributed evenhandedly. But in 1863 a sergeant at Falmouth, Virginia, reported the sale of fifty pairs of stockings at 33 cents a pair. When the soldiers found that the stockings contained tokens, verses, and pinballs, they wrote the knitters "pleasant notes informing them they had come by purchase into possession of their handiwork!" Knitters in Needham, Massachusetts, apparently expressed consternation. Bellows did his best to soothe them, writing:

. . . Colonel Ingalls, quartermaster of the United States Army, being destitute of stockings to cover the feet of men in the field applied for a loan (pending the arrival of stock) to our agent, who . . . as an act of humanity . . . loaned him what he wanted being 5000 pair. These stockings (being an extra issue) were sold to the soldiers in active service as they always are in such cases by the Government at the regular price [of] thirty-three cents a pair.

The stockings were to be returned when government stores arrived. The commission could not defend its agent. "We shall have to do much explaining," noted Bellows. "Such complaisance will not be allowed again." [3]

By 1862 most women of the North had been brought into direct relation with the commission. A steady flow of information and influence moved back and forth between Washington, the military outpost, and the most distant households of the United States. By correspondence the commission frequently spread news and corrected misinformation. Regular visitors at Washington headquarters were congressmen, more concerned with what the people at home were thinking than with what was happening at the front.

Branch headquarters kept in constant touch with aid societies. They did not always discuss supplies. Hurt feelings

[3] Box 709, Vol. I, p. 45. H. W. Bellows to Miss Abby M. May, March 25, 1863, New York.

called out for soothing; jealousies had to be allayed and anxieties calmed among the ignorant and impatient. Leaders were obliged to question without arousing suspicion, guessing the minor irritations of those who found difficulty in written expression. Daily they cheered the lonely and by anecdote brought the battle front to the family hearth. Prominent women had to make the small-town aid society feel that it counted; but reward came with cooperation from intelligent persons in rural areas.

Alfred J. Bloor of the Washington office disliked the bare bones of facts in Sanitary reports. The Northern woman, he said, wanted colorful writing. Reproduce battlefield and hospital experiences vividly, and she would understand Sanitary problems more fully. She wanted individual facts and instances round which to "cluster" her sympathies. The average man regarded feminine feeling as weak; but sentiment had its place, especially when women of sensibility saw to it that soldiers received proper care. In the East the *Sanitary Commission Bulletin*, whose first issue was published on November 1, 1863, was partly an effort to keep aid societies informed on general questions of relief. In the West the *Sanitary Reporter* performed the same service; but neither publication was remarkable for colorful prose.

The Sanitary Commission constantly studied new ways to encourage the flow of contributions. In 1862 it created associate memberships; these were conferred on four hundred men, leaders in their respective communities. They helped new aid societies, directed the labors of those already formed, and assisted women in working out methods and enlarging activities. Associate members were especially valuable in raising and collecting money and in the production of medical monographs. Women's councils gave and kept the commission in close touch with the public. Their first meeting was held at Washington in November, 1862. The Sanitary fairs in 1863 and 1864 spurred the drive to contribute. After the Metropolitan Fair many women in New York joined with others in Boston and Philadelphia, calling for the adoption of an embargo on costly foreign luxuries; but their campaign failed to catch the popular imagination.

Several Sanitary workers took a jaundiced view of women at the front. Here was the female braggart, she whose life was "as conducive to self-exploitation as to self-devotion." Mrs. Mary ("Mother") Bickerdyke was a case in point. This nurse of tremendous energy and conceit had the audacity of a tall story. She agreed to work under the Sanitary Commission for $50 a month; but with no idea of subordinating herself, as she used Sanitary stores for her greater glory. She made commissioners in the West uneasy; they could never be sure who was the bear and who was leading the bear. Mother Bickerdyke was "plain" and "pungent" in speech. No rules could bridle her tongue; in the heat of argument she was often "unscrupulously false." A Sanitary agent described the following scene:

. . . I informed her that we had been instructed . . . not to issue to her in bulk (and that is the wish of the surgeons, even of those who will give her many stores). I told her that I had tried to aid her in every way possible—but that she had made false statements against me frequently. She says, 'Do you mean to call me a liar?' I said 'I mean to say that you have often stated what was not true, but yet I appreciate your good work to the soldier and will do all I can to aid you.' She went off like a rockett, saying she would give me no more trouble—to which I replied, 'If you don't, I shall have accomplished all I want.' [4]

Disregarding red tape and protocol, she had no qualms about going straight to the commanding general, who generally listened to her. No labor seemed too heavy for Mother Bickerdyke; no sacrifice too much. The commission had reason for wanting to keep this singular ally within its system.

[4] Box 917, Letter 226. A. N. Read to J. S. Newberry, July 5, 1864, Acworth, Ga.

Those who stayed at home—the great unsung figures—moved the Sanitary Commission. Defeat and death made their contributions spasmodic; victories moved them to greater exertions. The commission found women immeasurably superior to men as collectors of supplies. The masculine attitude regarded money-making as real business; men viewed Sanitary work as sentimental and time-consuming. Women entered into the collection of supplies earnestly and as their particular affair. Their zeal more than made up the want of a countinghouse. By 1863, Olmsted could not find men to collect supplies. Most women contributors lived in comparative poverty; but the cash value of their gifts exceeded many times the money subscribed by the wealthy from coast to coast.

The commission often found women difficult to direct. Their zeal sometimes outran good sense, demanding trifling attentions and wasting time in chatter. Unable to understand organizational precautions, some became impudent and caustic if crossed; others could never see problems in the whole, but rushed as though panic-stricken into a sea of details. Prima donnas of benevolence caused trouble in camps. A Union general complained to a Sanitary inspector about the many "female-women" arriving with boxes of contraband goods. The Sanitary Commission never wholly succeeded in drawing the countryside and villages into its orbit. Her administrative success in the Woman's Central Association of Relief was only partial, said Louisa Lee Schuyler. She could not seem to impress on the majority of women the magnitude of their tasks. They would not examine its capabilities; they were unable to see "beyond the boxes and bales and into the hearts of the people." A love of tangible results limited their imaginations. The majority failed to think of Sanitary work as "the patriotic education of the people."

Women in their aid societies found the commission a means of making their influence felt. The country took what they offered without raising questions about their natural fitness for public service. The commission was an arena where women could work with men as equals. Nothing in history could compare with the Sanitary Commission, wrote a British admirer; for it had created a union of women, who molded and directed the "wills of the strongest."

The Sanitary Commission distributed stores by three ways of relief: general, special, and battlefield. General relief concerned the wants of men in general, field, and regimental hospitals, and of men in camp and on the march. The commission gave general relief (1) when the need was plain, (2) when the surgeon stated in writing that he had called for aid. The commission assigned an inspector to each army operating in Virginia and the Southwest; a staff of agents helped him. The commission furnished them a depot of supplies; it provided either horses and wagons or steamboats. Relief on a vast scale became the regular Sanitary business. Such was its system that the commission could successfully supply troops in Texas as well as those in Virginia; but dealing with base hospitals was easier than caring for the wants of remote field and regimental hospitals. The machinery worked successfully.

Olmsted drew up the plan for field relief on July 17, 1863. Apparently the Sanitary Commission was looking for new ways to offset the growing prestige of the Christian Commission. Dr. Douglas wrote: "We are informed from several quarters, from officers and privates this special work [of field relief], and of the influence the representatives of the Christian Commission are gaining by their attention to it. We want good working corps of this kind in the Army of the Potomac." [5]

The commission named Dr. L. H. Steiner chief inspector. In the Army of the Potomac six agents had men, horses, and

[5] L. H. Steiner MSS. J. H. Douglas to L. H. Steiner, Nov. 14, 1863, Washington, D.C.

wagons to carry out orders; they could call on a central supply base in addition to the Washington depot. The character of the agents was of first importance. Educated men volunteered for field relief at first. An applicant pledged himself to a definite period of service. The commission would not accept him "until disciplined and prepared by a subordinate service"; it drilled the agent in its principles and requirements and brought him as nearly under military service as this job would allow. The agent earned $45 a month; temporary and inexperienced help cost $100 a month, when the commission counted transportation. The agent lived in a tent, shared the soldier's life, making his headquarters with the ambulance corps for convenience. Many agents proved troublesome, but they were not the rule. The commission required that they swear loyalty to the United States. Being nonpartisan it received support from loyal Democrats and Republicans. The commission asked its agents to keep their political opinions to themselves and avoid scenes like the following:

An invited guest at a frugal and becoming table of the Agency of the Sanitary Commission at its depot in one of our chief armies was surprised at finding the prominent agent of the Commission engrossing the conversation in an excited tone as follows:

A guest unknown to me: 'General——has made himself very obnoxious at——by his arrogance and has acted like a scoundrel.'

Agent: 'An average sample of his party.' (the democratic)

The Writer: 'Ex uno disce omnes' is rather hard measure for so large a body of citizens . . . and political discussion is bad for digestion and is not good at dinner.'

Agent: 'Horatio Seymour is as much a traitor and richly deserves a halter around his throat as Jeff Davis (and a tissue of the same sort for several minutes).'

The company seemed astounded, but the speaker remained unterrified and went on.

The Writer: 'Governor Seymour is the executive of my state, my personal friend of thirty years nearly, and, I bear witness, a statesman, a patriot and a Christian.'

Agent [grows] still more violent.

The Writer: 'My friend, I came here as a guest, and I claim the privileges of a guest against personal . . . [abuse] of the Governor of my state and my friend. I am not a politician and have no party.' The company disperses.

Agent: "Things are right or wrong. I call things by their right names and claim the privilege of so doing.' [6]

Difficulties arose mainly over the large numbers of hired workers. It was not strange that some persons were ill-fitted and dishonest. If not autocratic, they were charged with lying and drinking. Their errors frequently resulted from stupidity. An agent described a lazy fellow as "so honest that he hesitates to take hold of work, fearing he may rob some other agent of his share." There were those who were plainly out for the excursion. Others were abusive and argumentative.

Early in the war Frederick Newman Knapp crawled into boxcars on a Washington siding where he fed soldiers suffering from fever. The sight of these abandoned Indiana volunteers opened his eyes to the need for special relief. Since the army had made no preparations to receive the abandoned sick, Knapp converted an empty sugar-cane factory on North Capitol Street into a rest home, where recruits received medicines, food, and care. Special relief gave board and lodging to the honorably discharged, and to the man dismissed from the general hospital. If he was subject to the delays of office and unable to procure papers and pay, special relief put him in communication with his former regiment; it even obtained the papers and pay for the convalescent too enfeebled to present his claims; it protected him from swindlers, bought his ticket, and saw that he reached home. Special relief

[6] Box 837, Vol. I, pp. 20–22. In the handwriting of J. F. Jenkins, Feb. 17, 1863, Washington, D.C.

watched the lately hospitalized to see that he did not desert; it ran houses to accommodate wives and mothers at military centers; it provided Washington hospitals with a thousand tons of fresh food. As part of special relief, the Sanitary Commission fought scurvy by planting hospital gardens at Murfreesboro, Nashville, Chattanooga, Knoxville, and New Bern.

The Sanitary Commission supported forty homes and lodges in the United States. It supplied over 1,000,000 nights' lodgings; it collected over $2,500,000 in wages for soldiers. At convalescent camps special relief distributed clothing among the needy; it gave the sick special food, furnished paper and postage, and wrote letters for patients. Special relief sent money home by draft at no cost to the soldier; it secured certificates of arrears of pay, and saw that erroneous charges were removed; it distributed reading matter; it telegraphed the friends of the very sick soldiers.

To Walt Whitman the special relief agents were among the wolves of the hospital inferno. Helpless patients turned their backs on these "hirelings," who were "well paid" but "always incompetent and disagreeable." The Sanitary Commission objected to a free lance like Whitman. Surgeons also disliked benevolence on a spree; they were too busy to act as policemen and save the patient from his friends.

. . . a . . . lady of more zeal than discretion sails into a ward full of miscellaneous patients, and . . . proceeds to a vigorous and promiscuous distribution of the well filled basket on her arm and the carriage load at the door. . . . She thrusts a pie into the hand and a green apple into the mouth of a man wasted away with diarrhoea . . . [and promises an Irishman a bottle of whisky (over which he will get drunk and abusive of his medical attendants) provided he will engage to take a Protestant Bible from her, which he does and never reads, not only because he will not but because he cannot].[7]

[7] Box 835, Vol. I, pp. 302–3, A. J. Bloor to Mrs. Emily Barnes, Oct. 20, 1862, Washington, D.C.

Prisoners became the commission's concern early in the war. For the length of the conflict the commission stationed at least one agent at Annapolis, and saw to it that the hospitals and camps there received supplies. By 1864 a Sanitary force headed by an inspector looked after Union prisoners as they arrived from Richmond. In October, 1861, it inspected living conditions for Southern sympathizers and Confederate soldiers at Fort Lafayette, Maryland, and Governor's Island, New York, respectively. In Illinois, Camp Douglas, for Southern prisoners, was "a disgusting hole," noted Bellows on July 1, 1862. The commissioners did not forget that the Confederate was also American. If the army sent prisoners to a Sanitary soldiers' home for lodging, the agent gave them rations and a quilt. After the great battles it helped nurse and care for Southern wounded in Union hands.

News of Confederate treatment of Union prisoners often reached Washington and New York through Sanitary headquarters. The Confederacy set aside Libby Prison and Belle Isle, where it cared for prisoners as well as its slender means allowed. Paroled soldiers denied reports of deliberate starvation and unkindness; Sanitary stores steadily reached Richmond, they said, and helped improve the appearance and morale of prisoners. The commission gave relief to returning Union prisoners on flag-of-truce boats. In the fall of 1863 the Sanitary agent at Norfolk managed this work with difficulty, until the army allowed him on the boat. By March, 1864, agents were sailing with paroled soldiers from Fortress Monroe to Annapolis. The commission later extended the same service to Union men released from Charleston and Savannah.

The return of the sick and emaciated in 1864 added vindictiveness to the prisoner problem. At Libby Prison a Union general asked for food but nothing bearing the Sanitary label. Either the rebels stole such articles or prisoners sold them. In March the Confederacy refused to receive anything further from the commission, but agreed to deliver packages from person to person. By October the commission had presented the public with the *Narrative of Privations and Sufferings of United States Officers and Soldiers while Prisoners of War in the Hands of the Rebel Authorities.* This pamphlet tried to prove that Confederate policy deliberately starved, froze, and killed by degrees the men it dared not "butcher outright." General Grant sent copies to General Lee. The Confederacy consequently invited the commissioners to investigate the camps, but their special committee postponed their Richmond journey because of military operations. The commission distributed thousands of copies of the report in Continental Europe and Great Britain. This diatribe ultimately placed it in the shadow of a false position. The commissioners lost their sense of fairness and objectivity, forgetting the suffering of Confederates in Northern camps.

In the autumn of 1862 the commission organized a group of clergymen as hospital visitors. They emphasized the individual; they would relieve his suffering from neglect, destitution, and pain whether in barracks, hospital, or prison. This corps struck a religious note, raising up the mind that had fallen on dejection. According to Dr. Newberry, hospital visitors went to the important hospitals of the West long before the Christian Commission came on the scene.

The constant switching of patients from one hospital to another baffled the civilian and the military. To help families and officers keep track of soldiers the commission established a hospital directory on September 16, 1862. It recorded over 600,000 names. Agents at the battlefield learned the wounded's identity, and notified his friends and relations. Those who asked about the missing gave his name, rank, and regiment, and where he had last been heard from. With these clues the agents could follow him through the directory. The commission answered 70 per cent of all such inquiries and

provided daily registrations and periodical bulletins of patients' names and conditions. To Washington, Louisville,
Philadelphia, and New York came returns from 233 military
hospitals. The directory cost $200,000. It gave order to a
mass of reports, cutting down hours of investigation to a
minute. The War Department adopted this system of hospital returns; the commission even prepared the blank forms
of government reports. The hospital directory would be a
necessary part of future warfare, thought the commissioners.
It enabled army officers to keep track of missing men; it
showed the heirs of dead soldiers how to get bounty, pay,
and pensions; it was the means of keeping families together.
Here could be seen at a glance the medical history of each
regiment. The hospital directory provided a unique collection
of medical statistics. In the opinion of many it was the most
humane of Sanitary successes; its force was not seen but felt.

The Sanitary Commission undertook the special inspection
of hospitals. With Dr. Henry G. Clark of Boston as inspector
in chief, it organized sixty physicians and surgeons. They
visited all general hospitals, their report covering 2,500 folio
pages by May, 1863. The doctors inquired into practical
management; their findings were apparently of value to Surgeon General Hammond. The army hospital system reached
an excellence not attained by any other country; but the
commissioners lamented that civilians did not build comparable hospitals. Bellows noted: "It is almost impossible
to find now in civil use what is known abroad with honor
and admiration as 'the American hospital' and this is a
disgrace to our intelligence and humanity (1877)." [8]

To the sanitarian the Bureau of Vital Statistics was of
permanent value; it was begun by Olmsted. The commission
collected and tabulated the returns of inspections. Camp inspections numbered 1,482; these represented about 870
regiments. The body of facts was of interest to students of

[8] *Johnson's New Universal Cyclopaedia* (1877), Vol. IV, Pt. I, p. 79.

anthropology, life insurance, and vital statistics. Printed reports had made the Sanitary Commission known to the scientific world; they had probably "added more new and valuable facts to the science of vital statistics than any other contribution at any time." [9]

The writing of the history seemed like one of the most difficult Sanitary tasks. It took place during windup of affairs, when new interests were diverting some of the writers. Agnew and Strong took exception to Knapp's story of special relief, which was never completed. Dr. Warriner never finished his report on the supply service, but the public received Stillé's *History of the United States Sanitary Commission* in 1866. Reviewers praised its lucidity, interest, and comprehensive scope. Bellows wrote the chapter on California; Strong contributed the one on finance. Not until 1871 did Newberry publish his report on the commission's work in the Mississippi Valley.

Up to May 1, 1866, the people had given the Sanitary Commission $4,962,014.26. The branches raised at least $2,000,000 more, but this they spent for their own needs. By the end of the war railroad and express companies were carrying supplies for nothing; telegraph companies were giving free communication. The aggregate of public services came to an estimated $25,000,000. Members of the commission drew no salaries; they were refunded their traveling expenses, nothing more. At some periods the Sanitary roster listed as many as 500 workers; the presence of doctors, cooks, and teamsters meant that its expenses were enormous. Those who believed in good deeds as their own reward were inclined to carp; but salaried men proved steadier and better disciplined than volunteers. After a great battle the commission accepted help from volunteers, when inexperienced hands seemed better than none. It did not try to arouse emotions and work on popular sympathies, but emphasized

[9] *Ibid.*

the constructive nature and economic value of Sanitary accomplishments.

Readers in Europe and America believed in the Sanitary success. To Joseph Mazzini, in 1865, the commission was the fitting means to transmit his romantic tribute to the United States. W. E. Gladstone, the British statesman, thought its operations "the most remarkable of all the characteristic circumstances of that unparalleled struggle." John Stuart Mill, the English philosopher, called it unique, a great "work of usefulness extemporized by the spontaneous self-devotion and organizing genius of a people, altogether independent of government."

But the organization never attained its full stature, said the commissioners. The indifference of the Lincoln administration was chilling, while the secretary of war suggested the black presence in the Chapel Perilous. He could not put out their taper, but did his best to hide its beams. Stanton left no detailed explanation of his detestation. According to Bellows, the secretary hated the commission "because it unwittingly crossed him in certain personal matters and hated it none the less because he did not dare to touch it, when he would gladly have crushed it under his foot." Hammond's "enlightened friendliness" ended when Stanton had him cashiered. In Surgeon General Barnes the secretary found one who was "jealous, uncooperative, and slyly injurious" to Sanitary plans.

The commission stood ready to command the best minds of science, said Bellows. Had it been permitted to pursue its scientific and advisory work, the fifth wheel would have furnished the Medical Bureau with the best results of hygiene and sanitary science. Allied, government and commission could have done "five times as much good" as the commission had accomplished in supply; but Stanton's "insane jealousy" made them competitors and rivals for the care of soldiers. The commissioners bore their vexations in silence, refusing in time of war to attack a member of the administration for fear of aiding the enemy.

Stanton apparently ignored and excluded the commission as much as possible. Elisha Harris implied that the secretary knew little of sanitary matters; he was reported as asking, "Who was the Lord [Sidney] Herbert we hear so much praised?" [10] This question called for much raising of eyebrows among sanitarians; but worse than his smattering of ignorance was the way Stanton sniped at the commission. Both the hospital directory and statistical bureau depended on the adjutant general's muster rolls, which contained the consolidated abstracts of monthly returns concerning losses and gains as well as the physical descriptions of soldiers. In March, May, and September, 1862, the commission had published its findings; E. B. Elliott incorporated them in his address to the Berlin Statistical Congress in 1863. The government viewed this work with favor.

For more than a month after Gettysburg and Vicksburg the commission was burdened with work. On August 22, 1863, the adjutant general temporarily barred agents from his office and refused to issue them passes to the army. Just before the spring campaign of 1864 the secretary of war stopped all passes to the Army of the Potomac. The Sanitary workers felt that the order ought not to have applied to relief, which was in danger of being crippled. The wounded soldier would be the only sufferer. When the commission finally got its stores through, they were too late for immediate benefit at the battles of the Wilderness and Spotsylvania. Dr. Steiner, chief inspector of the Sanitary Commission, wrote: "Truly the Commission has not the privileges it should have on the field. We are laboring under difficulties of the worst possible kind." [11]

Numerous complaints reached Sanitary headquarters con-

[10] Bellows MSS. E. Harris to H. W. Bellows, Jan. 12, 1866, New York.
[11] L. H. Steiner, *Diary* (MSS.), April 25, 1864.

cerning military hospitals. In November, 1864, the commission asked if its own inspectors could investigate them, but the secretary of war turned down the request; the act of 1862, he said, made Sanitary inspections unnecessary. He again denied the commission the right to use the records of the adjutant general and the Medical Bureau; this brought to an end the work on the hospital directory. In October, 1865, the War Department refused Sanitary statisticians access to government records. The commission had abused its privileges, said the adjutant general, and refused to revoke the order. Further research meant visits to state capitals, an expensive and laborious process. As late as 1867, Bellows tried to recapture the commission's lost privileges but all in vain.

The Sanitary Commission expected nothing from Surgeon General Barnes. He refused Dr. Benjamin Apthorp Gould * permission to take measurements of Confederate and Indian prisoners, calling it a work of doubtful scientific value. In June, 1865, Dr. Barnes warned surgeons against answering circulars and inquiries for the commission's medical report. Surgeons in the West quietly disobeyed their chief. They could not reveal hospital records, but they made up for this loss by direct observations. To many doctors the surgeon general seemed a petty tyrant who would monopolize the common property of science. But let Dr. Barnes turn into a dragon and sit on his hoard of paper, for he could do the commissioners no harm; they would behave as though he was their best friend and the Medical Bureau "a promoter of science and human improvement."

Could the commission prove Stanton's overt hostility? They were fully aware of this difficulty. When preparing the official history, C. J. Stillé visited Solicitor Whiting of the War Department. Stillé noted: "His account of the animus of the Secretary was very interesting and . . . confirmatory of all that we have been forced to believe hitherto. . . . I

am still unable to place my finger upon telling facts which
will prove in what special cases this animus was exerted to
our manifest injury." [12] The commissioners had no grievances
against the adjutant general; his manner had always been
frank and agreeable, and he had never complained about the
agents who visited his office. When he set impediments before their work, commissioners saw the hand of Stanton. To
regain their privileges they had to apply to the secretary of
war and even the president. Lincoln generally held aloof
from these contentions, for he seemed to think the secretary
of war should be master in his own house; but whenever the
president was "forced in," said Olmsted, he prevented some
"great injustice." Unfortunately Olmsted did not state the
occasions when Lincoln played peacemaker. Stanton, moreover, struck hardest after Olmsted left the commission.

The American people would never forget their organization, thought the Commissioners. But twenty years after the
conflict Stillé painfully admitted that his history made no
impression and that Americans had all but forgotten Sanitary
science and humanity. Now, the commission's story was only
one facet of the Civil War. To actors in the Sanitary drama
nothing could have been more exciting than their own roles;
but crowds in the main tent relished the sight of generals
putting their heads into the mouths of lions, while high over-
head Lincoln walked his precarious slack-rope. American
histories generally mentioned the commission in a few lines
or a footnote. That the organization influenced the birth of
the Red Cross has apparently meant little to the public.
Their imaginations have seized on Florence Nightingale and
Clara Barton; they have made solo parts of two inner voices
of the full orchestra. The Red Cross promised more extensive
operations than could be performed by a group organized for
inquiry, advice, and supply. The Sanitary Commission, more-

[12] Bellows MSS. C. J. Stillé to H. W. Bellows, Feb. 20, 1866, Washington,
D.C.

over, was not alone in its charity; innumerable agencies and persons succored the fallen on the American battlefield.

The commission was also an aspect of the larger public health picture. It made many aware of the benefits of hygiene. Military health problems gave sanitarians a chance to carry out their theories and substantiate their claims. Dr. Elisha Harris, a leader in the Sanitary Conventions before the war, became the secretary of the new American Public Health Association in 1872. After the conflict influential citizens connected with the Sanitary Commission demanded improvements in hospitals and the training of nurses. The commission stressed the immediate and practical; it had no concern with research in pure science. Victories in bacteriology and the dramatic conquest of epidemic disease after the seventies understandably eclipsed the commission's achievements. Today the sanitary idea does not command such great emphasis as formerly.

Members of the Sanitary Commission opposed anything that compromised its ideas of freedom and union. They banded together in Union League clubs. The *Nation* and the *Army and Navy Journal* expressed their point of view, while Bellows' *Unconditional Loyalty* and Stillé's *How a Free People Conduct a Long War* set out to kill defeatism. Foreign governments apparently valued Sanitary information on surgery, hygiene, and vital statistics; but Sanitary methods had little bearing in Europe. European and American societies were too unlike. European wars were generally short and in thickly settled areas, while the American Civil War ranged over uninhabited regions; but there were men who thought the Sanitary Commission "one of the chief stimulants to the study and admiration of political liberty and social equality" abroad.

To confirm the national feeling and reassert the people's confidence in themselves became cues to Sanitary action. Elected authorities were obliged to secure certain results;

but the commission would have Americans rely on extra-legal organizations to ensure responsible government. The commissioners stood ready to sacrifice their freedom for the duration of the crisis; but that government was still best that governed least, and peace must find the rights of citizens restored. Let the American forget the necessary evil of military life; he was strongest in his "popular, home-bred, and individual life" of peace.

The men and women who had faith in the Sanitary Commission worked for the oneness of humanity; they would pull down the barriers of prejudices and set aside harmful distinctions. Confidently they applied their ideas to the care of armies. "What chloroform is to surgery, humanity is to war," wrote Dr. Bellows to Henri Dunant. "It does not stop bloodshed, but it spares needless suffering." During the past ninety years the nations have benefited from the Geneva Convention of 1864; but the advantages they won have been more than offset by modern methods of dealing death and destruction. Has the optimism of men like Bellows and Dunant gone down to defeat? The humanitarian in the middle of our twentieth century cries out: "There cannot, at the present time, be any question of 'humanizing' war." [13]

Friends and critics of the Sanitary Commission were one in the preservation of liberty. At this point the present links hands with the past, and Walt Whitman's words become ours; for the world is struggling through the murk and longs to see

> . . . Freedom's features, fresh, undimm'd look forth—
> the same immortal face looks forth;
> (A glimpse as of thy mother's face, Columbia,
> A flash significant as of a sword,
> Beaming towards thee.)

[13] Albert Schweitzer, "The Problem of Peace in the World Today," *Christian Register*, Vol. 134, No. 1 (January, 1955), p. 12.

Biographical Notes

Cornelius Rea Agnew (1830–88), born in New York, received his M.D. from the College of Physicians and Surgeons in 1852. After a period of study abroad he was appointed surgeon at New York's Eye and Ear Infirmary in 1856. State surgeon general in 1858, Agnew directed the New York State Hospital for Volunteers before the outbreak of war. Along with Drs. Gibbs and Van Buren he helped establish the Judiciary Square Hospital, the model of pavilion hospitals. In the Sanitary Commission his opinion carried weight, although Olmsted thought little of Agnew's executive ability. In New York clinics and hospitals he advanced specialization in eye, ear, nose, and throat, inventing new instruments and operative procedures. From 1869 until his death Agnew taught classes in diseases of the eye and ear at the College of Physicians and Surgeons.

Godfrey Aigner, a German physician, had had experience in European military camps. He came to the Sanitary Commission from the New York City Dispensary to take the post at Cairo. Spring campaigns in 1862 brought a swamp of work as the sick poured into military hospitals. Aigner's single efforts were "too lilliputian" to produce satisfactory results. Chicago credited him with having first suggested floating hospitals; these were to keep pace with gunboats on the Southern waters.

Alexander Dallas Bache (1806–67), a native of Philadelphia, was graduated from West Point in 1825. He resigned from the army in 1828, when he accepted the professorship of natural philosophy and chemistry at the University of Pennsylvania. As president of Girard College (1836) he was sent abroad for two years to study educational institutions. His report, *Education in Europe* (1839), furnished the basis for reorganizing Philadelphia's public school system. In 1843 Bache was appointed superintendent of the United States Coast Survey, a position held until his death; in 1846 he was chosen regent of the Smithsonian

317

Institution. Having helped found the National Academy of Sciences (1863), he was elected its first president.

Known and honored in Europe, Bache served as adviser to Lincoln, Cameron, and Stanton during the Civil War. As vice-president of the Sanitary Commission he lent that body the prestige of his reputation. He was well liked by his colleagues, even though they sometimes felt that his official position kept him from assuming a bold uncompromising front.

His marriage to Miss Nancy Clarke Fowler of Newport (1828) was childless; but Bache and his wife seemed to live for each other, their hospitality free from the tyranny of etiquette. In manner Bache was genial and childlike; but his was the simplicity of great achievement.

In Surgeon General *Joseph K. Barnes* (1817–83) the commissioners met a bold antagonist. Barnes was the son of the Hon. Joseph Barnes, judge of the District Court of Philadelphia. The initial "K" did not represent a second name but stood complete in itself. Barnes had received his education at the Round Hill School of Northampton, Mass.; he later withdrew from Harvard because of illness. The University of Pennsylvania conferred an M.D. on him (1836). He became an assistant surgeon in the army (June 14, 1840) and served under Generals Taylor and Scott in the Mexican War. In the Civil War he was medical director for Generals David Hunter and Fitz-Greene Halleck successively in the Western Department. His period of duty in Washington began in May, 1862. Friendship with Stanton began at this time, when his rise became rapid and assured. Barnes received his colonelcy on Aug. 10, 1863; he took over direction of medical affairs on Sept. 3. The Senate confirmed his appointment as surgeon general on Aug. 22, 1864. Barnes became brevet major general on March 13, 1865. He was noted for his quickness of perception and soundness of judgment. Numerous learned bodies abroad counted him an honorary member. Described as "a man of fine physique and agreeable personality," he attended the two murdered presidents.

Theodore S. Bell (1807–84) of Kentucky worked fourteen hours a day as a tailor's apprentice, while his mother taught him history and science at night. Hearing Alexander Campbell preach, he became ambitious for larger usefulness. In leisure hours he studied medicine and began practice in Louisville. The University of Louisville appointed him professor of medicine and hygiene at the same time that he became editor of the Louisville *Medical Journal*. Bell emerged as a civic leader in founding many enterprises of a humanitarian and cultural character. Bell, said Strong, was "a kindly, cultivated, intelligent person of white-hot, steel-edged loyalty." Because of distances and the press of business he attended few meetings of the Sanitary Commission.

Henry Whitney Bellows (1814–82) was born in Boston, Mass., and was educated at the Round Hill School in Northampton and at Harvard. Before becoming a minister he taught school at Cooperstown, N.Y., and tutored the son of a wealthy planter in Louisiana. Not until he had spent a year preaching in Mobile did Southern life reveal its attractions. There was flattery in the service of a slave, but sensations of mastery did not lull Bellows into forgetting that the Negro had a soul. His dislike of abolition was sweeping, yet his mild criticism of slavery found no receptive audience in the South.

Ordained in 1837, Bellows quickly won recognition from older Unitarian leaders. In his twenty-fourth year came an invitation to take charge of the First Unitarian Church of New York. Bellows, equal to this heavy task, soon became a leader in the civic, social, and religious life of the city, helping to found the Century, Union League, and Harvard clubs. His fluent conversation won him a circle of admirers; his preaching, noted for its element of surprise, championed the heretical, the unpopular, and the misunderstood. He found time to publish the *Christian Inquirer* (1847), which finally merged with the *Christian Register*, and aid Antioch College at Yellow Springs, Ohio.

Bellows was best when inspiring others to work for a common purpose. East and West saw the growth of his reputation, as he lectured to large audiences on a variety of subjects. His concern with European advances in sociology and sanitation brought a response from New York advocates of sanitary improvement. Neither the work of Florence Nightingale at Scutari nor the reports of the English and French Sanitary Commissions in the Crimean War escaped his notice. Directing the United States

Sanitary Commission fitted Bellows as a leader for reorganizing the Unitarian society; he was responsible for founding the National Conferences of Unitarian Churches (1865) and the Ministers' Institute (1866). Editor of the *Christian Examiner* from 1866 to 1877, Bellows also became an enthusiastic supporter of Civil Service Reform.

Bellows did not lack critics. Some thought him a tangle of contradictions; others saw a monument of conceit and egotism, whose happiness was to see his name in the papers; others thought he treated people as though they were pawns in his own game of chess. But the captious never denied that Bellows was genuinely public-spirited, wise, and self-sacrificing.

In 1839, Bellows married Eliza Nevins Townsend, who died in 1869. In 1874 he married Anna Huidekoper Peabody.

The bare bones of biography tell little about Bellows. In his letters, however, he set himself down freely. As a boy he dreaded entering the world, only to discover later a greater kindness than he had anticipated. Success paid him more than he had ever expected. When the Civil War divided the country, Bellows found himself "in the very thick of care and at the very acme of . . . ambition with a tolerably calm and sober feeling."

Bellows girded himself in the armor of optimism, forged in the belief of "a divine ordering which achieves its plans by ways most seemingly opposed to the direct path . . ." Tempered in the conviction of human progress, it was riveted together by faith in the value of experiment and continual experience. He wrote his son Russell: "I hope I shall never join the class who think all wisdom dwells in the past or is the fruit of experience. The native fruit of the soil . . . in the successive generations of humanity is very sweet and precious to my palate." [1] Bellows readily poured his energies into socially useful crusades. His wife protested when he devoted himself to those who were "grasping, inconsiderate, and disposed to lean"; but Bellows believed he had no right to harden himself against human anguish. Responsibility did not crush him. "It always seemed to me that every man was responsible up to the fullest extent of his knowledge, light, and

[1] Bellows MSS. H. W. Bellows to Russell Bellows, June 23, 1861, New York.

ability and not a whit beyond." His was a simple boast of grand proportions: "I don't know that I have *one* wasted talent or *one* unemployed energy." [2]

Bellows took pride in himself as a judge of character. The commissioners quickly learned to know his qualities. Admitting he was not a good businessman, he gave up trying to pose. To Frederick Law Olmsted he confessed: "I wear the mask of one with some poor attempt at enacting the character in all this recent Sanitary Commission life of mine, but it is a very shameful hypocrisy on my part, and you and every other commissioner must have seen how constantly the mask is dropped, and how little of that sort it covers." Bellows acknowledged his inconsistencies and contradictions, claiming them as privileges of office. He begged Olmsted's indulgence: "You must allow me to prance around now and then on my official horse and wink at folly without publicly laughing." [3]

Bellows liked the useful. Christ to him was "the practical life-giver in the moral wilderness." Corrosive intellectuality alienated him; concern with ideas for themselves had no niche in his view of practicality. The language of science and the names of scientists struck him as out of place. Preaching should embody the results of highest learning, he said, but the terminologies of schollarship should be kept in the study. This common-sense conservative revolted at those transcendentalists who tried to pour the meaning of love into old bottles of guilt. Any "attempt to swim against the current of the great instincts and experiences of our universal humanity" irritated him.

Bellows knew the chilling effect of critical audiences. In 1862 he suffered three failures in public speaking at Brooklyn, Newark, and Philadelphia. He drew slight crowds but loud criticism. Some people thought him too casual in treating battlefield horrors; others believed him too flippant regarding the relations of the sexes. Returning from Manassas in March, 1862, Bellows exhibited "with great tenderness" a skull and a human bone to a group of spectators. He was startled that many were offended.

[2] Bellows MSS. H. W. Bellows to Mrs. H. W. Bellows, June 27, 1862, Cincinnati, Ohio.
[3] Box 746. H. W. Bellows to F. L. Olmsted, Oct. 8, 1862, New York.

Could he be growing emotionally calloused? To Mrs. Elizabeth Hamilton Schuyler he wrote: "It is very instructive to me that I, a tender chickenhearted creature, fastidious and easily offended by violations of taste, should be playing the *ghoul* and be wounding other sensibilities." [4]

As Bellows hated to offend, so was he quick to forgive. With the end of the war he readily forgave the South. In the last days of 1865 he felt as though the entire conflict had been a hurricane. Bellows could not cry revenge, seeing the South in ruins; but the victor's crude materialism distressed him. Cribbed in spirit was American life with its prosperity, comfort, luxury; cabined its intellectual range; confined to getting and gaining the United States in day-to-day existence laid waste its powers. American life had become "one of the most poverty stricken in the world," thought Bellows.

The nineteenth century was writing its gospel with figures that bore witness to the growth of industry, railroads, population, and agriculture. But Bellows did not consult these. He looked across democratic vistas; people were forgetting to be human. This was poverty—worse, it was sterility. Bellows protested: "The social, the religious, the domestic instinct of happiness, the knowledge how to live with and derive pleasure from other human beings seems to me sadly lost and wholly undeveloped." His countrymen led lives of mutual alienation. Pride, greed, and self-reliance were turning the home into a fortress. Sealed off from one another, families seemed selfish and hard. American village life offended both taste and religious principles, said Bellows. Its members were apathetic to "divine hopes and affections"; they were void of "all playfulness and all susceptibility on the side of worship." Bellows wanted something simple and human. Must wizened democracy peer out suspiciously from behind slats? he wondered. Must democratic individuality devastate all generous impulses? Bellows wrote: "I would sooner live in an ignorant Swiss canton where the peasants worshipped the Virgin and danced round the May Pole with some human dependence on each other and some awe-struck sense of God than in one of these intelligent

[4] Bellows MSS. H. W. Bellows to Mrs. E. H. Schuyler, April 5, 1862, New York.

villages where every individual reads, writes, cyphers, and is *bound up in his own skin* with as little feeling for his neighbor as a book has for its fellows on the same shelf." [5]

His family and friends considered Bellows a man of wit. He was devoted to his wife, and wrote letters which carried her into the current of all his concerns. In a lively style he described important people so that she might share his life more fully; but Mrs. Bellows became increasingly absorbed in herself and her children. In contrast, her husband rarely found himself alone. On July 15, 1866, he noted a "rare and not unprofitable season" of ten days of solitude. This was long enough. Bellows wrote: "It is always a strange and unnatural state for me, except when engaged in actual and set work. I think and meditate best within easy reach of those I love." [6]

Between himself and his son Russell he would admit no impediments. The father asked: "Is it possible anything could shut us up one to the other, or that anything could drive us to others sooner than to each other for sympathy, consolation, or advice in trouble or doubt?" [7] To perfect their accord Bellows gave freely of advice and pointed out weaknesses in the young man's character. His positive counsel stressed heroism and perfection. This Polonius cautioned against sowing wild oats, headaches, social vanities, and scholastic mediocrity. Music was a "good playmate but a bad business" and a cause of sin. He explained: "A musical career in this country in the earnest times for which we are preparing is a frivolous and degenerate life." [8] He urged Russell to kill all interest in it.

His daughter Anna complained of unpopularity at school. Her father returned difficult advice. Enjoy the popularity of others, he said, and remember that he in his youth had also met the obstacle of not being generally liked. "I thought it hard," he wrote in recollection of unhappy years. "But I have had my full share of sympathy, applause, and importance." [9] Distressed

[5] Bellows MSS. H. W. Bellows to Mrs. H. W. Bellows, July 9, 1865, New York.
[6] Bellows MSS. H. W. Bellows to C. A. Bartol, July 15, 1866, New York.
[7] Bellows MSS. H. W. Bellows to R. Bellows, April 14, 1861, New York.
[8] Bellows MSS. H. W. Bellows to R. Bellows, Oct. 20, 1862, New York.
[9] Bellows MSS. H. W. Bellows to Anna Bellows, June 22, 1862, New York.

about questions of theological belief, Anna asked what to believe. Here Bellows failed as her father and spiritual mentor. His words might just as easily have been turned against himself, when he wrote: "Correct views in regard to the disputed doctrines of theology . . . are neither possible nor important at your age." [10]

Bellows was strongly domestic. In spite of frequent absences, he loved his home. Bellows told his wife: "I am away so often that I suppose you think me hardened! But I am like hemp that grows softer the more it is beaten, not like gold that grows harder under the hammer." [11] Club life appealed to him, and Bellows belonged to the Century, Union League, and Harvard clubs. It was a pleasure to entertain men of talent in lavish fashion.

In literature Bellows was quick to appreciate individuality of style. He objected to criticism where the writer suffered for not fitting into an aesthetic bed of Procrustes. He did not know how to listen to music; each composer called up pictures, history, or social commentary. Mozart evoked scenes of playful kittens; Beethoven suggested prisoners shrieking in German dungeons; Mendelssohn brought Florence Nightingale's mission to Crimea. The last-named composer meant more to Bellows. He observed: "Mendelssohn seems to consecrate modern life as in the Wedding March, and I think will be the musical representative of our era a hundred years ahead." Yet Bellows could not understand music. Art had to be literal, direct, and immediate; music was too subtle an expression. He could never get over Platonic echoes: "[Music] is more sensuous in that it calls less on the soul to appreciate it, and it is incapable of ideas, being all feeling." [13] Paintings gave him experiences which in music he could not find, for they opened up unusual moral perspectives and ever a pleasant release from duties.

Bellows had troops of appreciative friends. Cyrus A. Bartol might have understood and valued his predilections and abilities best. He was familiar with the humanitarian emphasis of men like Bellows, and knew his friend preferred the church militant

[10] Bellows MSS. H. W. Bellows to Mrs. H. W. Bellows, March 25, 1862.
[11] Bellows MSS. H. W. Bellows to Mrs. H. W. Bellows, Jan. 25, 1863, New York.
[12] Bellows MSS. H. W. Bellows to R. Bellows, April 3, 1861, New York.
[13] Bellows MSS. H. W. Bellows to R. Bellows, March 21, 1861, not stated.

to the way of contemplation. The Sanitary Commission was an expression of his bent "for practical accomplishment, for inspiring men to be . . . cooperators for promoting a sort of contagion of humanity and putting Christian ideas into the swiftest and strongest gear." [14]

Mrs. Bellows thought he worked far too hard. If he was not running round, he was writing when he should have been resting. She confided in Russell: "I think Father isn't comfortable without a pen in his hand. I am sometimes afraid he will lose the power of resting his mind." [15] In April, 1862, she found life almost unbearable. Her husband was rushing back and forth between New York and Washington about the bill to reform the Medical Bureau, and came home too tired to talk. All she could learn came from scraps of information he would let fall or from letters he would leave carelessly around the house. Mrs. Bellows was sure her husband did a lot of good, but his absences left little home life. She could not help blurting out: "Ever since Kossuth's time you have been on a sort of rampage—flying around . . . like a top!" [16] Yet she clung to his buoyancy and serenity of mind which easily ignored minor irritations.

Horatio Stebbins, the Unitarian minister of Portland, Maine, drew on the optimism of Bellows for comfort. Thomas Starr King, an indefatigable Union worker in California, spoke of him as "one of the Titans." But Bellows had acid critics. To Katherine Prescott Wormeley he was a monument of self-praise. Mrs. Hamilton Fish dismissed him as avid for power. George Templeton Strong, on the other hand, took a more balanced view of Bellows. Because his delivery was clear, forceful, and compact, Bellows could command the attention of his audience for as long as an hour and a half. His speech was easy, fluent, and colloquial; with his sympathetic, effortless manner he could occasionally make an "immensely telling point." Strong honored Bellows for his usefulness and efficiency. What disgusted Miss Wormeley and Mrs.

[14] Bellows MSS. C. A. Bartol to H. W. Bellows, Aug. 7, 1861, not stated.
[15] Bellows MSS. Mrs. H. W. Bellows to R. Bellows, Oct. 20, 1861, New York.
[16] Bellows MSS. Mrs. H. W. Bellows to H. W. Bellows, Aug. 4, 1862, Walpole, N.H.

Fish formed part of the human animal for the treasurer of the Sanitary Commission. Bellows the man was a compound of the "unselfish, farsighted and wise" with the conceit of a publicity seeker; but his excellences were fortunately stronger than his weaknesses. In Strong's opinion sleep was the best time to catch the essential Bellows, who snored "in a vehement, spasmodic, passionate *Sturm und Drang* Byronic way, characteristic of the Romantic School."

Horace Binney, Jr. (1809–70), of Philadelphia, a graduate from Yale in 1828, studied law with his famous father, Horace Binney. He was admitted to the bar (1831) and practiced in Philadelphia, taking active interest in municipal politics. He served as president of the Philadelphia branch of the Sanitary Commission. A founder of the Philadelphia Union League, he was its president the year he died.

Alfred Janson Bloor (1828–1917) had a reputation at home and abroad as an architect, holding many offices and honors in his lifetime. Not only did he write extensively in architecture but also showed an active interest in poetry. In July, 1861, he entered the commission as assistant secretary. He furnished various branches and affiliated societies with information, drew up periodical reports, and superintended the Washington supply depot. His office involved the greeting and instruction of strangers; it called for the superintendence of offices, premises, employees, as well as the publication of documents. These were some of Bloor's routine duties; his special duties were more numerous. No one doubted his ability and loyalty, but he seemed morbidly jealous for spoken recognition of the Sanitary Commision and praise of himself. In a hysterical outburst he charged that an evil influence in the executive committee was working against him. Failure to retract the accusation resulted in his dismissal in September, 1864. A "talking person," he had grand ideas of himself as a prose stylist.

Of *William B.* and *Charles S. P. Bowles* little is known. William came to the commission with excellent recommendations. He organized the papers and accounts of special relief, and attended the wounded at Chancellorsville; after the war he became one of the managers of the commission's Lincoln Home for disabled veterans in New York. Charles had business ability. There were businessmen who believed in him, although impetuosity had early placed him "under a cloud." While he worked for the commission, Charles enjoyed his day in the sun, winning everyone's confidence in Europe, except that of the wealthy American bankers, whom he called "Copperheads." The Bowles Brothers Banking House had branches in Paris, London, Geneva, Nice, Boston, and New York. The European branches bought and stored objects for travelers; the firm also opened reading rooms for the entertainment of travelers. In December, 1872, the banking house failed through carelessness and dishonesty. According to the New York *Times* (Dec. 20, 1872), Charles had signed his name to letters "in which he negotiated the surreptitious pawning of the property of confiding clients"; this fact made his part "in the disreputable practices of Bowles Brothers unpleasantly plain." Arrested in Springfield, Mass., Charles characterized the frauds as "merely the grave faults of his extended management." Charles had "marvellous parts of speech," but George Strong could never trust "so prodigious a blower."

Thomas March Clark (1812–1903), a native of Newburyport, Mass., was graduated from Yale (1831) and later from the Princeton Theological Seminary. He changed to Episcopalianism and became rector of Grace Church in Boston in 1836. His election to the bishopric of Rhode Island came in 1854, an office he was to hold for forty-nine years. In 1899 he was named presiding bishop of the Episcopal Church in the United States.

Clark's simplicity and his sane and balanced judgments won him large followings. Not only was he a member of the Sanitary Commission, but he also served as occasional adviser to Lincoln. A broad churchman, he wrote extensively on religion and morals. His wit, said G. T. Strong, was "dry and caustic." It was said that he imitated the Saviour in the line: ". . . the Son of Man came eating and drinking."

George Washington Cullum (1809–92), a New Yorker, was graduated from West Point in 1833. Commissioned in the Engineer Corps, he helped construct the fortifications of Boston, New York, Newport, New London, Annapolis, and Charleston, and at West Point participated in setting up the buildings for military engineering. Holding the rank of major in 1861, Cullum served as aide to General Scott before he was raised to brigadier general of the volunteers. Two years following the war he spent as superintendent of West Point, but not until 1874 did he retire from the regular army. Cullum is best known for his *Biographical Register of the Officers and Graduates of the United States Academy.* Although he was a member of the Sanitary Commission, he apparently had little liking for it.

John M. Cuyler (1810–84), a native of Georgia, entered the army in 1834 as assistant surgeon, being among the first to pass the rigid examination set up in 1833. He saw active service in the Creek War of 1838, the Seminole War of 1840, and the Mexican War. In 1847, Cuyler received promotion as major and surgeon. From 1848 to 1855 the army stationed him at West Point. As senior medical officer at Fort Monroe during the first years of the Civil War, he proved an invaluable organizer. The army promoted Cuyler to lieutenant colonel and medical inspector; later he acted as inspector general. His zeal in upholding professional standards found favor with the Sanitary Commission. Brevetted brigadier general in March, 1865, he was made a colonel in June, 1876. After the war he served as medical director in important departments until retirement in 1882.

John Hancock Douglas (1824–92), a native of Waterford, N.Y., received his M.D. in 1847 from the University of Pennsylvania. In 1849 he went abroad for two years of further study. He chose New York City in which to practice from 1856 to 1862, editing twelve volumes of the *American Medical Monthly,* and from 1865 to 1866 three volumes of the *New York Medical Journal,* which was then a monthly. His numerous articles appeared in the *New Orleans Hospital Gazette,* the *New Orleans Medical and Surgical Journal,* the *Boston Medical and Surgical Journal* and other publications. Dr. Douglas was Grant's physician until the general's death in 1885.

One of the first inspectors, Douglas came to know all the important areas of Sanitary operations by 1864. Moodiness and bad temper kept him from suffering fools gladly. He was one of the most reliable workers in the commission.

An English journalist in his mid-thirties, *Frederick Milne Edge* might have stepped out of Dickens. He expressed jealousy of De Tocqueville and longed to play Lafayette to the "Second American Revolution" as well as Attila to the European aristocracy. Work became his mistress. Edge had a wife, but did she have a husband? His nights were passed at home but not in her company. He read during meals and spent the rest of the day writing. He was generally going to bed when she was getting up in the morning. To Henry Adams, Edge was a journalistic adventurer, whose good manners made him worth having to dinner. Keep Edge for a friend, cautioned Adams; but, remember, his large acquaintance was "fudge."

Edge's talents were stronger than his business habits; publication of *Slavery Doomed* (1863) brought him reputation and debts. To British politicians he seemed too exuberant and too American. Both parties in the United States supposedly drew on his arguments. Although correspondent for the London *Daily News* in 1863, Edge received $1,000 from the Union League clubs of New York, Philadelphia, and Boston to push their cause and the interests of the Sanitary Commission in Great Britain. Not until February, 1865, did he give up this work. The reward for his devotion to the Union was the debtor's prison; release came in November, 1865, when the commission paid his debts, amounting to £350.

Edge believed that America would inevitably outweigh Great Britain in world politics; but if they marched shoulder to shoulder, the two nations would reduce the possibilities of war to a minimum. Only aristocratic prejudices blinded his native land to its true role in history, said Edge. In *A Woman's Work: A Tribute to Florence Nightingale*, he described the work of the commission, vainly hoping to draw some word of praise from that great woman. Edge used the American issue in *England's Danger and Her Safety* in an attempt to upset the Palmeston ministry. *President Lincoln's Successor* was evidently an able exposition of the American political scene. Edge's pay was inadequate when compared with the value of his work, said Charles Bowles.

William Greenleaf Eliot (1811–87) brought important connections of wealth and influence from New England to the Western Sanitary Commission. Born in New Bedford, he was reared and educated in Washington. He was graduated from Columbia College in 1829, and received his theological degree from Harvard Divinity School in 1834. At St. Louis, Eliot organized the First Congregational Society (1835), helping to launch Washington University (1853), as well as the O'Fallen Polytechnic Institute, Smith Academy, and Mary Institute. A spokesman for gradual emancipation as early as 1834, he worked steadily to improve the Negro's lot after the Civil War. He advocated temperance, woman suffrage, and prevention of legalized prostitution.

Of little physical strength, the short and delicate man impressed men with his moral rectitude and benevolence. John Murray Forbes had "infinite confidence" in Eliot's heart "and almost as much in his head." Laboring among the wounded, Eliot never saw actual battle. One of his brothers was killed at Chancellorsville, while another lived to play an important part in Reconstruction. Eliot held high the standard of his principles and attacked all adversaries with pertinacity.

Ezekiel Brown Elliott (b. 1823) was graduated from Hamilton College, at Clinton, N.Y., in 1844. He spent some time teaching before turning to telegraphy. He was actuary for a Boston life insurance firm until 1861, when he performed the same service for the Sanitary Commission. Without common sense, he became the victim of his own irresponsibility. In 1863 he went to Berlin as a member of the International Statistical Congress. At the expiration of his leave of absence he did not report to the commission but stayed in England; no one knew where. Back in the United States, Elliott was surprised to learn that he was out of a job. In 1865 he became secretary to the commission on revision of revenue laws; in 1871 he served on the civil service reform commission. He was vice-president of the American Association for the Advancement of Science (1882), and was appointed actuary for the United States Treasury in 1887.

Clement Alexander Finley (1797–1879) was born at Newville, Pa., received an M.D. from the University of Pennsylvania (1818). He saw service in various parts of the Union. He served under Scott in the Black Hawk War (1832), when his action in the cholera epidemic won the general's praise. He went to Mexico with the Army of Invasion, acting for a time as Taylor's medical director and again in that capacity under Scott at Vera Cruz. From 1850 to 1860 he was frequently president of the medical examining board.

At age sixty-four he became surgeon general. He was described as one who recognized the value of immediate and satisfactory action, but his accomplishments in that office seemed hard to determine. He apparently disapproved of women nurses, but because the community wanted them, Finley was politic enough to tolerate their presence in army hospitals. He approved the introduction of medical cadets and the enlistment of civilians as nurses for general hospitals. He made proposals looking to the increased efficiency and strength of the medical staff in the regular army; he tried to harmonize the activities of his division with other staff divisions.

As a young man Finley was known as the handsomest man in the army. His well-proportioned six-foot body moved with military bearing; his eyes were blue, his complexion ruddy; with years his black hair turned silver-white. Military whiskers extended from the tips of his ears to the corners of his mouth. He liked to wear a military cape. Meticulous in observance of details in *Army Regulations,* his disciplinary strictness suggested the martinet. A deeply religious man, Finley was tenderhearted and lovable in family relations. To friends he was upright, generous, and courteous; his manners looked to the polish of an age since gone.

Oliver Wolcott Gibbs (1822–1908), born in New York City, received his M.D. from the College of Physicians and Surgeons in 1845. He enjoyed the next three years in Europe studying under the leading scientists. Back in America, Gibbs introduced German methods of laboratory research in chemical instruction. During the Civil War he continued research on platinum metals. He placed his extensive knowledge at the commission's disposal; he freely gave time to the administration, advising about tariff and scientific instruments. In 1863, Gibbs became Rumford professor at Harvard, directing the Lawrence Scientific School for eight years; in 1887 he retired to Newport, where he continued research for ten years in his own laboratory.

Gibbs dealt chiefly with inorganic compounds, analytical methods, and physiological chemistry. He was counted among the founders of the National Academy of Sciences; he was a member of the American Association for the Advancement of Science, the American Philosophical Society, and several European societies.

Benjamin Apthorp Gould (1824–96), mathematician and astronomer, was graduated from Harvard in 1844. A few years spent in Germany equipped him to found the *Astronomical Journal* (1849), which he conducted until the outbreak of the Civil War. Through his surveys the Sanitary Commission was able to present conclusions on the heights, ages, and physical characteristics of soldiers. More significant was his work in the Coast Survey, where he compiled a "standard catalogue" to determine star positions; here for the first time could Gould make systematic corrections of the various catalogues in use. His observations of stars in the southern heavens formed his greatest work, begun in 1870 and lasting fifteen years. Until his death Gould was active in scientific, historical, and social organizations.

William Alexander Hammond (1828–1900) was born in Annapolis, Md. He received his M.D. from the University of the City of New York (1848), entering the army as assistant surgeon after a year at Pennsylvania Hospital (1849). After completing three years of service in New Mexico, Hammond was granted leave because of illness. In Europe he observed hospitals and advanced medical developments. Back in America he served at forts in New Mexico, Florida, Kansas, Michigan, and the Military Academy at West Point. Untouched by the intellectual inertia of garrison life, he occupied himself with physiological and botanical investigations. In 1857 an essay, *Experimental Researches Relative to the Nutritive Value and Physiological Effects of Albumen, Starch, and Gum, when Singly and Exclusively Used as a Food,* won him a prize from the American Medical Association (1857). His other papers circulated abroad, where they were translated into French and German.

The University of Maryland offered him the chair of anatomy and physiology, a position he accepted after resigning from the army (October, 1859). His powers as speaker and doctor won him an enviable reputation in Baltimore. A Unionist in that strongly Confederate city, Hammond withdrew from teaching to re-enter the medical corps, where at the bottom of the list he was given no credit for his eleven years of service. At Hagerstown, Frederick, and Baltimore he organized general hospitals; at Wheeling he was made medical inspector of camps and hospitals. It was Hammond who put the Medical Bureau on its feet and gave it a stature never before enjoyed. He left the army in straitened circumstances (1864), but soon he assumed leadership in the practice and teaching of neurology in New York. Having acquired a fortune, he moved to Washington (1888), where he practiced until his death from cardiac disease.

Hammond wrote with ease. His *Treatise on Hygiene with Special Reference to the Military Service* appeared in 1863 when Hammond was carrying the heavy responsibilities of office. His other writings concerned wakefulness and sleep, insanity, spiritualism, and nervous diseases. He wrote novels dramatically; some critics believed *The Son of Perdition* the best novel ever written about the Christ. Hammond also found time to edit the *Maryland and Virginia Medical Journal*, the *Quarterly Journal of Psychological Medicine and Medical Jurisprudence*, the *New York Medical Journal*, and the *Journal of Nervous and Medical Diseases*.

Elisha Harris (1824–84), a native of Westminster, Vt., was graduated from the College of Physicians and Surgeons in New York. There he practiced medicine, becoming superintendent of the quarantine hospital on Staten Island. In 1859 he directed the construction of a floating hospital to be anchored below the Narrows. Prominent in the movement for sanitary reform, Harris belonged to the National Quarantine and Sanitary Association; he was also a member of the committee that prepared the "code of marine hygiene," a work containing the essentials of New York quarantine practice for many years thereafter.

A leader in municipal sanitation, Harris served as secretary to the Council of Hygiene of the Citizens' Association. When appointed city sanitary superintendent, he vigorously enforced the law of 1866, which provided for tenement inspection and regulation. He organized New York's first free public vaccination service (1869); he helped found the American Public Health Association (1872). Under the National Board of Health he was among the eight chosen to make seaport quarantine inspections. He became one of three original commissioners and secretary to the New York State Board of Health and also state superintendent for vital statistics (1880).

Besides helping to establish the Sanitary Commission, Elisha Harris was its leading sanitarian, writing *Hints for the Control and Prevention of Infectious Diseases in Camps, Transports, and Hospitals* (1863). The hospital car that he designed won an award in the Paris Exposition in 1867, and the Prussian Army used it in the Franco-Prussian War. He originated a system of recording deaths and burials of soldiers. He was also one of the editors of *The Sanitary Memoirs of the War of the Rebellion* (1867–69).

Strong and well built, Harris had been described as an "open-mouthed, white-whiskered man." Nearly everyone liked him, but he did not lack critics. To describe a slender idea he wrote interminable letters. He was a hard worker, and most useful to the Sanitary Commission.

Henry Stewart Hewit, born in Fairfield, Conn., Dec. 26, 1825, and died in New York City, Aug. 19, 1873. He was educated at Yale and received his M.D. from New York University in 1848. Entering the army in the autumn of that year, Hewit was stationed at Vera Cruz and at Fort Yuma, Calif. (1849). On resignation from the army (1852) Hewit went to San Francisco, where he practiced medicine for three years. He returned to New York and set himself up in his profession. In August, 1861, he re-entered the army as brigade surgeon of volunteers. As medical director for Grant, Hewit served at Fort Donelson, Shiloh, and Vicksburg. For gallant conduct the army brevetted him colonel in March, 1865. A convert to Roman Catholicism (1855), Hewit devoted himself to the charitable enterprises of his church. In New York he had charge of the House of the Good Shepherd, was director of St. Stephen's Orphan Asylum, and was president of the medical board of the Charity Hospital.[17]

[17] *Appleton's Cyclopaedia of American Biography*, edited by James Grant Wilson and John Fiske (New York, 1887), Vol. III, pp. 191–92.

John Healey Heywood (1818–80), born in Worcester, Mass., was graduated from Harvard (1832), received his degree in theology from Harvard Divinity School (1840), and was called to the First Unitarian Church in Louisville, Ky. There he strove for many years to secure a public school system of high order. Other labors resulted in the establishment of the Louisville Old Ladies' Home. For ten years he edited the Louisville *Examiner*, meanwhile contributing to the *Christian Register*, the *Unitarian Review*, and other periodicals. His pastorate in Louisville lasted for over forty years. With little publicity, Heywood worked for the Sanitary Commission, but he enjoyed the trust and confidence of its members.

A native of New Haven, Conn., *George Hoadly* (1826–1902) attended public schools in Cleveland, Ohio, and Western Reserve College. Following a year of legal study at Harvard, he completed his preparation for the bar in the office of Salmon P. Chase at Cincinnati. In August, 1847, he was admitted to practice. He presided for some fifteen years over the superior court of Cincinnati, resigning in 1866 to form the firm of Hoadly, Jackson, and Johnson. Hoadly was also known as an educator. His connection with the Cincinnati Law School lasted from 1864 to 1867, with interruptions. For a time he was also a trustee of the University of Cincinnati.

The slavery issue took him into the Republican party, but Hoadly was usually counted among the Democrats. In his term as governor of Ohio he showed no remarkable qualities as a politician in spite of his winning personality. Hoadly withdrew from politics in 1885, and two years later he established the firm of Hoadly, Lauterbach, and Johnson in New York. A leading corporation lawyer, he personally represented the Jefferson Davis estate.

Samuel Gridley Howe (1801–76), born in Boston, received his M.D. from Harvard in 1824. Conspicuous in the Greek rebellion against Turkey (1824–30), he became head of the Massachusetts School of the Blind in 1831. When he received the Perkins mansion as a gift, the school took the name Perkins Institute. Howe won a national reputation by his forty-four years of work among the blind.

One of the foremost among America's humanitarians, he helped Horace Mann fight for better public schools, aided Dorothea Dix in her campaign for improved treatment of the insane, and joined the antislavery movement. He was on good terms with Lincoln and Stanton. His name brought prestige to the Sanitary Commission, although he accused it of usurping the powers of government. In 1866 and 1867 Howe was active in raising funds to help the Cretans in their war for independence. In 1871 he was on the committee appointed by President Grant to report on the advisability of annexing San Domingo.

John Foster Jenkins (1826–82), a native of Falmouth, Mass., received his M.D. from the University of Pennsylvania in 1848. He practiced in New York City from 1849 to 1856, later removing to Yonkers. Jenkins was president of the Medical Society of the State of New York and vice-president of the New York Obstetrical Society. On his holidays in Europe he attended meetings of medical societies, visiting clinics, and haunting book stores. As a book collector he spent about $10,000 on classical medical literature, which at his death sold for $3,940. A large practice left him little time for reading and writing; he succeeded in producing three noteworthy treatises, one on war and science (1863), another relating to puerperal fever (1875), and a third dealing with umbilical hemorrhage. His signal contribution to sanitation was *Tent Hospitals*, a work he composed as general secretary of the Sanitary Commission. Jenkins died from renal or cardiac disease brought on by overwork.

His austerity was the subject of some complaint, but Jenkins proved his worth as a leader of medical men. An able inspector, he lacked self-confidence as an administrator; yet the Sanitary Commission had enough confidence to appoint him Olmsted's successor as general secretary in September, 1863.

Frederick Newman Knapp (1821–89), born in Jamaica Plain, Mass., was graduated from Harvard in 1843. After preparing for the ministry at Harvard Divinity School, he accepted a call at the Brookline Unitarian Church. Ill-health forced Knapp to give up the ministry in 1855, and not until 1869 did he resume pastoral duties in Plymouth. After 1874 he devoted himself to education for boys. This was no new field for him, having directed the Mili-

tary School in Engleswood, N.J. (1866), and established a home
school at Sutton (1867).

Knapp proved indispensable to the conduct of special relief.
Energetic and self-sacrificing at work in social relations, he was
shy, timid, and lacking in self-assertion. George Strong saw a
resemblance to Tom Pinch and Mark Tapley in *Martin Chuzzle-
wit*; but the frank, direct, and transparent manners of a child,
said Henry Bellows, his cousin, masked "a very calculating and
somewhat sly nature." Knapp was at his best in his dealings with
the soldier. As an administrator in the Sanitary Commission he
was wise and farsighted; prompt and swift in execution as well
as bold in assuming heavy responsibilities, he was the kind of
man who must lose his anxieties by helping others.

Jonathan Letterman (1824–72), a native of Canonsburg, Pa., received his M.D. from Jefferson Medical College in Philadelphia
(1849). Following graduation, he passed the army examination
and accepted an appointment as assistant surgeon. Letterman
spent the following twelve years on the Western and Southwest-
ern frontiers. Care and transportation of the wounded in Indian
warfare called for ingenuity and improvisation; here was excellent training for what was later to confront Letterman. In 1861
he was assigned to duty with the Army of the Potomac; McClellan
appointed him medical director in June, 1862. Letterman was
truly the organizer of the field medical service of the Union
Army. He created an effective ambulance service and mobile hospital organization. His basic plan of field hospitalization and
evacuation influenced that service in every modern army. The
latter part of the war he spent as inspector of hospitals in the
Department of the Susquehanna. He resigned his commission
in December, 1864, before taking up residence in San Francisco,
Calif.

Ezra Butler McCagg (1825–1908), a native of Kinderhook,
N.Y., moved to Chicago after admission to the bar (1847). Forming a law partnership with John Young Scammon, he built up an
extensive practice in real estate law. He succeeded Judge Skinner
in directing the Northwestern branch of the Sanitary Commission.
In 1869 he was appointed first president of the Lincoln Park Commission. He was a trustee of the Illinois Eastern Asylum for the

Insane, the University of Chicago, the Chicago Academy of Science, the Chicago Astronomical Society, and an incorporator of the Chicago Historical Society, and a president of the Chicago Bar Association. His house, an oasis of enlightenment, was destroyed by fire in 1871; with it were destroyed a library and valuable collection of early writings and letters of Jesuits. A brilliant and successful lawyer of scholarly tastes, McCagg was a man of broad interests.

John Strong Newberry (1822-92), born in Windsor, Conn., was graduated from the Cleveland Medical School in 1848. Having studied medicine and geology in France for three years, he settled in Cleveland until he received an appointment as assistant surgeon under Lieutenant R. S. Wilkinson, whose expedition explored the projected route for the Pacific Railroad from San Francisco to the Columbia River. He returned to prepare a report in Washington (1856), where began his association with the Smithsonian Institution; about the same time he was appointed to the chair of geology at Columbian College. In 1859 he became naturalist and physician to the expedition under Lieutenant J. C. Ives, then about to explore the Colorado River, and later that year joined a party surveying the Santa Fe region. After the Civil War he accepted a professorship at the newly created School of Mines at Columbia University.

Newberry's honors testified to his reputation in the American world of science. His activities as a member of the National Academy of Sciences, president of the American Association for the Advancement of Science (1867), vice-president of the Geological Society (1869), and president of the International Geological Congress (1891) were evidence of the esteem in which he was held. As secretary for the Western Department, Newberry helped the Sanitary Commission pursue a national course through the reefs of Western sectionalism.

Frederick Law Olmsted (1822-1903), a native of Hartford, Conn., emerged as a man of letters and a powerful critic of the Old South with the appearance of *A Journey in the Seaboard Slave States* (1856), *A Journey Through Texas* (1857), *A Journey in the Back Country* (1860). His writing lacked the denunciation and the rhetoric that obscured many accounts of Negro slavery. His lucidity attracts the modern reader. In him were married practical intelligence and foresight. A pioneer in the preservation of natural resources, he had much to do with making Yosemite Valley in California a state reservation, thus saving it from the ravages of commercial and industrial exploitation. Perhaps most Americans know Olmsted's works better than his name, for his creative imagination has stamped their lives. Whether they romped through Boston's Public Gardens or made love in New York's Central Park; whether they pushed a perambulator through South Park in Chicago or with age retired to within a comfortable walking distance of Golden Gate Park in San Francisco, the vistas they enjoyed were of his design or influence.

Olmsted always had staunch friends. He also made bitter enemies, the natural lot of one who held decided views. Professional people especially admired him. Miss Katherine Wormeley, bathed in the glow of her sensibility, wrote: "His face is generally very placid with all the expressive delicacy of a woman's, and would be beautiful were it not for an expression which I cannot fathom . . ." Detecting a note of severity—never truculence—she noticed that his face had a remarkable range of expression, "sometimes stern, thoughtful, and haggard; at other times observing and slightly satirical" and then again "an inspired look of goodness and power." Struck by Olmsted's self-will, she tempered her criticism, calling him an enlightened autocrat and noting his "deep, calm thoughtfulness." [18]

Olmsted had a "lovely though peculiar nature," said Mrs. Elizabeth Hamilton Schuyler. Would wartime Washington be the place for him? she wondered. A Jeffersonian granddaughter of Alexander Hamilton, Mrs. Schuyler praised Olmsted's energy and swiftness of action, his sincerity and earnestness; but she was critical of Olmsted's political thinking and his love of centralized organization. He was not alone in this, for many active young men thought as he did. Mrs. Schuyler explained: "All tend now toward centralization, unconstitutional and illegal, or despotic measures. A national act of emancipation to begin with, or a revolution at home, and a dictator." Was this but the impatience of those who would not bide the answer? Or was it "that prophecy

[18] Katherine Prescott Wormeley, *The Other Side of War* (1889), p. 63.

of the future which can be read in the rough by studying the tendencies of the new generation?" [19]

Bellows regarded himself as the only person who understood Olmsted's administrative genius. Bellows wrote:

Mr. Frederick Law Olmsted is of all the men I know the most comprehensive, thorough, and minutely particular organizer. He is equally wonderful in the management of principles and . . . details. His mind is patient in meditation, careful and acute, his will inflexible, his devotion to his principles and methods confident and unflinching. He looks far ahead and his plans and methods are sometimes mysterious.[20]

A man with Olmsted's drive did not work well in a team of "shrewd, worldly wise, self-opinionated managers." They found him obstinate and self-willed, said Bellows.

They think . . . him impracticable, expensive, slow, when he is only long headed with broader deeper notions of economy than themselves and with no disposition to hurry what if done satisfactorily must be done thoroughly. My feeling is that Olmsted is an admirable governor but an uncomfortable subject. He loves power and is fit to hold it.[21]

Olmsted would exhaust all means to capture success and produce astonishing results, but these he won with friction. He would not bring "peace, comfort, daily satisfaction" to supervisory boards.

Olmsted thought he had good reason for accepting the position of secretary general of the Sanitary Commission. On the Central Park Commission of New York he had a personal antagonist who jealously blocked his plans. By leaving New York, Olmsted believed he might have more influence on the development of Central Park than if he stayed. Only his health stood in the way of his working with the Sanitary Commission. The consequences of a broken leg subjected him to much nervous strain. Bellows wondered whether Olmsted would last long under stress, telling him to save his strength by hiring a carriage. A few days before

[19] Bellows MSS. Mrs. E. H. Schuyler to H. W. Bellows, Sept. 10, 1861, Dobbs Ferry, N.Y.
[20] Bellows MSS. H. W. Bellows to J. Miller McKim, Aug. 18, 1865, Walpole, N.H.
[21] *Ibid.*

the first battle of Bull Run, Bellows spoke for the commissioners, when he wrote: "We are all anxious for your health and comfort, and none of us can think of sparing you at this crisis in our affairs." [22]

Before and after joining the commission, Olmsted thought about applying for a government post to manage those Negro slaves who had fled from the South to Union. Not dissatisfaction but belief that the days of the commission were numbered caused him to think of looking for other work. Once he became secretary general, Olmsted was quick to catch the significance of the commission, owning: "It is a good big work I have in hand, giving me absorbing occupation and that sort of connection with the work of the nation without which I should be very uncomfortable." [23]

The commission quickly showed the results of Olmsted's strong lead. His work was thorough, noted the commissioners, and the army greeted their association with growing respect. Bellows proposed meeting the salary paid Olmsted in New York, for without him the commission's usefulness would have been impaired.

As a result of devotion to the Sanitary cause, Olmsted frequently overworked. Whenever fatigue got the best of him, the "logic of his despondency" became "crushing and terrible." Olmsted was "wary, shrewd, and never sanguine," said George Templeton Strong, and ought to have directed the War Department. His enthusiasm radiated from the hub to the rim of the fifth wheel, noted Dr. Steiner, infusing his assistants "with a zeal that ambition or hope of pecuniary reward never could have excited." Bellows impressed the Sanitary matter with its initial form, but Frederick Law Olmsted provided the efficient cause. Under him the commission reached its greatest effectiveness.

Fairman Rogers (b. 1833) of Philadelphia was graduated from the University of Pennsylvania in 1853. He taught civil engineering there from 1855 to 1870. As a volunteer officer in the Engineers he completed the survey of the Potomac River under the Coast

[22] Box 727. H. W. Bellows to F. L. Olmsted, July 18, 1861, New York.
[23] Olmsted MSS. F. L. Olmsted to Bertha Olmsted, Jan. 28, 1862, Washington, D.C.

Survey in 1862. Rogers was a member of the American Society of Civil Engineers and of the American Philosophical Society. He was an original member of the National Academy of Sciences. In the Sanitary Commission he was active but not conspicuous.

Louisa Lee Schuyler (1837–1926) was a great-granddaughter of Alexander Hamilton from both sides of her family. She was a leader in welfare work, and at twenty-three she became a volunteer teacher for the Children's Aid Society. The Civil War brought her to the fore as a leader in the Womans' Central Association of Relief. Here she developed her executive ability and organized information as well as express services. Recuperating from the strain of Sanitary work, she spent seven years in Europe and Egypt following the war. During the seventies Miss Schuyler assumed leadership in local and state charities. The State Charities Aid Association, a project of her own, promoted the visiting and inspection of public poorhouses by private citizens. At New York's Bellevue Hospital she succeeded in opening a nurses' training school, the first in America. Because of her campaign to improve the lot of the insane, the state in 1890 transferred these unfortunates from county poorhouses to well-administered state hospitals. As a trustee of the Russell Sage Foundation, she worked to prevent blindness in children, only to lose her own sight in old age. Colleagues and admirers described Miss Schuyler as having "the mind of a lawyer and the will-power of a captain of industry."

Alexander Eakins Shiras (1812–75), a native of New York, was graduated from West Point in 1833 and served on the frontier until 1839. He taught at West Point for four years; from 1847 until his death he held a post in the Bureau of Subsistence. Shiras took little part in Sanitary affairs; Strong dismissed him as an "inveterate red tapist."

Mark Skinner (1813–87), born in Manchester, Vt., was graduated from Middlebury College in law. He settled in Chicago (1836), was elected city attorney (1839), was appointed U.S. District Attorney for Illinois (1844), was elected to the legislature (1846), and became judge of the Cook County Court of Common Pleas (1851). Prominent in many civic and humanitarian activities, Skinner was chosen president of the Illinois General

Hospital (1842) and the Chicago Home for the Friendless (1860); he was first president of the Chicago Reform School and one of the founders of the New England Society of Chicago. He was active in railroads, participating in building the Galena and Chicago Railroad and acting as a director of the Chicago, Burlington, and Quincy. Originally a Democrat, Skinner helped found the Anti-Nebraska party (1854) and was a member of the Republican party from its organization (1856). He was a valuable representative for the commission in the West. With tact and understanding he reconciled the tugs between Sanitary nationalism and Western sectionalism.

Edwin McMasters Stanton (1814–69), a native of Steubenville, Ohio, entered the Washington scene in 1856. He appeared constantly before the Supreme Court and won a national reputation. Few questioned his love for the Union, although his politics could run with the hares and hunt with the hounds. Southern Democrats and abolitionists smiled on him simultaneously. Stanton entered Buchanan's cabinet as attorney general. With Jeremiah S. Black he helped constitute a Union block. In this office of trust he did not hesitate to tell cabinet secrets to the Republicans. When Lincoln came to office, Stanton as a private citizen condemned the administration as fatuous. Ingratiating himself with McClellan, he acted as his legal adviser and confident. As Simon Cameron's legal adviser, he framed the annual report. The section recommending that slaves be armed gave Lincoln offense. As a result, Cameron found himself out of the cabinet, while on January 20, 1862, Stanton entered upon the duties of secretary of war.

Little did the Sanitary know of false, fleeting, prejudiced Stanton. Jeremiah Black denounced him as "sycophant"; James Buchanan recalled his candied tongue, which flattered "ad nauseam." General McClellan set him down as one who turned Judas pale with innocence. President Johnson was to find trust betrayed to radical Republicans through the agency of his secretary of war. Stanton's ambition appeared to sweep away obstacles by unscrupulous means. He was noted for brutality of manner and despotic behavior toward subordinates; his outbursts of rage were said to have been akin to madness. He was nothing if not critical. In

Lincoln's War Cabinet, Burton J Hendricks had written: "The positive qualities chiefly associated with Stanton's name were fierce determination, instantaneous decision and execution, remorseless concentration, and a savage capacity for labor that despite perpetual ill-health made him . . . the greatest lawyer of his time, and . . . the most dynamic, if not the most admirable, member of Lincoln's cabinet."

This restless asthmatic of medium height and thick set walked with a quick, jerky step. A wide stern mouth balanced large eyes and nose; a patriarchal beard of coarse black whiskers covered jaws and chin. He looked on the world coldly and without trust, regardless of deep religious convictions. Though never threatened personally, he was wont to carry a sheathed dagger under his waistcoat. He was preoccupied with death to the point of contemplating the physical remains of those he loved. His eccentricities showed marks of the pathological, which threw a shadow over his great abilities.

Lewis Henry Steiner (1827–92), a native of Maryland, received his M.D. from the University of Pennsylvania in 1849. Until the Civil War he taught such subjects as medicine, chemistry, botany, and pharmacy in the schools of Maryland and the Colleges of Washington, D.C. A prominent Republican at the end of the hostilities, he made the education of Negro children his concern. As a state senator he was one of the Maryland delegation that helped elect Hayes in 1876. His editorship of the Frederick *Examiner*, begun in 1873, came to an end in 1884, when Enoch Pratt hired Steiner as librarian of Baltimore's free public library. Steiner was remarkable for his range of interests. A member of the Reformed Church, he wrote about spiritualism and religion; a student of physics and medicine, he translated German writings in chemistry, wrote stories for children, and edited D. D. Smyth's *History of Guilford, Connecticut*. Steiner belonged to many scientific societies. He was one of the founders of the American Academy of Medicine (1876) and became its president in 1878.

Steiner was one of the most capable of Sanitary inspectors. To Bellows he united "taste and knowledge, an eye to see and tongue to tell what he sees." Commissioned inspector in August, 1861, Steiner was assigned to the Army of the Shenandoah. Summer,

1862, took him among the wounded at Harrison's Landing, Bull Run, and Antietam. Chief inspector in May, 1863, he organized the Field Relief Corps, the model for similar relief corps in other armies. His proposed system of relief for Union prisoners in Richmond (1864) was not carried out, owing to General Butler's disapproval. He foresaw the need of an auxiliary relief corps, which was organized by Frank Fay of Chelsea, Mass. Steiner was in the thick of Grant's spring campaign in 1864. Because of antagonisms within the Sanitary Commission, he resigned in July, 1864.

Charles Janeway Stillé (1819–99), a graduate of Yale in 1839, studied law with Joseph Reed Ingersoll and was admitted to the bar. The enlightened patriotism of his pamphlet, *How a Free People Conduct a Long War* (1862), sold over half a million copies in the North. As corresponding secretary of the executive committee, Stillé was instrumental in founding the Union League Club of Philadelphia, and promoted the local Sanitary fair. After the war he became official historian of the commission, his careful if somewhat stilted book appearing in 1866.

That same year Stillé was appointed professor of literature and belles lettres at the University of Pennsylvania, where no changes had been made in curriculum for one hundred years. He immediately urged elective courses, and his proposal was adopted in 1867 for upper classes. In 1868 he became university provost, a post he held for twelve years. Stillé created the new departments of science (1872), music (1877), and dentistry (1878). As the scope of the university expanded, he made a start toward putting it on a sound financial basis, augmenting the endowments for science, library, and scholarships. On retiring from the provostship (1880) he devoted himself to history, writing *Studies in Medieval History* (1882), *The Life and Times of John Dickinson* (1891), and *Major General Anthony Wayne and the Pennsylvania Line in the Continental Army* (1893).

George Templeton Strong (1820–75), a native of New York, was graduated from Columbia College in 1838. Admitted to the bar in 1841, he became a partner in the firm of Strong, Bidwell, and Strong on Wall Street. In Ellen Ruggles, Strong found a wife with similar tastes, their home becoming a center for people of fashion and culture. As a trustee of Columbia (1853) he advocated bringing equipment and curriculum into line with the times; he proposed developing new departments to convert the college into a university. As a vestryman Strong served Trinity Church with devotion. During the Civil War he helped establish the Union League Club, while as treasurer of the Sanitary Commission he accepted the responsibility for the accounting system and for receiving and disbursing large sums of money. Day after day he performed his "peculiar, anxious, and persistent" duties, meeting at 3:00 P.M. with four other members of the executive committee in New York. Strong did not originate ideas, but combined the lawyer with the financier in the transaction of Sanitary affairs.

"Thank God that a miserable, nearsighted cockney like myself can take part in any work that strengthens and helps on the national cause," wrote the treasurer of the Sanitary Commission.[24] George Templeton Strong enjoyed noblesse oblige. Ever correct, he seemed innately modest and self-effacing. He erred by not holding himself in high esteem, thought the worldly-wise. He made few demands of men; he made no display of affection, but kept his distance and let others make the advances. To guard against unwanted intrusion he turned to irony and a gentle ridicule. A keen and articulate judge of men, Strong was a snob but never a knave or a fool.

In his love of the old, Strong suggested Goldsmith's Mr. Hardcastle. The medieval world of church, art, music, and symbolism offered him greater richness of mind than the crude and pedestrian nineteenth century. Strong prized the private life. Here the man of taste found study its own reward; here he learned that ambition was made of sterner stuff than public applause. Strong believed in purposeful activity, but he shunned the appearance of busyness.

In his diary what was bottled up flowed with a sparkle. His Unionism shone valiantly, as he tried to explain basic principles and differences. Aristocratic and conservative, he nevertheless hated that Southern oligarchy which would tear his United States

---

[24] Strong, George Templeton, *The Diary of George Templeton Strong*, edited by Allan Nevins and Milton Halsey Thomas, New York, 1952, Vol. III, p. 246.

to tatters. It was not surprising that he should write: "This war will soon be universally recognized as waged by an effete corrupt aristocracy of slave breeders against the cause of Progress, Democracy, Free Thought, and Equality, (for which, by the by, I have no great respect, though I certainly prefer them to the semi-barbarous system of Mississippi and South Carolina), and the sympathies of Christendom will begin to array themselves against Southern treason." [25] He blamed the South for the national catastrophe and the North for its readiness to offer sops to Southern views.

A stanch Episcopalian, Strong felt chagrin when in September, 1862, the Protestant Episcopal Church declined to take a firm Union stand. He explained:

I think this shows the existence of a latent anti-democratic or aristocratic feeling as a constituent element of the Protestant-Episcopal or Anglo-American Church. Not a conservative spirit, founded on tradition, inherited from the English Church and dating back to the days of the Stuarts . . . but a revolutionary spirit as against our democratic institutions. . . . I have no special liking for democratic institutions; but "the powers that be" and that are ordained of God rest on those institutions, and the Church is bound to uphold them.[26]

In his diary Strong set down a remarkable picture of Civil War New York and Washington. Since little was lost on him, his record gave texture to the period; he re-created a world in which people lived at the same time that they were making history. Strong had a sense of immediacy; this he combined with a critical grasp of literature. He was consciously mid-Victorian; but this son of the comic spirit loved to search out foibles and pomposities, even when he himself was the target of laughter. Often he let his moral biases blunder into aesthetic matters, saying: "Byron is stronger than Cowper. But if we know of two men only this, that one delighted in Cowper and the other in Byron, I think we should infer that the former was the healthier-minded of the two." [27] He drew the same fallacious parallel between Haydn (health) and Beethoven (moral disease).

[25] *Ibid.*, p. 142.   [26] *Ibid.*, p. 263.   [27] *Ibid.*, p. 92.

Strong the snob may amuse or bore the reader of his diary; but when he describes his musical experiences one is drawn into his world of pleasure, even though one may not share his point of view. Strong felt at home with Haydn and Mozart. Wagner's *Tannhäuser* he thought unmusical, an opinion shared by many of his generation. Bach failed to interest him; Berlioz sounded "flashy and flagrant." His criticism of Gounod's *Faust* would startle a box office. "The opera has its good points but is, on the whole, a bore," wrote Strong. "Gounod does his best, but he cannot write melodies, and three hours and a half of unmelodic music are severe." [28] Strong's musical opinions are still interesting, because he listened to music as music; he looked for neither pictures nor social significance in major and minor scales.

Charles Stuart Tripler (1806–66), born in New York City, received his M.D from the College of Physicians and Surgeons in 1830. Tripler was first stationed on the Michigan frontier after entering the medical corps. As medical director to General Twiggs he served at several Western outposts in the Mexican War. The opening of the Civil War found him medical director for General Patterson in the Shenandoah Valley. McClellan appointed him to the same position in the Army of the Potomac, where he organized its medical service. From the Peninsular campaign he was sent to Michigan; later he was brevetted brigadier general and chosen chief officer of the Department of Ohio. His death in Cincinnati resulted from epithelioma.

William Holme Van Buren (1819–83), a native of Philadelphia, received his M.D. from the University of Pennsylvania in 1840. Joining the army medical corps as assistant surgeon, Van Buren served in Florida and then on the Canadian frontier. In 1845 he resigned from the army and settled in New York, where he built up a large practice and joined the staff at Bellevue Hospital. Professor at the University of the City of New York from 1851 to 1866, Van Buren also held the chair of surgery in Bellevue Medical College from 1866 until his death.

The year 1859 brought Van Buren the vice-presidency of the New York Academy of Medicine; in 1876 he was elected to the presidency of Bellevue Medical College. The Medical Bureau

[28] *Ibid.*, p. 384.

respected him because of his understanding of its ways and limitations. Without him, said Bellows, the commission would have lacked its "balance wheel, if not its medical mainspring."

Joshua Huntington Wolcott (1804–91) of Connecticut, grandson of Oliver Wolcott, "the Signer," entered the textile commission house of Amos and Abbott Lawrence when he was seventeen. So well did he prosper that by 1865 he was living on Beacon Street in Boston. A member of the Sanitary Commission, he was also treasurer of its Massachusetts branch. His stern looks belied a pleasant nature. He wore black broadcloth, a standing white collar, and black bow tie. Tall and erect, his dark eyes and red cheeks contrasted with rather long, wavy hair and white beard. Wolcott always bore traces of his lack of schooling; after meals he used to extract from a little gold box a quill toothpick, which he applied in public. Olmsted hoped that Wolcott would become financial director upon election to the Sanitary Commission.

Robert Crooke Wood (d. 1869) was brother-in-law to Jefferson Davis, whom he detested. An assistant surgeon in 1825, Wood ultimately rose to the rank of brigadier general in 1865. Timid and cautious, he could always be expected to side with the conservative medical corps; his rigid conventionality did not help him win the coveted office of surgeon general. Woods was "grey and impassive, unsmiling and cold," said Bellows; his manner was devoid of energy and earnestness. Although a member of the Sanitary Commission, he spent most of his time in opposition to it.

Daughter of a rear admiral in the British Navy, *Katharine Prescott Wormeley* (1830–1908) spent the first eighteen years of her life abroad, where she saw much of the best of English and French society. Miss Wormeley wrote the letters comprising *The Other Side of War* during the Peninsular campaign. Her sketch of the Sanitary work and purposes found many readers in Great Britain. Miss Wormeley refused to own authorship of the 1863 edition; since most women contributors to the commission's cause were unknown, she chose anonymity also; her reasoning seemed quixotic to the leading commissioners. At Portsmouth Grove, R.I., Miss Wormeley served as superintendent of a hospital for convalescents. The years after the war saw her active in Newport affairs, especially those relating to sanitation, charity, and education for women.

Miss Wormeley's translations of Paul Bourget, Alexandre Dumas, Alphonse Daudet, the Duc de Saint-Simon, Axel Fersen, and Sainte-Beuve brought her general recognition. Balzac was her favorite; thoroughly immersed in *La Comédie Humaine*, Miss Wormeley rose to his defense at any suggestion of criticism. To her went the tribute most translators prize, for "she was never enslaved to her text, but conveyed spirit as well as actual meaning."

James Erwin Yeatman (1818–1901), president of the Western Sanitary Commission, was a native of Tennessee and identified himself in St. Louis with almost every public and humanitarian movement. Banker, civic leader, and philanthropist, he was educated at New Haven Commercial School. Living abroad for a time, Yeatman settled at St. Louis in 1842. His honesty in business and prominence in charitable enterprises placed him among the foremost in civic attention. His activities in the Merchant's National Bank, the Missouri Pacific Railroad, the St. Louis Mercantile Library Association, the St. Louis Asylum for the Blind, Washington University, the Missouri Botanical Garden, and the St. Louis Medical College reveal the scope of his interests. Yeatman performed important work in the Western Sanitary Commission, giving it effective and energetic organization. He understood the Southerner deprived of the prop of slavery; but Negro bondage looked hateful, while ignorance in the emancipated slave stirred his pity. Inevitably the freedman's problem drew him to give aid in every way possible. After the war he helped influence legislation which established the Freedmen's Bureau. Affectionately known as "Old Sanitary" to the soldiers, Yeatman stood six feet in height, impressing people by his courtliness and geniality. He cared nothing for money and, although he inherited much, died with only a few hundred dollars in the bank.

Sources

Manuscript Collections

New York Public Library

Files of the United States Sanitary Commission.
Medical Committee Archives: Boxes 1–20.
New England Women's Auxiliary Association: Box 50.
Executive Committee of Boston Associate Archives: Books 54–60;
75–76.
California Branch Archives: Books 80–81.
English Branch Archives: Box 339.
Philadelphia . . . Agency—Pennsylvania Branch Archives: Books
570–74; 587–89; 590–95.
New York Archives: Boxes 636–58; 667–81; 709–14.
Washington . . . Archives: Boxes 729–32; 735; 738–48; 755–72;
775; 796; 833–42.
Western Department Archives: Boxes 909–19 (912 missing).
Condensed Historical Material: 1025; 1026; 1029; 1086.

The medical archives are in poor condition, while the Western
Department kept its letters in a slovenly manner. The branch
files open up the problems of aid societies and present a picture
of the Christian Commission as a rival. The English branch
archives give the Sanitary history abroad, although these are
incomplete. Letter press books from 709 to 714 have occasional
items of importance; more useful for my purpose were the press
copies in 833 to 842.

The following collections also were used at the New York Public
Library:

S. B. Ruggles MSS.
William Frothingham MSS.

Maria Lydig Daly MSS.
Miscellaneous Civil War items.

Library of Congress

With the exception of the Olmsted MSS., the following collections yielded an occasional item of importance:

Jane Addams (1860–1935)
Robert Anderson (1805–71)
Alexander Dallas Bache (1806–67)
Samuel J. Baird (1817–93)
George Bancroft (1800–91)
Thomas F. Bayard (1828–98)
John Bell (1797–1869)
Jeremiah S. Black (1810–83)
James G. Blaine (1830–93)
Breckinridge family (1752–1904): Examined from V, 136 (Dec. 2, 1849), through V, 240 (April 11, 1865)
Benjamin F. Butler (1818–93)
Charles Butler (1802–97)
Simon Cameron (1799–1889): Boxes 9–17
John Dean Caton (1812–95)
William E. Chandler (1835–1917)
Zachariah Chandler (1813–79)
Salmon Portland Chase (1808–73)
John F. H. Claiborne (1809–84)
John M. Clayton (1796–1856)
Schuyler Colfax (1823–85)
Cyrus B. Comstock (1831–1910)
Roscoe Conkling (1829–88)
William W. Corcoran (1798–1888)
Samuel Wylie Crawford (1829–92)
John J. Crittenden (1787–1863)
Benjamin R. Curtis (1809–74)
Caleb Cushing (1800–79)
John A. B. Dahlgren (1809–70)
Charles A. Dana (1819–97)
Henry Laurens Dawes (1816–1903)

Thomas Ewing (1789–1871)
William P. Fessenden (1806–69)
Hamilton Fish (1808–93)
Andrew Hull Foote (1806–63)
John W. Forney (1817–81)
William B. Franklin (1823–1903)
Louis M. Goldsborough (1805–77)
Horace Greeley (1811–72)
Duff Green (1791–1875)
Adam Gurowski (1805–66)
James Allen Hardie (1823–76)
Benjamin Harrison (1833–1901)
Samuel Peter Heintzelman (1805–88)
Ethan Allen Hitchcock (1798–1870)
Andrew Johnson (1808–75)
Reverdy Johnson (1796–1876)
Horatio King (1811–97)
Thomas Lawson (*ca.* 1781–1861)
Francis Lieber (1800–72)
John A. Logan (1826–86)
George B. McClellan (1826–85)
Hugh McCulloch (1808–95)
Edward McPherson (1830–95)
Willie P. Mangum (1792–1861)
Manton M. Marble (1835–1917)
Absalom H. Markland
Justin Smith Morrill (1810–98)
Thomas H. Nelson (*ca.* 1823–96)
Helen Nicolay
John G. Nicolay (1832–1901)
Fitz-John Porter (1822–1901)
John M. Schofield (1831–1906)
Carl Schurz (1829–1906)
Philip H. Sheridan (1831–88)
John Sherman (1823–1900)
Edwin M. Stanton (1814–69)
Thaddeus Stevens (1792–1868)
Lyman Trumbull (1813–96)

Benjamin F. Wade (1800–78)
Elihu B. Washburn (1816–87)
Walt Whitman (1819–92)
Henry Wilson (1812–75)
Frederick Law Olmsted MSS.

Massachusetts Historical Society

Henry Whitney Bellows MSS.
Orville Dewey MSS.
Samuel Gridley Howe MSS.

New York Historical Society

Alfred Janson Bloor Letter Book. These letters are copies of those in the files of the commission.
Alfred Janson Bloor Diary. Interesting but of little consequence.
Louisa Lee Schuyler—Angelina Post MSS. A small but important collection. To guard the feelings of certain women, Miss Schuyler removed these letters from the files of the Woman's Central Association of Relief.

Maryland Historical Society

Lewis Henry Steiner MSS. and Diaries.
F. N. Knapp MSS. in the possession of Mr. Gersham Bradford.

Bibliography

I. *Dictionaries of Biography, Encyclopedias, Reports, Etc.*

Appleton's Cyclopedia of American Biography. J. G. Wilson and John Fiske, eds. Vols. I-VI. New York, 1887–89.

National Cyclopedia of American Biography. 35 vols. N.Y.: J. T. White, 1892–1949.

Dictionary of American Biography. A. Johnson and D. Malone, eds. 22 vols. New York, 1928–44.

Who's Who in 1917.

A Cyclopedia of American Medical Biography from 1610 to 1910. H. A. Kelly, M.D., ed. 2 vols. Philadelphia and London, 1912.

American Medical Biographies. H. A. Kelly and W. L. Burrage, eds. 1920.

Rebellion Record. Frank Moore, ed. 11 vols. 1861–65.

The Medical and Surgical History of the War of the Rebellion 1861–1865. J. K. Barnes *et al.*, eds. 6 vols. Washington, 1870–88.

War of the Rebellion: a Compilation of the Official Records of the Union and Confederate Armies. R. N. Scott *et al.*, eds. 130 vols. Washington, 1880–1901.

Numbers and Losses. T. J. Livermore, ed.

Historical Register and Dictionary of the United States Army . . . 1789–1903. F. B. Heitman, ed. 2 vols. Washington, 1903.

Encyclopaedia of Social Sciences. E. R. A. Seligman, ed. 15 vols. New York, 1930–34.

Congressional Globe, 37th Congress, 2nd Session; 45th Congress, 2nd Session.

U.S. Sanitary Commission Bulletins 3 vols., nos. 1–40, Nov. 1, 1863–Aug. 1, 1865. New York, 1866.

U.S. Sanitary Commission Documents. 2 vols. New York, 1866.

Minutes of the U.S. Sanitary Commission. Sessions 1–22. Washington, 1861–65.

Miscellaneous Documents. 4 vols. Formerly belonging to H. W. Bellows. Specially bound.

Surgical Memoirs of the War of the Rebellion. F. H. Hamilton, ed. 3 vols. New York, 1870–71.

II. *Secondary Sources*

Adams, G. W. *Doctors in Blue.* New York, 1952.

Adams, H. *The Letters of Henry Adams.* W. C. Ford, ed. 2 vols. Boston and New York, 1930–38.

Ashburne, P. M. *A History of the Medical Department of the United States Army.* New York, 1929.

Barton, W. E. *The Life of Clara Barton: Founder of the American Red Cross.* 2 vols. Boston, 1922.

Brockett, L. P. and M. C. Vaughan. *Woman's Work in the Civil War: A Record of Heroism, Patriotism, and Patience.* Boston, 1867.

Curti, M. *The Growth of American Thought.* New York and London, 1943.

Duncan, L. C. *The Medical Department of the U.S. Army in the Civil War.* Washington, 1914.

Eliot, Mrs. C. C. *William Greenleaf Eliot, Minister, Educator, Philanthropist.* Boston and New York, 1904.

Ellis, J. J. *Leaves from the Diary of an Army Surgeon: or Incidents of Field, Camp, and Hospital Life.* New York, 1863.

Forbes, J. M. *Letters and Recollections of John Murray Forbes.* S. F. Hughes, ed. 2 vols. Boston, 1899.

Forman, J. G. *The Western Sanitary Commission: A Sketch.* St. Louis, 1864.

Greenbie, M. L. *Lincoln's Daughters of Mercy.* New York, 1944.

Hancock, C. *South after Gettysburg: Letters of Cornelia Hancock from the Army of the Potomac, 1863–1865.* H. S. Jacquette, ed. Philadelphia, 1937.

Hendricks, B. J. *Lincoln's War Cabinet.* Boston, 1946.

Henshaw, Mrs. S. E. *Our Branch and Its Tributaries.* Chicago, 1868.

Letterman, J. *Medical Recollections of the Army of the Potomac.* New York, 1866.

Livermore, Mrs. M. A. *My Story of the War: A Woman's Narrative of Four Years' Personal Experience as a Nurse in the Union Army.* n.p., n.d.

Meneely, A. H. *The War Department, 1861.* New York, 1928.

Mitchell, B. *Frederick Law Olmsted, a Critic of the Old South.* Baltimore, 1924.

Morison, S. E., and H. S. Commager. *Growth of the American Republic.* 2 vols. New York, 1942.

Moss, L. *The Annals of the U.S. Christian Commission.* Philadelphia, 1868.

Newberry, J. S. *The Sanitary Commission in the Valley of the Mississippi.* Cleveland, 1871.

Nutting, A. M., and L. L. Dock. *A History of Nursing.* 4 vols. New York, 1907–17.

Olmsted, F. L. (ed.) *Hospital Transports: A Memoir.* Boston, 1863.

Packard, F. R. *A History of Medicine in the United States.* 2 vols. New York, 1931.

Randall, J. G. *Civil War and Reconstruction.* Boston and New York, 1937.

Rhodes, J. F. *History of the Civil War 1861–1865.* New York, 1917.

Sandburg, C. *Abraham Lincoln: The War Years.* 4 vols. New York, 1939.

Shannon, F. A. *The Organization and Administration of the Union Army, 1861, 1865.*

Shryock, R. H. *The Development of Modern Medicine: An Interpretation of the Social and Scientific Factors Involved.* Philadelphia, 1936.

Smith, Adelaide W. *Reminiscences of an Army Nurse During the Civil War.* New York, 1911.

Smith, Mrs. C.-W. *Florence Nightingale.* New York, 1951.

———. *The Reason Why.* New York, 1953.

Stillé, C. J. *History of the United States Sanitary Commission, Being the General Report of its Work During the War of the Rebellion.* Philadelphia, 1866.

Strong, G. T. *The Diary of George Templeton Strong.* A. Nevins and M. H. Thomas, eds. 4 vols. New York, 1952.

Vulliamy, C. E. *Crimea, The Campaign of 1854–56.* London, 1939.

Wendte, C. W. *Thomas Starr King: Patriot and Preacher.* Boston: Beacon Press, 1921.

Whitman, Walt. *The Wound Dresser: A Series of Letters Written from the Hospitals in Washington during the War of the Rebellion.* R. M. Buck, ed. Introduction by Oscar Cargill. New York, 1949.

Woolsey, J. *Hospital Days.* New York, 1868.

Wormeley, K. P. *The Other Side of War.* Boston, 1889.

———. *The United States Sanitary Commission.* Boston, 1863.

III. *Magazines, Pamphlets, Etc.*

Bellows, Russell N. *Recollections of Henry Whitney Bellows.* Keene (N.H.) Printing Co., 1898.

Bellows, H. W. *In Memoriam: Tribute to the Character and Services of George Templeton Strong, Oct. 27, 1875.* Found among the S. B. Ruggles MSS.

———. "Origins, Struggles, and Principles of the United States Sanitary Commission," *North American Review* (January, 1864). Reprint contained in the *Miscellaneous Documents,* 1864, Part I.

———. "Sanitary Commission," *Johnson's New Universal Cyclopaedia.* F. A. P. Barnard and A. Guyot, eds. Vol. IV, Part I, pp. 73–81. New York, 1884.

———. *Unconditional Loyalty.* New York, n.d.

Bowles, C. S. P. *Report . . . Upon the International Congress at Geneva . . .* London, n.d.

Chadwick, J. W. *Henry Whitney Bellows, his life and character: A Sermon.* New York: Green's, 1882.

Davis, G. W. "The Red Cross, Its Origin and Development," *American Red Cross Bulletin* (April, 1910).

———. "The Sanitary Commission—The Red Cross," *American Journal of International Law* (July, 1910).

Reprints of both articles are among the Olmsted MSS.

Duncan, L. C. "The Strange Case of Surgeon General Hammond," *Military Surgeon,* Vol. 64 (January, 1929), pp. 98–114, and (February, 1929), pp. 252–67.

Eliot, E. C. *An Address Upon the Laying of the Corner Stone of the James E. Yeatman High School,* June 6, 1903.

Eliot, W. G. "Western Sanitary Commission," *North American Review* XCVIII (April, 1864), pp. 370–419.

Knapp, F. N. *Frederick Newman Knapp: Memorial Tributes.* Boston, 1891.

Olmsted, F. L. *Books and Papers Relating to the Concerns of the United States Sanitary Commission in the War of the Rebellion.* 1890. A pamphlet in Olmsted MSS.

———. *Report on the Demoralization of the Volunteers.* Washington, 1861.

Pilcher, J. E. Three articles in *Military Surgeon:*

"Brevet Brigadier General Clement Alexander Finlay, Surgeon General of the United States Army, 1861–1862," XV (1904), 59–66.

"Brigadier General William Alexander Hammond, Surgeon General of the United States Army, 1862–1864," XV (1904), 145–55.

"Brevet Major General Joseph K. Barnes, Surgeon General of the United States Army, 1864–1882," XV (1904), 219–24.

Reed, W. H. *The Heroic Struggle of the United States Sanitary Commission.* 1910.

Steiner, L. H., *A Sketch of the History, Plan of Organization and Operations of the United States Sanitary Commission.* Philadelphia, 1866.

Steiner, W. R. "A Physician's Experiences in the United States Sanitary Commission during the Civil War," *Proceedings of the Charaka Club,* X (1941), 172–191.

Wolcott, Roger. *Family Jottings.* Boston, 1939.

Index